Counseling Families Across the Stages of Life

Counseling Families Across the Stages of Life

A Handbook for Pastors and Other Helping Professionals

Andrew J. Weaver, M.Th., Ph.D.
Linda A. Revilla, Ph.D.
Harold G. Koenig, M.D.

Abingdon Press
Nashville

COUNSELING FAMILIES ACROSS THE STAGES OF LIFE
A HANDBOOK FOR PASTORS AND OTHER HELPING PROFESSIONALS

Copyright © 2002 by Abingdon Press

This book is printed on elemental-chlorine–free paper.

Library of Congress Cataloging-in-Publication Data

Weaver, Andrew J., 1947–
   Counseling families across the stages of life : a handbook for pastors and other helping
   professionals / Andrew J. Weaver, Linda A. Revilla, Harold G. Koenig.
      p. cm.
   Includes bibliographical references and indexes.
   ISBN 0-687-08415-6 (alk. paper)
   1. Church work with families. 2. Pastoral counseling. I. Revilla, Linda A., 1960- II. Koenig, Harold George. III. Title

   BV4438 .W43 2002
   259'.12—dc21

                                                                         2001045995

All scripture quotations are taken from *The New Revised Standard Version of the Bible*, copyrighted © 1989, Division of Christian Education of the National Council of the Churches of Christ in the United States of America. Used by permission. All rights reserved.

02 03 04 05 06 07 08 09 10 11—10 9 8 7 6 5 4 3 2 1

*To Louise Starrett Stapleton
and the late Major General Carl W. Stapleton
and his valiant comrades of the 364th Fighter
Group of the U.S. Army Air Corps who fought
for our liberty from 1943 to 1945.
God bless them—AW*

*To my husband, Gregory Yee Mark, and our
children, Kellen and Alexa, for making every day
an adventure—LR*

*To Doris Spicknall with love and appreciation
—HK*

Acknowledgments

We are very grateful to the
Reverend Carolyn L. Stapleton for her invaluable
help. Her exceptional editing and research skills
added immeasurably to the quality and usefulness of
the text. We are thankful for her ministry. We are
grateful to Rabbi Mychal Springer for her helpful
suggestions.

For surely I know the plans I have for you, says the L ORD*, plans for your welfare and not for harm, to give you a future with hope.*

—Jeremiah 29:11

Contents

PART III: SUMMARY

recently read an article titled "Relationship Centered Care" in which the author, Beth Wiltrogen McLeod, refers to a "culture of caring" that she sees emerging in our society.[1] She declares that "no longer are we willing to put our faith in professionals who cannot afford to listen and care." McLeod's intention is to confront the growing gap between technology, managed health care—which is economically driven—and face-to-face relationships. Stating that "we want to be heard," she sees an early end to all forms of health care that are not relationship-centered.

My reading of that article coincided with the invitation to write this preface to *Counseling Families Across the Stages of Life: A Handbook for Pastors and Other Helping Professionals*, a book that can be seen as another call for a culture of caring and a description of one in formation. The authors, all people of faith, state that "in this time of widespread concern about the demise of the family, it is especially important that pastors and others in ministry understand how to help guide persons through life passages," a goal that involves, in McLeod's words, "maintaining relationships over time" (p. 39). The purpose of these authors is to present the scientific evidence that durable relationships enhanced with "non-punitive, nurturing religious beliefs and practices" serve both preventive and curative functions. The heart of the book is a description of therapeutic methods and the faith community's resources, which, when applied, can provide relief and healing for twenty life passages.

These two documents are fascinating to me. Although they represent different philosophies, the first a social/spiritual/scientific perspective, the other a religious/psychological/pastoral perspective, both reflect a sensitivity to, and need for, a transformation of our cultural consciousness about caring. They share the view that we need to move from the mechanical to the personal, from management to empathy. Both also identify impediments to the development of a healing caregiving. For McLeod, the major obstacle is a technology without heart, which she associates with impersonal managed-care practices. To overcome this obstruction to healing, she champions the necessity of sustained relationship-centered, face-to-face contact. Weaver and colleagues confront social isolation and punitive religious practices as obstacles to healing, and they emphasize the positive potential of nurturing beliefs, pastoral care and counseling, and participation in a faith community. What fascinates me is that the common factor identified as essential for healing is a caring relationship between the caregiver and the care-receiver. This is a logical connection that seems self-evident, but its apparent absence impels the writers to call for a correction.

The call for a "culture of caring," which actualizes the curative power of relationship, reflects, to my mind, a radical transition in worldviews that arises in a culture where technological progress is expanding exponentially. It is also an intuition that technology, while opening the doors to the mysteries of the human psyche and the functions of the human body and offering near miracle cures for all manner of diseases, has unexamined limits without the inclusion of the personal. What a paradox that no matter how elegant medical science, it is inefficient and ultimately ineffectual without the empathic presence of the heart of healing!

However, the worldview challenged by the philosophy of relationship-centered care has its own reason for being. Originating in the Enlightenment in response to the medieval world, it attempted to replace magic, incantation, and prayer—the personal—with observation, experimentation, and reason, leading eventually to a rational science of a mechanical world. In a sense, it replaced an ancient view of the universe as an organism with that of it as a machine. The understanding of the unity of the whole was replaced by a view of the whole as composed of separate parts in interaction, but not in relationship. While this mechanization of the world de-spiritualized the human, it also freed the personal from oppressive dogma, which inhibited the study of the body and the spirit, thus enabling the rise of modern medicine, psychology, and technology, which, in turn, has freed humans from the ravages of disease, mental illness, and early death.

Now, it seems we are coming full circle, and the cycle is correcting itself with a move in the other direction—seemingly the way change occurs both at the collective and at the personal levels. The mechanistic physics of the nineteenth century, which gave us a view of the world as a machine, is being replaced by twenty-first-century quantum physics and molecular biology, which is beginning to portray the world as an organism. The separate but interacting parts of the machine turn out to be points of intersection in a tapestry of relationships. The spiritual dictum that "we are one" is echoed by the quantum vision of a "unified field." In the context of this emerging consciousness, the call for a culture of caring and the power of participation in a faith community makes sense both ontologically and practically. The value of relationship is not merely a sentiment or an important condition for healing, however; relationship is the primal fact that makes "face-to-face caring" and "counseling families" moral imperatives. In this new situation, technology humanized by empathic caring can become the oscillating poles of the healing continuum.

The research and recommendations of Andrew Weaver and his colleagues in this handbook are an important and instructive development of the emerging culture of caring. Although it is designated as a manual for pastors and other helping professionals, it is more than that, in three ways: First, it is a response to the danger of depersonalization by curative technologies unmoderated by dynamics of care. Second, it is a documentation that would be comforting to McLeod, who calls for a culture of caring, because she would be introduced to an enormous network of caring resources already in place and in operation. The authors state that over 350,000 ministers, rabbis, and priests staff "500,000 places of worship with a presence in almost every U.S. community," which "approximately 60 percent attend monthly . . . [with] 90 percent of Americans want[ing] some sort of religious education for their children . . . [and whose] most common prayer is for the 'well-being of their family'" (pp. 37–42). What is this but a massive culture of caring?

Third, this handbook is not only an encyclopedia of human needs across the life span, but also a virtual workbook of recommended counseling responses to human needs and suffering as they appear in families. With candor and authenticity, the authors point out a discrepancy between family needs and the training of clergy to address them. Nevertheless, the authors demonstrate with impressive statistics that more people consult religious professionals than all other mental health specialists combined. They interpret this phenomenon by asserting that religion offers hope and a means of coping—necessary complements to technological expertise. After explaining that the new model of family diagnosis is based on strengths rather than pathology, they identify the factors that contribute to family strength such as commitment, affirmation, stability, resilience, faith, connection to community, effective communication, and conflict management. To support the development of these qualities, the authors call for a revised social policy that allows families quality and quantity time to develop these resources, a reform that would indeed create a culture of caring.

Most of this book is devoted to twenty situations that illustrate common issues experienced by families. These include premarital counseling, dual-earner families, new and single parents, blended families, troubled teens, serious mental illness, alcohol abuse, divorce, and domestic violence. In addition, the authors deal with special conditions, such as sudden job loss, infertility, disability, Alzheimer's disease, nursing home placement, terminal illness, and homelessness. Each situation is concretized by a clinical example, an appropriate response, and the value of belonging to a faith community and the indications for referral.

In conclusion, the authors have compiled a comprehensive and instructive book that will be valuable to any clergyperson or other religious professional who inevitably will be called upon to minister to the life problems of families. It is a valuable illustration of an operational culture of caring and a model for the evolution of this ethic into the whole of society. I recommend this book to every clergyperson as a valuable guide for ministry to the special and universal needs of families. No clergyperson should be without it, and any helping professional will be informed and instructed by it.

—Harville Hendrix

---

1. McLeod, B. W. (1999, April–July). Relationship centered care. *Noetic Sciences Review, 48,* 37–42.

Harville Hendrix, Ph.D., an ordained minister in the American Baptist Church, earned his Ph.D. in psychology and religion at the University of Chicago and formerly taught pastoral care and counseling at Perkins School of Theology, Southern Methodist University. He is the author of *Getting the Love You Want: A Guide for Couples* and *Keeping the Love You Find: A Personal Guide*; and co-author with his wife, Helen LaKelly Hunt, of *Giving the Love That Heals: A Guide for Parents*.

How to Use This Book

Counseling Families Across the Stages of Life: A Handbook for Pastors and Other Helping Professionals is designed to be a text for those in training for pastoral ministry, as well as a practical resource for those engaged in ministry with families. The volume addresses family transition issues (e.g., becoming a parent, divorce, sudden job loss, chronic illness, retirement, untimely death) and related mental health problems that may be experienced over the life span. In this time of widespread concern about the demise of the family, it is especially important that pastors and others in ministry understand how to help guide persons through life passages.

Part I offers information about the important role that clergy and the faith community serve in the mental health care of families. This section spells out the need for special expertise by pastors and other religious professionals in recognizing and addressing important transitional life span issues and related family problems. We summarize the scientific evidence that nonpunitive, nurturing religious beliefs and practices serve both preventive and healing functions. Finally, there is a review of the factors that cultivate strong and resilient families in spite of adversity.

The heart of the book is found in Part II, which is presented in a format that uses real-life situations while highlighting practical implications for pastoral care. They reflect recent research on relevant issues and recognize that the demands on a family change over time in the life cycle. The case studies are multidisciplinary in approach, integrating clinical knowledge in pastoral care, psychology, family medicine, psychiatry, nursing, gerontology, sociology, social work, and marriage and family therapy, along with current scientific findings on the role of religion in mental health care. The volume recognizes that the difficulties that families face do not stand in isolation from one another but are interrelated. For example, the chapters involving chronic illness also address caregiver stress and depression.

The book is designed so that a reader can easily locate information on specific issues and related mental health problems for which families seek pastoral counsel. It is a practical, easy-to-use guide on how to assess problems and how to respond to them. The table of contents provides the subjects of twenty situations that illustrate common issues experienced by families.

Each case provides an example of a family member with a specific problem and in need of help. Included in each chapter is information about how a pastor or colleague in ministry would assess the problem, certain aspects of the case that are most important, how to identify the major issues, specific directions that the pastor and congregation can take, when to refer for professional assistance, and information about resources that can provide help. National organizations (often with toll-free numbers and Internet addresses) that supply information and support for families facing these issues are identified for each concern addressed. Cross-cultural aspects are noted and discussed as well. Technical terms are defined in the glossary at the end of the book.

The text is written for people of all faiths, with an appreciation for the richness of the intergenerational and multicultural diversity found in religious communities. The authors are people of faith with specialties in mental health.

Dr. Weaver is a clinical psychologist, licensed marriage and family therapist, and ordained United Methodist minister who has served rural and urban parishes. He has written over 70 scientific articles and book chapters and has coauthored 6 books. Dr. Revilla is a United Methodist laywoman and developmental psychologist who specializes in working with ethnic families. She also teaches at the University of Hawaii in the Ethnic Studies Department. Dr. Koenig is professor of psychiatry and internal medicine, as well as director of the Center for the Study of Aging, Religion/Spirituality and Health at Duke University Medical Center. He has written over 170 scientific articles and book chapters and has authored or coauthored 9 books.

PART ONE

Introduction

Clergy, Faith, and Family Issues

Religious community is important to the lives of most Americans—4 out of 5 believe religion strengthens their family (Abbott, Berry, and Meredith, 1990). There are nearly 500,000 places of worship with a presence in almost every U.S. community (Bradley, Green, Jones, Lynn, and NcNeil, 1990). About 40 percent of Americans attend one of these places of worship weekly, and approximately 60 percent attend monthly (Gallup, 1996). More than 90 percent of Americans want some form of religious education for their children (Hoge, 1996). Ninety percent consider religion "very important or fairly important" in their lives and indicate that their most common prayer is for the "well being of their family" (Gallup, 1996). The 353,000 Christian and Jewish clergy serving congregations in the United States (4,000 rabbis; 49,000 Catholic priests; and 300,000 Protestant ministers, according to the U.S. Department of Labor, 1998) are among the most trusted professionals in society. This data has remained fairly constant over the past sixty-five years (Gallup, 1996).

The 22,000 members of the American Association of Marriage and Family Therapists are outnumbered by clergy sixteen to one (Weaver, Koenig, and Larson, 1997). Not surprisingly, clergypersons serve as marriage and family counselors for millions of Americans, based on accessibility alone. In thirteen separate studies conducted between 1979 and 1992, it was found that those who seek pastoral counsel bring concerns predominantly related to marriage and family issues (Weaver et al., 1997). Wasman, Corradi, and Clemens (1979) report that 85 percent of parish-based clergy indicated that family problems were the most frequent and most difficult counseling issues they were asked to address. In a survey of 405 pastors in 10 geographical regions of the United States, Benner (1992) found that 84 percent of the clergy reported marriage and divorce as the most commonly presented problems. Frequent church attendees in the midwestern U.S. are seven times more likely to seek clergy for help with marriage and family problems (86 percent) than to turn to the assistance of nonreligious mental health specialists (12.5 percent), according to Privette, Quackenbos, and Bundrick (1994).

Clergy perform 3 out of 4 American wedding ceremonies, and almost all of them report that they formally counsel couples before they officiate at an average of 8.6 weddings a year (Jones and Stahmann, 1994). Young engaged couples in the general public who were surveyed are three times more likely to prefer counseling from a clergyperson than from a mental health specialist, and the rate is much higher among those who are religiously committed. Engaged couples report that they believe clergy are trustworthy advisers and are to be taken seriously when they make referrals for premarital counseling (Williams, 1992). However, only one half of mainline Protestant pastors have any formal training in premarital counseling (Jones and Stahmann, 1994).

Other professionals see clergy as important community resources that offer valuable counsel to families. A survey of 438 members of the American Academy of Family Physicians found that more than 8 in 10 referred or recommended their patients to clergy for counseling, and 30 percent of the family doctors indicated that they do so more than ten times a year. About 73 percent of the physicians listed marital and family counseling as the reason for their patient referral to clergy (Daaleman and Frey, 1998). Other studies indicate that the diverse areas in which clergy are asked to provide counseling include: genetics education (Steiner-Grossman and David, 1993); child maltreatment (Weaver, 1992); addiction treatment (Turner, 1995); HIV/AIDS (Crawford, Allison, Robinson, Hughes, and Samaryk, 1992); rehabilitation (Walters and Neugeboren, 1995); and hospice care (Millison and Dudley, 1992).

Regrettably, many clergy are unprepared to address the family, marital, and emotional problems of those who seek their help. In a comprehensive national study of almost two thousand United Methodist pastors, in which 95 percent of the sample supported had some counseling training in seminary, only about 2 in 5 felt competent in the area of marriage and family counseling (Orthner, 1986). When ranking ten aspects of ministerial skill, marriage and family counseling was the lowest area of perceived competency among the surveyed pastors (Orthner, 1986). Interestingly, unlike growth in other areas of ministry (e.g., preaching, administration, teaching), pastors indicate that no matter how long they serve in parishes, they believe that their counseling skills do not improve without continuing education. When experienced Christian and Jewish clergy are asked to name training areas in which they could use the most help, the great majority of their responses involve marriage and family issues (Ingram and Lowe, 1989; Lowe, 1986).

Although clergy have limitations in diagnostic and referral skills (Weaver, 1995), when a group of 233 young adults was asked to compare clergy to psychologists and psychiatrists, clergy were perceived to be significantly better at interpersonal skills (including warmth, caring, stability, professionalism) and about the same for listening skills (Schindler, Berren, Hannah, Beigel, and Santiago, 1987). Not surprisingly, in a study conducted over a thirteen-year period, college students indicated that they were as likely to seek a clergyperson for help as a psychologist or psychiatrist (Rule and Gandy, 1994). When compared to other professionals working with seniors, pastors score higher in their acceptance and approval of the elderly—factors very important to counseling success (Gulledge, 1992). Most surveyed clergy take their pastoral counselor role seriously, see the need for additional training, and respond positively when it is offered (Weaver, 1995). One of the primary reasons for writing this book is to give pastors and other religious professionals information about marital and family issues, which will assist them in becoming more effective helpers.

Family Difficulties and Religious Coping

Religion plays a vital role in the lives of family members across the life span, especially in times of crisis and chronic illness (Pargament, 1997). Religious beliefs and practices provide a means of coping with illness and loss, and faith communities provide social as well as spiritual support (Koenig and Weaver, 1997). In a study of 124 parents who lost an infant to sudden infant death syndrome, McIntosh, Silver, and Wortman (1993) found that greater religious participation was related to increased perception of social support and increased meaning found in the loss. Furthermore, the positive coping effects of religious participation and its importance were related to greater well-being and decreased distress in those grief-stricken parents eighteen months after the infant's death.

A second study analyzed stress and coping in families of children with severe birth defects. The fathers and mothers who were members of the Spina Bifida Association all reported that "having a belief in God" was the most important family coping strategy among thirteen choices presented and that attending church was among the most helpful activities (Samuelson, Foltz, and Foxall, 1992). In a separate study, fathers of children being treated for cancer in a hematology hospital clinic were asked about the frequency and effectiveness of various methods of coping. Among twenty-nine separate coping strategies used, prayer was both the most common and most helpful for the fathers (Cayse, 1994).

Religious beliefs are an essential component of hope for many people. In one study, 59 of the 60 seniors surveyed indicated that spiritual beliefs and practices were a source of hope in their daily living (Herth, 1993). Hope is especially important for patients undergoing the acute stress of new or worsening physical illness. Religious beliefs and practices have been found to be helpful to older adults when facing the psychological stress of poor health and disability. Studies indicate that one quarter to one third of the elderly find religion to be the most important factor in enabling them to cope successfully with physical illness, mental illness, and life stressors (Koenig and Weaver, 1997). Hospitalized seniors who practice their faith are less likely to become depressed and recover faster from depression than their nonreligious peers, shortening the time spent in the hospital (Koenig and Larson, 1998).

Family caregivers of the chronically ill elderly with dementia or terminal cancer cope better if they have a strong faith (Rabins, Fitting, Eastham, and Zabora, 1990). Religious teachings often foster an ethos of care and responsibility that is an important resource for facing the stress of providing long-term care. Those caregivers who have an active faith tend to have a better relationship with the care recipients than do their nonreligious counterparts, which can reduce the risk of depression (Chang, Noonan, and Tennstedt, 1998). In addition, the regular practice of religion (i.e., worship attendance) is associated with better health outcomes and lower mortality rates (Strawbridge, Cohen, Shema, and Kaplan, 1997; Hummer, Roger, Nam, and Ellison, 1999).

Religion and Marital Commitment

In the 1990s, about half of U.S. marriages ended in divorce. If the trend continues, that figure will climb to 2 out of 3 marriages ending in divorce by the early decades of the twenty-first century (Martin and Bumpass, 1989). Every year, more than one million children in the U.S. experience the divorce of their parents, and the emotional impact is distressing and long-lasting for many (Larson, Sawyers, and Larson, 1995). Because of the negative impact on society, scientists have become interested in understanding the factors that lead to satisfying, enduring marriages and stable family life.

Researchers are rediscovering the truth of the adage that those who pray together are, in fact, more likely to stay together. Commitment to a nurturing faith community can enhance family life and marital stability. In a national survey of 4,587 married couples, results showed that when spouses attended church together regularly, they had the lowest risk of divorce among all married groups (Call and Heaton, 1997). This study suggested that shared participation in church gives the couple a sense of purpose and mutual values that increase family commitment and an integrated social network of friends and relatives. Other research studies have found that religious involvement is an important predictor of marital satisfaction, happiness, and adjustment (Hansen, 1992). Andrew Greeley, Roman Catholic priest and sociologist (1991), discovered that religious involvement can play an important part in sexual satisfaction in marriage. He found that praying together was strongly related to being sexually playful and adventurous within the marriage.

A study based on national data found that even a simple measure, such as church attendance, was the strongest predictor of marital satisfaction when considering seven other independent variables in a statistical analysis: occupational prestige, family income, years of schooling completed, age, age at first marriage, number of children at home, and wife's employment status (Glenn and Weaver, 1978). Married couples report that faith provides moral guidance, facilitates decision making, minimizes conflicts (Robinson, 1994), increases tolerance, and improves adjustment (Hunt and King, 1978). In addition, active religious involvement increases marital commitment (Larson and Goltz, 1989) and is a consistent predictor of long-term marriage (Robinson and Blanton, 1993).

Couples who had been married for more than thirty years indicated that religion figured prominently in their lives. Many spoke of the spiritual support and comfort that faith offered during difficult times (Robinson and Blanton, 1993). Their religious faith also encouraged commitment through the value placed on the marital bond in their religious teachings. About 2 in 3 of surveyed couples indicated that similar religious beliefs had been essential to long-term marital stability and satisfaction (Kaslow and Robison, 1996).

Faith and Family Resilience

What are the factors that contribute to high resilience in American families struggling with serious difficulties? What helps families rebound from adversity and become more resourceful? What are the protective factors that enable young people who face problems to have positive, productive lives?

With remarkable consistency, religion has been found to have a positive influence on young people and their families at risk for social and personal problems. In a comprehensive study of 225 Hispanic and Anglo families in California, religious involvement was associated with general well-being, social support, shared values, family solidarity, and social control mechanisms that reduced family members' "at risk" behaviors through positive expectations and social sanctions (Ransom, Fisher, and Terry, 1992).

A study of 33,397 high school students in 112 different communities measured sixteen problem behaviors in seven areas: tobacco use, sexual activity, alcohol use, antisocial behaviors, school problems, illicit drug use, depression, and suicide. Analysis revealed that the number of youth involved in structured activities or otherwise connected to religious institutions was strongly related to community health. Those communities with a majority of high school students attending religious services at least once a month were twice as likely to be among those with the least problem behaviors among youth (Blyth and Leffert, 1995). A study using national data found that with the single exception of personal violence by males, there was an inverse relationship between frequency of religious attendance and youth involvement in four problem areas: suspension/ expulsion from school, theft, violence, and drug use (Ketterlinus, Lamb, Nitz, and Elster, 1992).

Depression is one of the most common emotional problems in young people. Experts estimate that about 1 in 20 adolescents is depressed, and suicide has been linked to depression (Reynolds, 1995). Religion can protect children and their parents against depression by acting as a buffer against stressful events. According to researchers at Columbia University, children whose mothers are religiously committed are less likely to suffer depression (Miller, Warner, Wickramaratine, and Weissman, 1997). The study found that the daughters of mothers who valued religion were 60 percent less likely to have a major depression over a ten-year period.

Religious involvement has many positive social benefits for family members. Youth who practice their faith increase their pro-social values and caring behaviors. Among the 3 in 4 teens who are members of a religious group, 62 percent are community volunteers and 56 percent make charitable financial contributions. Of those who have no religious affiliation, only 44 percent are volunteers and 25 percent are contributors (Gallup and Bezilla, 1992). Other researchers have found that the importance of religion and regular worship attendance in a young person's life is associated with a greater concern for the poor and more frequent helping behaviors than their nonreligious peers (Benson, Williams, and Johnson, 1987).

Religion and Ethnic Minority Families

The mental and physical health benefits of religious practices and beliefs for African-Americans (Levin, Chatters, and Taylor, 1995), Hispanic-Americans (Levin, Markides, and Ray, 1996), Asian-Americans (Holtz, 1998; Lubben, Chi, and Kitano, 1987), and Native Americans (Spangler et al., 1998) have been documented across the life span. For example, a study of 326 Mexican-American youth in a drug abuse intervention program found that both family support and religious involvement were significantly related to reduction of problem behaviors, such as drug and alcohol use, school problems, and involvement with the legal system (Barrett, Simpson, and Lehman, 1988). In a survey of older Mexican-Americans in San Antonio, Texas, 82 percent reported that they had attended church that week, and 88 percent regularly used prayer to cope with stress or sadness. Overall, 78 percent stated that their faith was a "very important" sustaining resource in their lives, while only 4 percent indicated that religion had not been helpful (Maldonado, 1994). Mexican-Americans are more than twice as likely to seek help with personal problems from clergy than from psychologists and psychiatrists combined (Chalfant et al., 1990). In fact, the study found that the degree of identification with Mexican ethnicity was strongly related to seeking pastoral help as a primary resource. In a survey of 1,805 Hispanic-Americans (the majority of Mexican, Cuban, or Puerto Rican heritage) over the age of fifty-five, researchers discovered that individuals were twice as likely to seek help from the church than from any other community service when addressing family problems, depression, worry, or fear (Starrett, Rogers, and Decker, 1992).

Historically, the church has promoted social and psychological support in the African-American family. Church support can reduce the burden of bias on family members and may counter social isolation and stigmatization. The church is an important resource within the African-American community where there is often little distinction between church and extended family (Johnson and Barer, 1990). Three of 4 African-American adults surveyed responded "very often" or "often" to the statement "The religious beliefs I learned when I was young still help me" (Seaborn-Thompson and Ensminger, 1989). In an extensive study of 635 African-American churches in the northern United States, a remarkable 38 percent of the congregations had a working relationship with the local mental health department, while one half of the churches had family support programs (Thomas, Quinn, Billingsley, and Caldwell, 1994).

In a national sample of older African-Americans, about 80 percent reported receiving emotional and/or financial support from fellow church members in times of need (Taylor and Chatters, 1986). The risk of suicide is much lower for African-Americans who have strong religious beliefs and a personal devotion than for their peers without an active faith (Needleman, Wessely, and Lewis, 1998). African-Americans, especially in later life, are more likely to seek help for emotional problems from their religious community than from mental health specialists (Husaini, Moore, and Cain, 1994) and to express general satisfaction with the help ministers offer (Neighbors, Musick, and Williams, 1998). In 1986, Mollica, Streets, Boscarino, and Redlich found that African-American pastors were more likely to go into the community and seek out people in crisis than their non-African-American colleagues were. These authors summarized their study, published in the *American Journal of Psychiatry*, with the comment "Parish-based clergy, especially the black clergy, function as a major mental health resource to communities with limited access to professional mental health services" (p. 223).

Summary

At a time of widespread concern about the demise of the family, it is especially important that pastors and their colleagues in ministry better understand how to help guide families through the passages of the life cycle. Despite limitations in training, clergy act as marriage and family counselors for millions of Americans. Clergypersons consistently report that those who seek their counsel bring problems predominantly related to marriage and family concerns. There is strong scientific evidence that faith involvement has both preventive and healing benefits that act to preserve and support family life. Religious beliefs and practices provide a means of coping with illness and loss, and faith communities provide social and spiritual support. Clergy need additional training in family counseling skills, and pastors indicate a high interest in continuing education in the area.

References

Abbott, D. A., Berry, M., and Meredith, W. H. (1990). Religious belief and practice: A potential asset in helping families. *Family Relations, 39,* 443–448.

Barrett, M. E., Simpson, D. D., and Lehman, W. E. K. (1988). Behavioral changes of adolescents in drug abuse intervention programs. *Journal of Clinical Psychology, 44(3),* 461–473.

Benner, D. G. (1992). *Strategic Pastoral Counseling: A Short-term Structure Model.* Grand Rapids: Baker Press.

Benson, P. L., Williams, D., and Johnson, A. (1987). *The Quicksilver Years: The Hopes and Fears of Early Adolescence.* San Francisco: Harper & Row.

Blyth, D. A., and Leffert, N. (1995). Communities as contexts for adolescent development: An empirical analysis. *Journal of Adolescence Research, 10(1),* 64–87.

Bradley, M. B., Green, N. M., Jones, D. E., Lynn, M., and McNeil, L. (1990). *Churches and Church Membership in the United States, 1990.* Atlanta: Glenmary Research Center.

Call, V. R., and Heaton, T. B. (1997). Religious influence on marital stability. *Journal for the Scientific Study of Religion, 36(3),* 382–392.

Cayse, L. N. (1994). Fathers of children with cancer: A descriptive study of the stressors and coping strategies. *Journal of Pediatric Oncology Nursing, 11(3),* 102–108.

Chalfant, H. P., Heller, P. L., Roberts, A., Briones, D., Aguirre-Hochbaum, S., and Farr, W. (1990). The clergy as a resource for those encountering psychological distress. *Review of Religious Research, 31,* 305–313.

Chang, B., Noonan, A. E., and Tennstedt, S. L. (1998). The role of religion/spirituality in coping with caregiving for disabled elders. *The Gerontologist, 38(4),* 463–470.

Crawford, I., Allison, K. W., Robinson, W. L., Hughes D., and Samaryk, M. (1992). Attitudes of African-American Baptist ministers towards AIDS. *Journal of Community Psychology, 20(4),* 304–308.

Daaleman, T. P., and Frey, B. (1998). Prevalence and patterns of physicians' referral to clergy and pastoral care providers. *Archives of Family Medicine, 7,* 548–553.

Gallup, G. H. (1996). *Religion in America: 1996.* Princeton, NJ: The Gallup Organization, Inc.

Gallup, G. H., and Bezilla, R. (1992). *The Religious Life of Young Americans*. Princeton, NJ: The George Gallup International Institute.

Glenn, N. D., and Weaver, C. N. (1978). A multivariate, multisurvey study of marital happiness. *Journal of Marriage and the Family, 40,* 269–282.

Greeley, A. (1991). *Faithful Attraction: Discovering Intimacy, Love, and Fidelity in American Marriage*. New York: Tom Doherty Associates.

Gulledge, J. K. (1992). Influences on clergy attitudes toward aging. *Journal of Religious Gerontology, 8(2),* 63–77.

Hansen, G. L. (1992). Religion and marital adjustment. In J. F. Schumaker (Ed.), *Religion and Mental Health* (pp. 189–198). New York: Oxford University Press.

Herth, K. (1993). Hope in older adults in community and institutional settings. *Issues in Mental Health Nursing, 14,* 139–156.

Hoge, D. R. (1996). Religion in America: The demographics of belief and affiliation. In E. P. Shafranske (Ed.), *Religion and the Clinical Practice of Psychology* (pp. 21–41). Washington, DC: American Psychological Association.

Holtz, T. H. (1998). Refugee trauma versus torture trauma: A retrospective controlled cohort study of Tibetan refugees. *Journal of Nervous and Mental Disease, 186(1),* 24–34.

Hummer, R., Roger, R., Nam, C., and Ellison, C. G. (1999). Religious involvement and U.S. adult morality. *Demography, 36,* 273–285.

Hunt, R. A., and King, M. B. (1978). Religiosity and marriage. *Journal for the Scientific Study of Religion, 17,* 399–406.

Husaini, B. A., Moore, S. T., and Cain, V. A. (1994). Psychiatric symptoms and help-seeking behavior among the elderly: An analysis of racial and gender differences. *Journal of Gerontological Social Work, 21(3),* 177–195.

Ingram, B. L., and Lowe, D. W. (1989). Counseling activities and referral practices of rabbis. *Journal of Psychology and Judaism, 13,* 133–148.

Johnson, C. L., and Barer, B. M. (1990). Family network among older inner-city blacks. *The Gerontologist, 30,* 726–733.

Jones, E. F., and Stahmann, R. F. (1994). Clergy beliefs, preparation, and practice in premarital counseling. *Journal of Pastoral Care, 48,* 181–186.

Kaslow, F., and Robison, J. A. (1996). Long-term satisfying marriages: Perceptions of contributing factors. *The American Journal of Family Therapy, 24(2),* 153–170.

Ketterlinus, R. D., Lamb, M. E., Nitz, K., and Elster A. B. (1992). Adolescent nonsexual and sex-related problem behavior. *Journal of Adolescence Research, 7(4),* 431–456.

Koenig, H. G., and Larson, D. B. (1998). Use of hospital services, religious attendance, and religious affiliation. *Southern Medical Journal, 91(10),* 925–932.

Koenig, H. G. and Weaver, A. J. (1997). *Counseling Troubled Older*

Adults: A Handbook for Clergy and Religious Caregivers. Nashville: Abingdon Press.

Larson, D. B., Sawyers, J., and Larson S. (1995) *The Costly Consequences of Divorce.* Rockville, MD: National Institute for Healthcare Research.

Larson, L. E., and Goltz, J. W. (1989). Religious participation and marital commitment. *Review of Religious Research, 30,* 387–400.

Levin, J. S., Chatters, L. M., and Taylor, R. J. (1995). Religious effects on health status and life satisfaction among black Americans. *Journal of Gerontology, 50B(3),* S154–S163.

Levin, J. S., Markides, K. S., and Ray, L. A. (1996). Religious attendance and psychological well-being in Mexican Americans: A panel analysis of three-generations data. *The Gerontologist, 36(4),* 454–463.

Lowe, D. W. (1986). Counseling activities, and referral practices of ministers. *Journal of Psychology and Christianity, 5,* 22–29.

Lubben, J. E., Chi, I. C., and Kitano, H. H. L. (1987). Exploring Filipino American drinking behavior. *Journal of Studies on Alcohol, 49,* 26–29.

Maldonado, D. (1994). Religiosity and religious participation among Hispanic elderly. *Journal of Religious Gerontology, 9,* 41–61.

Martin, T. C., and Bumpass, L. L. (1989). Recent trends in marital disruption. *Demography, 26,* 37–51.

McIntosh, D. N., Silver, R. C., and Wortman C. B. (1993). Religious role in adjustment to a negative life event: Coping with the loss of a child. *Journal of Personality and Social Psychology, 65,* 812–821.

Miller, L. F., Warner, V., Wickramaratine, P., and Weissman, M. (1997). Religiosity and depression: Ten-year follow-up of depressed mothers and offspring. *The Journal of the American Academy of Child and Adolescent Psychiatry, 36(10),* 1416–1425.

Millison, M., and Dudley, J. R. (1992). Providing spiritual support: A job for all hospice professionals. *The Hospice Journal, 8(4),* 49–66.

Mollica, R. C., Streets, F. J., Boscarino, J., and Redlich, F. C. (1986). A community study of formal pastoral counseling activities of the clergy. *American Journal of Psychiatry, 143,* 323–328.

Needleman, J., Wessely, S., and Lewis, G. (1998). Suicide acceptability in African and White Americans: The role of religion. *Journal of Nervous and Mental Disease, 186(1),* 12–16.

Neighbors, H. W., Musick, M. A., and Williams, D. R. (1998). The African American minister as a source of help for serious personal crises: Bridges or barriers to mental health care? *Health Education and Behavior, 25(6),* 759–777.

Orthner, D. K. (1986). *Pastoral Counseling: Caring and Caregivers in The United Methodist Church.* Nashville: The General Board of Higher Education and Ministry of The United Methodist Church.

Pargament, K. I. (1997). *The Psychology of Religion and Coping: Theory, Research, Practice.* New York: Guilford Press.

Privette, G., Quackenbos, S., and Bundrick, C. M. (1994). Preferences for religious and nonreligious counseling and psychotherapy. *Psychological Reports*, 75, 539–546.

Rabins, P. V., Fitting, M. D., Eastham, J., and Zabora, J. (1990). Emotional adaptation over time in care-givers for chronically ill elderly people. *Age and Aging*, 19, 185–190.

Ransom, D. C., Fisher, L., and Terry, H. E. (1992). The California Family Health Project: II. Family world view and adult health. *Family Process*, 31, 251–267.

Reynolds, W. M. (1995). Depression. In V. B. Van Hasselt and M. Hersen (Eds.), *Handbook of Adolescent Psychopathology* (pp. 297–348). New York: Lexington Books.

Robinson, L. C. (1994). Religious orientation in enduring marriage: An exploratory study. *Review of Religious Research*, 35, 207–218.

Robinson, L. C., and Blanton, P. W. (1993). Marital strengths in enduring marriages. *Family Relations*, 42, 38–45.

Rule, W. R., and Gandy, G. L. (1994). A thirteen-year comparison in patterns of attitudes toward counseling. *Adolescence*, 29(115), 575–589.

Samuelson, J. J., Foltz, J., and Foxall, M. J. (1992). Stress and coping in families of children with myelomeningocele. *Archives of Psychiatric Nursing*, 6(5), 287–295.

Schindler, F., Berren, M. R., Hannah, M. T., Beigel, A., and Santiago, J. M. (1987). How the public perceives psychiatrists, psychologists, nonpsychiatric physicians, and members of the clergy. *Professional Psychology: Research and Practice*, 18(4), 371–376.

Seaborn-Thompson, M., and Ensminger, M. E. (1989). Psychological well-being among mothers with school age children: Evolving family structures. *Social Forces*, 67, 715–730.

Spangler, J. G., Bell, R. A., Knick, S., Michielutte, R., Dignan, M. B., and Summerson, J. H. (1998). Church-related correlates of tobacco use among Lumbee Indians in North Carolina. *Ethnicity and Disease*, 8(1), 73–80.

Starrett, R. A., Rogers D., and Decker, J. T. (1992). The self-reliance behavior of the Hispanic elderly in comparison to their use of formal mental health helping networks. *Clinical Gerontologist*, 11, 157–169.

Steiner-Grossman, P., and David, K. L. (1993). Involvement of rabbis in counseling and referral for genetic conditions: Results of a survey. *American Journal of Human Genetics*, 53(6), 1359–1365.

Strawbridge, W. J., Cohen, R. D., Shema, S. J., and Kaplan, G. A. (1997). Frequent attendance at religious services and mortality over 28 years. *American Journal of Public Health*, 87(6), 957–961.

Taylor, R. J., and Chatters, L. M. (1986). Patterns of informal support to elderly Black Americans: Family, friends, and church members. *Social Work*, 31, 431–438.

Thomas, S. B., Quinn, S. C., Billingsley, A., and Caldwell, C. (1994). The characteristics of northern black churches with community health outreach programs. *American Journal of Public Health*, 84, 575–579.

Turner, W. H. (1995). Bridging the gap: Addressing alcohol and drug addiction from a community health perspective. *American Journal of Public Health*, 85(6), 870–871.

United States Department of Labor. (1998). *Occupational outlook handbook: United States Department of Labor*. Washington, DC: Bureau of Labor Statistics.

Walters, J., and Neugeboren, B. (1995). Collaboration between mental health organizations and religious institutions. *Psychiatric Rehabilitation Journal*, 19(2), 51–57.

Wasman, M., Corradi, R. B., and Clemens, N. A. (1979). In-depth continuing education for clergy in mental health: Ten years of a large scale program. *Pastoral Psychology*, 27, 251–259.

Weaver, A. J. (1992). The distressed family and wounded children. *Journal of Religion and Health*, 31, 207–220.

Weaver, A. J. (1995). Has there been a failure to prepare and support parish-based clergy in their role as front-line community mental health workers? A review. *The Journal of Pastoral Care*, 49, 129–149.

Weaver, A. J., Koenig, H. G., and Larson, D. B. (1997). Marital and family therapists and the clergy: A need for clinical collaboration, training and research. *Journal of Marital and Family Therapy*, 23(1), 13–25.

Williams, L. M. (1992). Premarital counseling: A needs assessment among engaged individuals. *Contemporary Family Therapy*, 14, 505–516.

What Makes a Family Strong?

Family Strengths

With the many pressures on family life and the high rate of divorce today, clergy and their colleagues in ministry need to better understand the dynamics of well-functioning families. There is now a movement among mental health professionals toward a strengths-based model of understanding and treating families. This model comes from a wellness perspective, rather than the conventional pathology viewpoint, and is more interested in how families succeed than in how they fail. The strengths-based view seeks to identify and support the key ingredients that enable a family to cope and even thrive in spite of crises and persistent problems. This model directs attention toward the protective and preventive elements that fortify. What makes it possible for some families to bounce back from difficulties while other families cannot? The following strengths have been identified by current research and can be useful in assessing the hardiness of a family. Families with these strengths tend to function better across the life cycle and better manage stress than those without these qualities.

Commitment

Strong families take pride in their identity as a unit. They know they can depend on one another and can work together to solve common problems. Commitment is demonstrated by the fact that the members invest much of their time and energy together. Because they enjoy one another's company, they plan activities that promote togetherness and enjoyment. They share family rituals such as regular meals, bedtime routines, and intentional communication with extended family. They have traditions and a sense of family history, celebrating important occasions including birthdays, anniversaries, and holidays. Family rituals are one expression of a general sense of stability and predictability in the family (Stinnett and DeFrain, 1985). It should be noted that one of the chief complaints even of healthy families today is the limited time for communication (Stinnett, Sanders, DeFrain, and Parkhurst, 1982).

Affirmation

Strong families effectively nurture one another by expressing care and affection that foster trust and confidence (Stinnett and DeFrain, 1985). Caring families strive to be sensitive to each other's needs. Members are encouraged to be individuals, and yet they are expected to contribute to the common good. They affirm and support each other in an environment that enhances an atmosphere of love, warmth, and respect. Stronger families report using fewer "put-downs," while weaker families use more "put-downs" and belittling humor (Wuerffel, DeFrain, and Stinnett, 1990). Healthy families are able to appreciate, encourage, and support the individuality and growth of each member.

Effective Communication and Conflict Management

Strong families have positive communication patterns, are good listeners, and are willing to negotiate as issues arise. Communication in these families is clear and open, encouraging persons to take responsibility for their thoughts, feelings, and actions. Strong families quarrel and get angry at each other, but they get the conflict out in the open and are able to talk it over. They share their feelings about the conflict and are successful in discussing alternative ways to deal with differences and in selecting a solution that is best for everyone.

When families do not know how to protect the positive aspects of their relationship from destructive patterns of conflict, the negative behaviors will grow over time and erode positive feelings. Happy families are those who have learned how to protect the good in their relationship and to limit the effects of the negative. Couples and families who can share their feelings and have effective communication skills are good at problem solving, which is particularly important in adverse times. The most powerful predictors of marital distress and divorce are destructive, negative patterns of behavior used by couples when addressing conflict and disagreement (Markman and Hahlweg, 1993).

Community Connections

Strong families work to develop and maintain relationships beyond the family unit that give the members a sense of being valued and appreciated (McCubbin and McCubbin, 1986). Robust families maintain close involvement with institutions such as school, church, and other local organizations that promote the well-being of the community and family. Marriages are more likely to endure and strengthen when they are supported by communities of people committed to their growth. Faith-based organizations are the largest group of institutions in our society that have a vested interest in fostering strong marriages and families.

Faith

There is strong empirical evidence that faith has positive benefits for many families (Weaver, Koenig, and Larson, 1997). Active religious involvement increases marital commitment (Larson and Goltz, 1989) and can be a strong deterrent to instability and divorce (Heaton, 1984). Researchers studying coping strategies that families utilize over the life span found that the most important overall strategy was seeking spiritual support (Olson, 1989). Well-functioning families adhere to deeply felt values (Stinnett and DeFrain, 1985). Good parents not only teach but also, more importantly, model positive values and beliefs.

Stability and Flexibility

Families require consistent and egalitarian roles and norms that are not static over time. Members need to know what is expected of them and what they can expect from one another. Well-functioning families appreciate the evolving process of family life, recognizing the stages from children growing up and leaving home to parents growing older and dying. Family strengths have changing patterns of adaptation at different times in the life cycle to meet the various developmental phases. In families with small children, for example, close and protective bonds are required for children to become secure. While during the teen years there is a necessary shift in dynamics to enable more autonomy for the adolescent.

Resilience

Resilience is the capacity to endure and grow in response to crisis and challenge. It is being able to bounce back after adversity (Barnard, 1994). Members of strong families model for one another the effective management of crises or long-term stresses. Many robust families report that after weathering a crisis together, their relationships become more caring and compassionate than prior to the adversity. They believe that they can influence both good and bad things that happen; they are not victims of circumstances. Resilient family members are not afraid to reach out to others for help in a time of need.

Needed Social Policy Reform

The most important factor in strengthening families is creating social policy that supports family life. This point is addressed by Don Browning and his colleagues (1997) in a thoughtful book titled *From Culture Wars to Common Ground: Religion and the American Family Debate*. The authors give several examples of how social policy needs to be reformed to better nurture families, such as by reducing the workweek.

More people are working longer hours and have less time to be with their families than ever before. American businesses have increased workloads, extended hours, and reduced staff to remain competitive. In 1992, Americans worked 320 hours more than German and French workers (Browning et al., 1997). According to psychologist Mary Pipher (1996), parents now spend 40 percent less time with their children than their parents did in the 1950s. American families need both quality time and quantity time together in order to become strong and resilient, and this will require changes in social policy.

Summary

When pastoral care assessments and treatments are developed and implemented, it is important to take into account the strengths families and individuals have as resources in facing these problems. The strengths-based approach can help a person involved in family ministry be more aware and supportive of the protective and preventive elements that fortify and restore a family.

References

Barnard, C. P. (1994). Resiliency: A shift in our perception. *The American Journal of Family Therapy, 22(2)*, 135–144.

Browning, D. S., Miller-McLemore, B. J., Couture, P. D., Lyon, K. B., and Franklin, R. M. (1997). *From Culture Wars to Common Ground: Religion and the American Family Debate*. Louisville: Westminster John Knox Press.

Heaton, T. B. (1984). Religious homogamy and marital satisfaction reconsidered. *Journal of Marriage and the Family, 46*, 729–733.

Larson, L. E., and Goltz, J. W. (1989). Religious participation and marital commitment. *Review of Religious Research, 30*, 387–400.

Markman, H. J., and Hahlweg, K. (1993). The prediction and prevention of marital distress: An international perspective. *Clinical Psychology Review, 13*, 29–43.

McCubbin, H. I., and McCubbin, M. A. (1986). Resilient families, competencies, supports and coping over the life cycle. In L. Sawyers (Ed.), *Faith and Families* (pp. 65–88). Philadelphia: Geneva Press.

Olson, D. H. (1989). *Families: What Makes Them Work*. Newbury Park, CA: Sage Publications.

Pipher, M. B. (1996). *The Shelter of Each Other: Rebuilding Our Families*. New York: G. P. Putnam's Sons.

Stinnett, N., and DeFrain, J. (1985). *Secrets of Strong Families*. Boston: Little, Brown, & Co.

Stinnett, N., Sanders, G., DeFrain, J., and Parkhurst, A. (1982). A nationwide study of families who perceive themselves as strong. *Family Perspective, 16(1)*, 15–22.

Weaver, A. J., Koenig, H. G., and Larson, D. B. (1997). Marital and family therapists and the clergy: A need for clinical collaboration, training and research. *Journal of Marital and Family Therapy, 23(1)*, 13–25.

Wuerffel, J., DeFrain, J., and Stinnett, N. (1990). How strong families use humor. *Family Perspective, 24(2)*, 129–141.

Garland, D. R. (1999). *Family Ministry: A Comprehensive Guide.* Downers Grove, IL: InterVarsity Press.

Hendrix, H., and Hunt, H. (1998). *Giving the Love That Heals: A Guide for Parents.* New York: Pocket Books.

Markman, H., Stanley, S., Blumberg, S. L., and Edell, D. S. (1994). *Fighting for Your Marriage: Positive Steps for Preventing Divorce and Preserving a Lasting Love.* San Francisco: Jossey-Bass Publishers.

Olson, D. H., and DeFrain, J. (1996). *Marriage and the Family Systems, Diversity, and Strengths.* Mountain View, CA: Mayfield Publishing.

Walsh, F. (1998). *Strengthening Family Resilience.* New York: Guilford Press.

Resources

Diversity in American Families

Demographic changes in recent decades mean the United States quickly is becoming a multiracial, multicultural, and multilingual society. Current racial and ethnic minorities are projected to become the majority by 2010 (Sue, 1991). The 2000 census paints a stunning portrait not only of the decline of the traditional two-parent American family and the rise of single-parent households, but also of ethnic diversity transforming a culture once dominated by descendants of European immigrants into a complex but rich society of multiethnic faces. Both immigration patterns and differential birth rates among racial and ethnic groups are behind this phenomenon (Aponte and Crouch, 2000; Sue, Arredondo, and McDavis, 1995). These changing demographics may be reflected in the ethnic composition of congregations around the country.

Religious groups and their leaders have often been at the forefront of social movements that seek to better the lives of ethnic minorities. Many of the leaders of the civil rights movement were ministers of African-American churches. African-American religious leaders continue to be the most recognized spokespersons for their communities. Presbyterian and other churches played a large role leading and supporting the Asian-American movement of the 1960s and 1970s in its efforts to bring attention to the issues and needs of immigrant groups. The Catholic Church was, and continues to be, supportive of the needs of many Hispanic constituencies, from ministering to migrant workers in the agricultural fields of California to providing sanctuary for undocumented residents. These long-term, positive relationships between faith and ethnic communities provide a basis for developing and strengthening the consultation and communication between minority groups and religious professionals.

One of the most trusted occupations in this country is clergy, and they are often the only professionals consulted for mental health problems (Weaver, 1995). This is especially true for members of many ethnic groups that seldom utilize mental health services for a variety of reasons. Most problems brought to pastors revolve around marriage, family, and parenting issues (Weaver, Koenig, and Larson, 1997). Thus, it is important that clergy are familiar with some of the background issues for minority persons whom they may have opportunities to counsel. The purpose of this chapter is to provide basic information on the four major ethnic groups in the

United States, with a goal toward positively affecting pastoral counseling with persons from these communities.

Understanding Diverse Families

Families come together in a specific culture and people and through shared assumptions, values, norms, and beliefs, recognize who they are. The strength of a culture is in its ability to socialize and shape identity, both personal and social. While there are many historical experiences that ethnic groups share, it is important to remember that there are also differences within the same communities.

We believe that all families have strengths as well as limitations and that both must be held in tension for a full and accurate assessment. Diversity across the spectrum—ethnicity, gender, age, status, religion, etc.—is positively valued. Preventive strategies and programs that build on family and cultural strengths provide a needed balance to most social programs that are remedial in scope and that focus only on family dysfunction with limited capacity for lasting change (Schorr, 1988; 1997).

In the following sections, we highlight some of the strengths and differences gleaned from demographics among and within several ethnic groups.

African-Americans

According to the U.S. census, African-Americans numbered thirty-one million in the 1990s—about 12 percent of the total population. More than one half of them lived in the South. Their median age was twenty-eight years, with one third of the population under the age of eighteen and 8 percent over the age of sixty-five. Eighty-two percent of adults had completed at least four years of high school, and 12 percent were college graduates. Seventeen percent of men and 24 percent of women worked in managerial and professional specialty occupations. In terms of family structure, 47 percent were married-couples, 45 percent were families headed by women without husbands, and 8 percent were maintained by men without wives. Thirty-six percent of children lived with two parents, and 16 percent of African-American families had five or more members. Forty-eight percent of all married-couple families had incomes of $50,000 or more, and 46 percent of African-American heads of households were homeowners. Twenty-nine percent of African-American families were poor, while 48 percent of those families maintained by a woman lived below the poverty line (U.S. Department of Commerce, 1993; 2000). Their history of suffering has given birth to a full and rich bodily spirituality evidenced in religious and secular music, art, political and scientific accomplishments, letters, and athletic prominence. American pop culture is virtually dominated by African-American artists. Many of their religious leaders have been on the forefront in challenging and disclosing their struggles against the racism that pervades our society.

Hispanics

Hispanics include persons of Mexican, Puerto Rican, Central and South American, and Cuban ancestry. According to the U.S. census, the Hispanic population is growing faster than the rest of the American population due to high birthrates and immigration levels. By 2050, it is projected that 1 in 4 Americans will be Hispanic. Hispanics numbered twenty-seven million in the 1990s—about 10 percent of the total population. Their median age was twenty-six years. But for those of Mexican origin, the median age was twenty-four years, and for those of Cuban origin, it was forty-three years. Over one third of Hispanics were foreign-born. Fifty-one percent of adults had completed at least four years of high school, and about 9 percent were college graduates. Eleven percent of men and 16 percent of women worked in managerial and professional specialty occupations. In terms of family structure, 68 percent were married couples, and 25 percent were families headed by women without husbands. Eleven percent of Hispanics were unemployed, with a range of 7 percent for Cubans to 14 percent for Puerto Ricans. Overall median income for Hispanics was $23,670 in 1993. Twenty-seven percent of families were poor, ranging from 17 percent of Cuban families to 35 percent of Puerto Rican families (U.S. Department of Commerce, 1995). Obviously, there are variations within the Hispanic groups in terms of immigration status, age, educational attainment, and socioeconomic status. Other variations include cultural heritage, ethnic identity, and language. Their culture's mystical spirituality beautifully emerges in their architecture, music, and works of art and fiction. The strength of their ties to religion and family affiliations have bolstered hope in their struggles to overcome the oppressive poverty and political forces to which they have been subjected.

American Indians and Alaska Natives

According to the U.S. census, American Indians and Alaska Natives numbered 2.4 million in the year 2000—about 0.9 percent of the total population. About one half of them live in the West. The states with the largest American Indian and Alaska Native populations were California, Oklahoma, Arizona, New Mexico, Washington, and Alaska. Their median age was twenty-seven years. Sixty-six percent of adults had completed at least four years of high school, and 9 percent were college graduates or higher. Eighteen percent worked in managerial and professional specialty occupations. In terms of family structure, 65 percent were married couples, 26 percent were families headed by women without husbands, and 9 percent were maintained by men without wives. American Indians and Alaska Natives had a median household income of $30,784 in the late 1990s. The poverty rate was 25 percent (U.S. Census Bureau, 1995; 2000). Their cultures are replete with an ecological spirituality that views all of life as connected. Their appreciation of the earth as a living being entrusted to their care echoes the beliefs of many indigenous peoples. The devastation of the natural environment and the confining of tribal groups to barren reservations have cut them off from the source of their spiritual power that is tied to the land.

Asian-Americans and Pacific Islanders

Asian-Americans and Pacific Islanders, also called Asian Pacific Islanders (APIs) by the federal government, include many groups. Some of the largest Asian-American populations are Chinese, Filipino, Japanese, Asian Indian, Korean, Vietnamese, Thai, Cambodian, Laotian, and Hmong. The Pacific Islanders category includes such groups as Hawaiians, Samoans, Tongans, and Micronesians.

According to the U.S. census, Asian Pacific Islanders numbered 10.9 million in 1999—about 4 percent of the total population. More than half of this population lived in the West, while one fifth lived in the South and another fifth resided in the Northeast. The vast majority of APIs (96 percent) lived in metropolitan areas. Their median age was thirty-one years, with 29 percent of the population under the age of eighteen and 7 percent over the age of sixty-five. Eighty-five percent of adults had completed at least four years of high school, and 42 percent were college graduates. Only 4 percent of the population is unemployed. Thirty seven percent of men and 36 percent of women worked in managerial and professional specialty occupations. In terms of family structure, 80 percent were married couples, 13 percent were families headed by women without husbands, and 7 percent were maintained by men without wives. Twenty-three percent of families had five or more members, and 16 percent of those maintained by women had five or more members. The range of income levels within the API population is wide. While one third of families had incomes of $75,000 or more, one fifth had incomes of less than $25,000. Thirteen percent of all API families were poor. Among families maintained by a woman with no husband, 29 percent lived below the poverty line (Humes and McKinnon, 2000; U.S. Department of Commerce, 1995). API groups differ in language, culture, and generation, or length of residence in the United States.

Although the statistics above may lead to the general impression that APIs are doing well in the United States, it is necessary to examine data between subgroups to get a clearer picture. The more "successful" APIs in terms of education, occupation, and income level tend to be Chinese-,

Japanese-, and Filipino-Americans, whose families have been in this country for several generations. The less educated and poorer groups tend to be the ones that immigrated within the last two or three decades or that came to this country as refugees. For many Asian-Americans and Pacific Islanders the common bond is the experience of racism and discrimination as ethnic groups in this country. Asian-American culture is a social-centered system in which the individual is understood not autonomously but within a network of extended family relationships and affiliations. Their cultural values of pragmatism, dedication to education, and dutiful obedience to authority are grounded in tradition. Pacific Islander youth are undergoing a renaissance in their language and cultural traditions. They are being taught ancient navigating skills, or "way-finding," to journey out into the ocean, guided by only the winds, stars, and tides.

Summary

Hispanics and Asian-Americans may also be refugees from politically unstable or war-torn countries. Despite the federal categorizations and similar histories and experiences among African-Americans, Native Americans, Hispanics, Asian-Americans, and Pacific Islanders, it bears repeating that there exist differences within groups in regard to cultural background, language, religion, socioeconomic status, condition of health, educational achievement, family structure, immigration history, and geographical residence, among other variables. They face many of the same stressors as European-Americans of education, jobs, housing, marriage, and health. However, there are the additional stressors of racism, prejudice, and oppression (Aponte and Johnson, 2000). Racism is thought to be a factor in substance abuse problems for African-Americans, Hispanics, and American Indians. It may also be a factor in child abuse and suicide for American Indians and in domestic violence for Asian-Americans (Aponte and Johnson, 2000). For all of these groups, traditional social support in the forms of extended families and flexible roles may not be enough to effectively counter all the stressors (Aponte and Crouch, 2000).

Multicultural Counseling

A basic premise of family and multicultural counseling perspectives is that an individual is shaped by his or her family and culture. In order to understand a person, one must consider the family and culture of origin (Gushue and Sciarra, 1995). An individual's or family's behavior can therefore only be understood from within the social and cultural context in which it occurs (American Counseling Association, 1991). For example, a family member's silence in one culture may mean agreement; in another culture, silence may be a way of disagreeing in deference to the family relationships and to the need for "saving face." Clergy counseling with an individual need to try to understand the person's family of origin and its behaviors, values, and communication patterns, or in the very least, recognize the limits of their own experience. Counselors are trained about the dangers of "cultural encapsulation," or the stance that there is only one set of cultural values and assumptions. To make absolute one's own cultural worldview would be to argue for the superiority of one language, one view of the world, and one race out of the many diverse ways of being human.

In particular, clergy who are counseling an individual need to try to understand the person's family of origin and its behaviors, values, and communication patterns. These can then be compared to "typical" family patterns within the same culture. Next, the counselor can look at cultural differences within the family itself. Various family members can be at different places on the road of cultural transition. In the past, ethnic families of all classes have been compared to middle-class European-American families and deemed inadequate. Similarly, it is not helpful to assume that all "Mexican-American" or "Chinese-American" families, for example, are alike.

Gushue and Sciarra (1995) provide a multidimensional approach to working with diverse families. Dynamics to consider include: (a) acculturation level, which is the degree to which members of a minority group have learned the dominant culture. Often, age and exposure to the American culture are significant here. For example, in a Vietnamese immigrant family, parents who work in a factory with other Vietnamese immigrants are usually less acculturated, less familiar with American ways, and less proficient in English than their children who go to school and come in contact daily with American peers. It is common for children of immigrants to become translators for their parents in everyday situations, such as at the doctor's office or grocery store. It is also common for conflict to occur between less acculturated parents and their more Americanized children over the children's behaviors in areas such as dating and socializing. Differing levels of acculturation can affect the ways that family members react to counseling; (b) identity issues. Racial or cultural identity is "an individual's psychological orientation to membership in both the dominant and nondominant cultures in the United States" (Gushue and Sciarra, 1995, p. 591). This includes what persons think about themselves, about members of the minority group, about other minority groups, and about the dominant group. Ethnic minorities may experience identities on a continuum from having a positive racial identity to feeling self-hate as a result of racism; and (c) language ability. Family members often have different levels of fluency in the language of origin and in English. There are frequently problems when children have increased power in the family because of their English skills.

Mental health professionals have developed competencies or guidelines for those who strive to address the challenges of working with diverse individuals. Characteristics of a culturally skilled counselor include: (a) actively becoming aware of his or her own assumptions about human behavior, values, biases, preconceived notions, personal limitations, and so forth; (b) actively attempting to understand the worldview of his or her culturally different client without negative judgments; and (c) actively developing and practicing appropriate, relevant, and sensitive intervention strategies and skills in working with his or her culturally different client (Sue and Sue, 1990).

Referral to a Mental Health Specialist

Ethnic minorities have low rates of mental health services utilization. They have high premature termination rates caused by such reasons as distrust of, or misunderstandings about, mainstream social institutions, fear of treatment, lack of medical insurance, and inability to afford such services. Racism and stereotyping within the mental health system have led to a fear of treatment for some. Cultural factors, such as the lack of bicultural staff at mental health centers and the individual's use of culture-based coping practices, also serve to prevent ethnic minorities from seeking help. Practical matters, such as lack of information on the availability of services or lack of health insurance, also come into play (see Kurasaki, Sue, Chun, and Gee, 2000, for a brief review).

Clergy can take steps to alleviate some of these barriers. They should try to familiarize themselves with, and feel comfortable about, referring people to mental health agencies that are located in ethnic communities and that have bilingual, bicultural staff and program goals and services that match the community's needs. Clergy also can identify parishioners or professionals who can act as interpreters. Formal and informal connections between churches and mental health agencies positively affect ethnic groups' awareness of services and make the groups more likely to use the agencies when needed (Aponte and Bracco, 2000). These can take the form of reciprocal presentations, community forums, community health fairs, classes, workshops, support groups, or other forms of outreach involving clergy and mental health professionals. The identification of "culture brokers," key informants from the parishioner's culture, to consult with is also helpful (Fadiman, 1997). Seeking insight into persons' culture via social groups and cultural societies from their ethnic background will provide an array of resources for supporting the family.

In recent years, healthcare systems have begun to open up their biomedical perspective in acknowledging and including religious and cultural concerns in the standards by which health care facilities are accredited and in the classification of mental illness (DSM-IV). It is a recognition that an understanding of human nature and the human person is not exhausted by a biological living systems approach but must include concerns about culture as well as that of the human spirit for meaning, transcendence, and connection (or in their religious formulations: faith, hope, and love). Clergy stand at an important cultural and religious convergence, making them prime candidates to influence and support multiethnic care in the wider community.

Resources

—American Psychological Association (APA), Public Interest Directorate, Office of Ethnic Minority Affairs, 750 First Street, NE, Washington, DC 20002; (202) 336-5500; www.apa.org/pi/oema. Website for the office whose goals include increasing the public knowledge of special psychological resources and of mental health needs in communities of color. Has brochures and books that can be ordered on-line.

—National Association of Social Workers (NASW), 750 First Street, NE, Suite 700, Washington, DC 20002; (800) 638-8799; www.naswdc.org/DIVERSTY.htm. Website for the association has a section on the topic of "diversity." Includes newsletters of the NASW caucuses for the four major ethnic groups and for topics on lesbian, gay, and bisexual issues, as well as women's issues.

—United States Census, www.census.gov/pubinfo/www/hotlinks.html. Website with information on the four major ethnic minority groups.

References

American Counseling Association. (1991). Special Issue: Multiculturalism as a Fourth Force in Counseling. *Journal of Counseling and Development, 70(1)*.

Aponte, J. F., and Bracco, H. F. (2000). Community approaches with ethnic populations. In J. F. Aponte and J. Wohl (Eds.), *Psychological Intervention and Cultural Diversity* (pp. 131–148). Boston: Allyn & Bacon.

Aponte, J. F., and Crouch, R. T. (2000). The changing ethnic profile in the United States. In J. F. Aponte and J. Wohl (Eds.), *Psychological Intervention and Cultural Diversity* (pp. 1–17). Boston: Allyn & Bacon.

Aponte, J. F., and Johnson, L. R. (2000). The impact of culture on the intervention and treatment of ethnic populations. In J. F. Aponte and J. Wohl (Eds.), *Psychological Intervention and Cultural Diversity* (pp. 18–39). Boston: Allyn & Bacon.

Fadiman, A. (1997). *The Spirit Catches You and You Fall Down: A Hmong Child, Her American Doctors, and the Collision of Two Cultures*. New York: Farrar, Straus, and Giroux.

Gushue, G. V., and Sciarra, D. T. (1995). Culture and families: A multidimensional approach. In J. G. Ponterotto, J. M. Casas, L. A. Suzuki, and C. M. Alexander (Eds.), *Handbook of Multicultural Counseling* (pp. 586–606). Thousand Oaks, CA: Sage Press.

Humes, K., and McKinnon, J. (2000). The Asian and Pacific Islander Population in the United States: March 1999. U.S. Census Bureau, Current Population Reports, Series P20–529, U.S. Government Printing Office, Washington, DC.

Kurasaki, K. S., Sue, S., Chun, C., and Gee, K. (2000). Ethnic minority intervention and treatment research. In J. F. Aponte and J. Wohl (Eds.), *Psychological Intervention and Cultural Diversity* (pp. 234–249). Boston: Allyn & Bacon.

Schorr, L. B. (1989). *Within Our Reach: Breaking the Cycle of Disadvantage*. New York: Anchor Books, Doubleday.

Schorr, L. B. (1998). *Common Purpose: Strengthening Families and Neighborhoods to Rebuild America*. New York: Anchor Books, Doubleday.

Sue, D. W. (1991). A conceptual model for cultural diversity training. *Journal of Counseling and Development, 70*, 99–105.

Sue, D. W., Arredondo, P., and McDavis, R. J. (1995). Multicultural counseling competencies and standards: A call to the profession. In J. G. Ponterotto, J. M. Casas, L. A. Suzuki, and C. M. Alexander (Eds.), *Handbook of Multicultural Counseling* (pp. 624–644). Thousand Oaks, CA: Sage Press.

Sue, D. W., and Sue, D. (1990). *Counseling the Culturally Different: Theory and Practice*. New York: John Wiley & Sons.

U.S. Census Bureau (1995, August). Selected social and economic characteristics for the 25 largest American Indian Tribes. http://www.census.gov/population/socdemo/race/indian/ailang2.txt.

U.S. Census Bureau (2000, October 23). American Indian Heritage Month: November 2000. CB00-FF.13. http://www.census.gov/Press-Release/www/2000/cb00ff13.html.

U.S. Department of Commerce (1993, March). Black Americans: A Profile. Bureau of the Census Statistical Brief/93-2. http://www.census.gov.

U.S. Department of Commerce (1995, September). The Nation's Hispanic Population—1994. Bureau of the Census Statistical Brief/95-25. http://www.census.gov.

U.S. Department of Commerce (1995, November). The Nation's Asian and Pacific Islander Population—1994. Bureau of the Census Statistical Brief/95-24. http://www.census.gov.

U.S. Department of Commerce (2000, February). Profile of the country's African-American Population Released by the Census Bureau. http://www.census.gov/Press-Release/www/2000/ch00-27.html.

Weaver, A. J. (1995). Has there been a failure to prepare and support parish-based clergy in their role as front-line community mental health workers? A review. *The Journal of Pastoral Care, 49(2)*, 129–149.

Weaver, A. J., Koenig, H. G., and Larson, D. B. (1997). Marital and family therapists and the clergy: A need for clinical collaboration, training and research. *Journal of Marital and Family Therapy, 23(1)*, 13–25.

PART TWO

Case Studies

Case 1

Marriage Preparation

"They Were Planning the Wedding"

Charlene and William met at the church young adult group. The twenty-five-year-olds had dated for a year and now came to see Pastor Hobb about preparing for their wedding. The couple knew that the church required marriage preparation sessions at least six months before the ceremony. Both came from families where there had been a divorce and were motivated to participate in the marriage preparation program. This was the first marriage for these psychologically minded college graduates.

Pastor Hobb explained that the congregation saw the ministry of marriage preparation as a primary mission. After years of watching marriages that began with great joy and promise and ended tragically in divorce and pain, the church decided to research what could be done to prevent marital distress. They found scientific evidence that certain types of marriage preparation can lower the risk of marital difficulties and divorce. Studies indicate that couples can learn skills and enhance ways of thinking prior to marriage that significantly increase the likelihood of marital success (Hahlweg, Markman, Thurmaier, Engl, and Eckert, 1998). The clergy and laity of the church, along with several other congregations in the community, developed a comprehensive, scientifically based marriage preparation program.

The pastor explained that experts have found that a waiting period of six or more months from the engagement to the service maximizes the learning process involved in marriage preparation. This is true because as the time of the wedding approaches, romantic feelings overshadow the reality of a relationship and leave less opportunity for reflection and learning new skills.

Pastoral Assessment

During the first premarital counseling session, Pastor Hobb explained the importance of the program in creating an atmosphere in which to talk openly about their relationship and in providing concrete issues to work on. Its primary goals are to teach communication and conflict-management skills and to enhance the positive dimensions of a relationship, especially commitment. The program is designed to help a couple handle their issues respectfully and to aid them in clarifying and evaluating expectations. Many studies show that unhappy couples interact more negatively than happy ones.

Pastor Hobb emphasized that after several years of experience, the church had found that the program boosted couples' understanding of their commitment and enhanced the positive bonding that comes from fun, friendship, and faith. Early in a marriage, patterns are formed for communicating, resolving conflict, and negotiating differences that influence long-term marital satisfaction. When couples do not know how to protect the positive aspects of their relationship from destructive patterns of conflict, these patterns will grow over time and erode the positive feelings. Happy couples are those who have learned how to protect the good in their relationship and limit the effect of the negative. Pastor Hobb emphasized that the church's role is not to judge if a couple should marry but to assist them in their decision making.

Relevant History

Charlene and William share several characteristics that have been shown to lower the risk of marital distress and divorce, including similar levels of education, marriage after age twenty-two, lack of premarital cohabitation (Bumpass, Martin, and Sweet, 1991), shared religious beliefs and practices (Maneker and Rankin, 1993), knowing the partner for over a year before marriage, and similar attitudes toward life (Kurdek, 1993). However, they share one factor that has been shown to increase the risk of marital difficulties and dissolution, which is parental divorce (Glenn and Kramer, 1987). The most powerful predictors of marital problems and divorce are destructive, negative patterns of behavior used by couples when addressing conflict and disagreement (Markman and Hahlweg, 1993).

Diagnostic Criteria

In the U.S., couples have a nearly 50 percent chance of divorcing—one of the most stressful events that a person can experience (Kitson and Morgan, 1990). Marital distress and dissolution are major risk factors for emotional problems in both children and adults. In the past several decades, the number of children affected by divorce has increased dramatically; nearly 1 in 3 children born in the U.S. in the 1990s will experience the disruption of a divorce, as compared to 1 in 10 in 1970 (Norton and Miller, 1992). About one third of all children of divorce have long-term emotional difficulties (Kurtz, 1994).

In 1970, 69 of 100 couples who married were doing so for the first time, while the remaining 31 involved the remarriage of one of the partners. By 1995, 54 in 100 were first marriages for both, and 46 in 100 involved partners who were remarrying. Clergy are much more likely to perform weddings and premarital counseling for those who are remarrying than they were a generation or two ago. Couples who are remarrying often face different and more complex issues than those in first marriages, such as how to form a blended family and stepparenting demands.

An alternative to treating the problems of divorce and marriage difficulties is to provide preventive care while the couple are in the early stages of building a relationship. With a large range of problems traceable to marital distress and divorce, increasing attention is being paid to prevention (Sayers, Kohn, and Heavey, 1998). Several years after their involvement, couples participating in one marriage preparation program (Prevention and Relationship Enhancement Program [PREP]) were found to have at least a 50 percent lower rate of negative interactions, greater satisfaction in their relationship, and lower risk of physical aggression than those who had not participated in the premarital program (Markman, Renick, Floyd, Stanley, and Clements, 1993).

The church designed its marriage preparation program after the PREP approach, created by psychologists Howard Markmann, Scott Stanley, and colleagues at the University of Denver. The PREP model is based on fifteen years of research and has demonstrated effectiveness through its focus on teaching couples skills to improve their communications (Sayers et al., 1998). The church offers the PREP, a twelve-hour program, in one Saturday and three weeknight sessions or in a full weekend schedule. Groups of three to five couples meet together with two facilitators to minimize the cost. The group facilitators are laymembers of the congregation who have taken special training for this ministry. The sessions use a mini-lecture, discussion, and interpersonal skill practice format in which couples work together and with the facilitator. Most of the program focuses on communication skills and conflict resolution. Dysfunctional patterns are identified and functional ones are practiced with role-playing methods using concrete examples that the couples bring to the sessions. An important part of the program addresses the meaning of Christian marriage and commitment. Communal meals and worship allow for fellowship with other couples and for reflection on their faith and marital commitment.

During the marriage preparation program, Charlene and William were able to work on an issue that had caused problems in their relationship. William had a tendency to withdraw and not want to talk to Charlene about what was going on with him. When an issue was important to her, his avoidance was frustrating and made her want to pursue it even more vigorously. Sometimes this escalated into angry name-calling and hurt

Response to Vignette

feelings. During the marriage preparation, they worked on some agreed-upon techniques and strategies for dealing with this problem. The communication skills they developed in the program gave them guidelines for keeping their conversations safer and under control. They also gained more empathy for one another when they understood that men and women are socialized to communicate differently and that the patterns of withdrawal in men and pursuit in women are common. Men (or women) who tend to avoid talking things out with their spouses are actually more likely to be avoiding conflict than intimacy. When both partners in a marriage agree on ways to handle difficult issues, frustrating cycles such as one pursuing and the other withdrawing can be changed.

The church also offers couples an aftercare program. Mentoring couples from the congregation are available to continue working with Charlene and William after the wedding, if they want more practice with their new skills or need support and counsel. The pastor makes an appointment to see each couple six months after the wedding to find out how they are doing as the reality of married life progresses.

Treatment Within the Faith Community

Marriages are more likely to endure when they are supported by communities of people committed to them. Faith-based communities are the largest group of institutions in our society that have both a vested interest in preventing marital breakdown and the capability to deliver premarital (and marital) counseling and education. Three out of 4 weddings are performed in a church or synagogue, and the great majority of clergy offer some type of premarital counseling. Since 1995, nearly all of the 175 Catholic dioceses in the U.S. have required marriage preparation (Sayers et al., 1998).

Although almost all Protestant clergy require counseling sessions prior to performing a wedding, only one half of mainline Protestant clergy have formal training in premarital counseling (Jones and Stahmann, 1994), and many lack confidence in addressing premarital counseling issues. In a national sample of almost 2,000 United Methodist pastors, only 41 percent felt they were competent as premarital or marriage counselors (Orthner, 1986). In a separate study of Protestant clergy from five states, less than half (46 percent) indicated that they felt adequately trained in premarital counseling. On a hopeful note, the majority reported that they had participated in post-seminary training in premarital counseling to enhance their skills. A nearly unanimous 99 percent thought course work in premarital counseling should be required during seminary—where it is frequently not included (Wylie, 1984).

At the same time, engaged couples indicate that they are three times more likely to prefer counseling from clergypersons than from mental health specialists, and this rate is much higher among those who are religiously committed. Engaged couples report that they believe clergy are trustworthy advisers and are to be taken seriously when they make a referral for additional premarital assistance or counseling (Williams, 1992). The obvious trust that the public places in clergy to be good counselors and advisers highlights the obligation the faith community has to more effectively trained clergy in the area of marriage preparation.

Couples who are involved in physical or psychological abuse must be referred to a mental health professional for additional counseling before a wedding is performed. Psychological abuse may include intimidation, extreme jealousy, and terrorizing. Physical abuse may include pushing, slapping, kicking, and the use of a weapon. Physical violence and psychological abuse are never acceptable, and every person has a right to be safe and respected.

Indications for Referral

In the United States, stepfamilies are fast becoming the most common family form. Remarriages outnumber first marriages by 3 to 2 (Norton and Miller, 1992), and about 30 percent of weddings performed by clergy involve them (Jones and Stahmann, 1994). Remarriages are at higher risk for dissolution than first marriages, and those with children present from a prior relationship are even more prone to divorce than those with no children (White and Booth, 1985). Many couples enter married life with either overly optimistic expectations that their stepfamily will rapidly develop a close bond or with little planning regarding the unique problems inherent in stepfamily living. Most remarried couples need to revise their preconceptions and construct a realistic model of married life. A mental health specialist trained to work with stepfamilies about expectations prior to forming a blended family can be an important preventive adjunct to traditional premarital counseling.

Treatment by Mental Health Specialist

A high-risk group for divorce and marital distress is the several hundred thousand interfaith couples married in the U.S. each year. For example, between one third to one half of all Jewish-Americans will choose a partner who is not born Jewish (Greenstein, Carlson, and Howell, 1993). In a California study, it was found that when both individuals in the marriage are Jewish, 70 percent remain married five or more years; when one of the partners is Jewish and one is non-Jewish, only 53 percent remain married five years or more (Maneker and Rankin, 1993). The issue of significant differences in faith needs to be addressed in marriage preparation.

Cross-Cultural Issues

National Resources

Resources

—Engaged Encounter, Catholic Family Services; (800) 788-4616; www.encounter.org; is an offshoot of Marriage Encounter weekends created in the Roman Catholic Church in the 1960s. Through a series of topics (romance, disagreements, decision making, expectations/attitudes, careers, family life, children, money, sexuality, the church, and society) presented by priest and married-couple leaders, engaged couples are encouraged to dialogue. The primary emphasis is on communication as a couple explores mutual strengths and weaknesses. Communal meals and worship allow for fellowship with other couples. Engaged Encounter is Catholic in focus, but anyone may attend. United Methodist, Lutheran, Presbyterian, Episcopal, and Assembly of God Engaged Encounter groups exist in some locations.

—Enrich Canada Inc; Postal Bag 2042, Saint Albert, Alberta T8N 2G3; (888) 973-3650; 105035.2236@compuserve.com; is the Prepare/Enrich Program in Canada.

—FOCCUS (Facilitating Open Couple Communications, Understanding, and Study) Family Life Office, 3214 North Sixtieth Street, Omaha, NE 68104; (888) 874-2684; www.foccusinc.com; has developed a widely used premarital inventory, which asks couples to react to issues of communication, conflict resolution, finances, faith, family and friends, leisure, sexuality, and role relationship within the future marriage.

—Marriage Savers, Inc; 9311 Harrington Drive, Potomac, MD 20854; (301) 469-5873; www.marriagesavers.org; is a national faith-based organization designed to help prepare, strengthen, and restore marriages. Churches agree to a minimum of four months' marriage preparation with at least four counseling sessions in which a premarital inventory is used and mentor couples are trained in each church to work as role models and counselors with engaged couples. Pastors also agree to meet with newlyweds twice in their first year of marriage and to encourage all married couples to attend a couples retreat such as Marriage Encounter. The group has helped the clergy of 30-plus denominations in 108 cities adopt Community Marriage Policies in the U.S. and Canada.

—PREP (Prevention and Relationship Enhancement Program), P.O. Box 102530, Denver, CO 80250-2530; (800) 366-0166; prepinc@aol.com; has books, videos, audiotapes, and workshops available for those who wish training. PREP and Christian PREP offer three-day training workshops for mental health professionals, pastors, and layleaders interested in helping couples build strong marriages. Participants learn to conduct premarital/marital PREP workshops in their churches or communities. The techniques can also be used in counseling settings to counteract destructive relational patterns.

—Prepare/Enrich, P.O. Box 190, Minneapolis, MN 55440-0190; www.lifeinnovation.com; works with professional counselors and clergy to provide premarital counseling and marriage enrichment using the Prepare/Enrich Program. Couples take an inventory and meet with a counselor in three to six sessions to receive feedback based on the results of the inventory. Over five hundred training workshops are offered each year.

Self-Help Resources

Becoming Married: Family Living in Pastoral Perspective (Herbert Anderson and R. Cotton Fite, Louisville: Westminster John Knox Press, 1993).

Before the Wedding: Look Before You Leap (Michael E. Cavanagh, Louisville: Westminister John Knox Press, 1994).

Fighting for Your Marriage: Positive Steps for Preventing Divorce and Preserving a Lasting Love (Howard Markman, Scott Stanley, Susan L. Blumberg, and Dean S. Edell, San Francisco: Jossey-Bass Publishers, 1996). The book shows that commitment, communication, and conflict resolution are three critical skills for effective married living and that skill-building in these areas can be taught. It has a clear, readable presentation of solid research findings.

Getting the Love You Want: A Guide for Couples (Harville Hendrix, New York: Henry Holt & Co., 2001).

The Interfaith Family Guidebook: Practical Advice for Jewish and Christian Partners (Joan C. Hawxhurst, Kalamazoo, MI: Dovetail Publishing, 1998). Over one million Jewish/Christian couples in the United States face the challenges and opportunities inherent to their decision to marry. This balanced and open-minded book is for families living with two faiths in one household. It offers these families a look at the many questions they will face and the resources available to help them find their own answers.

A Lasting Promise: A Christian Guide to Fighting for Your Marriage (Scott Stanley, Daniel W. Trathen, and B. Milton Bryan, San Francisco: Jossey-Bass Publishers, 1998). This is an evangelical Christian version of the book *Fighting for Your Marriage*.

Marriage Savers: Helping Your Friends and Family Avoid Divorce (Michael J. McManus, Grand Rapids: Zondervan, 1995).

Premarital and Remarital Counseling: The Professional's Handbook (Robert F. Stahmann and William J. Hiebert, San Francisco: Jossey-Bass Publishers, 1997). This is a very helpful book for clergy. It discusses issues related to counseling those marrying for the first time, as well as to the increasing numbers of individuals who remarry.

The Seven Principles for Making Marriage Work (John Mordechai Gottman and Nan Silver, New York: Crown Publishers, 1999).

References

Bumpass, L. L., Martin, T. C., and Sweet, J. A. (1991). The impact of family background and early marital factors on marital disruption. *Journal of Family Issues, 12,* 22–42.

Glenn, N. D., and Kramer, K. B. (1987). The marriages and divorces of the children of divorce. *Journal of Marriage and the Family, 49,* 811–825.

Greenstein, D., Carlson, J., and Howell, C. W. (1993). Counseling with interfaith couples. *Individual Psychology, 49,* 428–437.

Hahlweg, K., Markman, H. J., Thurmaier, F., Engl, J., and Eckert, V. (1998). Prevention of marital distress: Results of a German prospective longitudinal study. *Journal of Family Psychology, 12*, 543–556.

Jones, E. F., and Stahmann, R. F. (1994). Clergy beliefs, preparation, and practice in premarital counseling. *Journal of Pastoral Care, 48(2)*, 181–186.

Kitson, G. C., and Morgan, L. A. (1990). The multiple consequences of divorce: A decade of review. *Journal of Marriage and Family, 52*, 913–924.

Kurdek, L. A. (1993). Predicting marital dissolution: A 5-year prospective longitudinal study of newlywed couples. *Journal of Personality and Social Psychology, 64*, 221–242.

Kurtz, L. (1994). Psychosocial coping resources in elementary school-age children of divorce. *American Journal of Orthopsychiatry, 64*, 554–563.

Maneker, J. S., and Rankin, R. P. (1993). Religious homogamy and marital duration among those who file for divorce in California, 1966–1971. *Journal of Divorce and Remarriage, 19*, 233–247.

Markman, H. J., and Hahlweg, K. (1993). The prediction and prevention of marital distress: An international perspective. *Clinical Psychology Review, 13*, 29–43.

Markman, H. J., Renick, M. J., Floyd, F. J., Stanley, S. M., and Clements, M. (1993). Preventing marital distress through communication and conflict management training: A 4- and 5-year follow up. *Journal of Consulting and Clinical Psychology, 61(1)*, 70–77.

Norton, A. J., and Miller, L. F. (1992). *Marriage, Divorce, and Remarriage in the 1990s.* U.S. Bureau of the Census, Current Population Reports, Series P-23, No. 180. Washington, DC: U.S. Government Printing Office.

Orthner, D. K. (1986). *Pastoral Counseling: Caring and Caregivers in The United Methodist Church.* Nashville: The General Board of Higher Education and Ministry of The United Methodist Church.

Sayers, S. I., Kohn, C. S., and Heavey, C. (1998). Prevention of marital dysfunction: Behavioral approaches and beyond. *Clinical Psychology Review, 18(6)*, 713–744.

White, L., and Booth, A. (1985). The quality and stability of remarriage: The role of stepchildren. *American Sociological Review, 50*, 689–698.

Williams, L. M. (1992). Premarital counseling: A needs assessment among engaged individuals. *Contemporary Family Therapy, 14(5)*, 505–516.

Wylie, W. E. (1984). Health counseling competencies needed by the minister. *Journal of Religion and Health, 23(3)*, 237–249.

Dual-Earner Families

"I'm Not Supermom"

Grace is a clerk in a department store, the mother of two boys, and the wife of Brandon. She works full-time; and her husband, a partner in a small business, usually works long hours. The children often come home to an empty house where twelve-year-old Brent is supposed to watch over seven-year-old Danny, but often they fight instead. The boys complain that no one has time for them. Grace feels guilty because, although she loves being employed, she is unhappy about not being as good a wife and mother as she would like. The house is not as clean as she would choose, she sometimes gets take-out food for dinner instead of cooking, and she is pressed to find time to accompany the boys to their various after-school activities. She has asked Brandon if he will take more responsibility at home and with the boys. Although Brandon says he is willing to be more involved, he does not follow through, using his business as an excuse for his lack of time and energy for his family. Grace is frustrated with him about this. "I want it all, but I'm not getting it right. I'm tired and stressed out all the time. Something's got to give," she told Pastor Westfall. But Grace did not know what could possibly be changed.

Pastor Gloria Westfall has known the family for a long time. Grace has always been active in the church and other volunteer activities. When she returned to work, she did not cut back on any of her outside commitments. Grace finds support in the church women's group—where some of her friends convinced her to talk to the pastor about her problems. Brandon has not cut back on his work hours, although the extra income that Grace brings in would allow him to do so.

Pastoral Assessment

Grace was a stay-at-home mother until both children were in school. She then got a job at the local shopping mall. She wanted to work, not

Relevant History

57

only to earn extra income but also to have a life outside of the home. Grace enjoys having a career and the social aspects of work. However, she often compares herself to her own mother, who was not employed outside the home. Grace believes that she should be the kind of traditional mother that she experienced as a child, in addition to a full-time employee.

Diagnostic Criteria

Cutting across all class and ethnic lines, approximately 60 percent of marriages in the United States are dual-earner couples in which both spouses are employed outside the home (Schwartz and Scott, 1994). The work patterns can have many different configurations. For example, one spouse may work part-time while the other works full-time. Another variation is a dual-career couple, in which both spouses are employed full-time and are highly invested in, and committed to, their profession (Schwartz and Scott, 1994). Dual-earner families are defined as married family units with children and two employed parents. These families must balance many aspects of their work and family life. In the United States, dual-earner families are now the norm rather than the exception (Hammer and Turner, 1990).

The increase in the number of such families over the past few decades is usually attributed to the nature of the economy (Hamilton, 1999), the women's movement, and personal reasons, such as the search for meaning and identity (Gottfried, Gottfried, and Bathurst, 1988). However, as women have increased their presence in the workplace, the workplace has not changed much. Most work settings are inflexible to the needs of parents, and most men have not adjusted to the changes that women have made as employees (Hochschild, 1990). Conventional career paths are designed for those who can put in long hours, are able to relocate, can separate their work from personal responsibilities, and can put their job above family. Furthermore, the childbearing years coincide with those that are key for career development and advancement (Deutsch, 1999). Working mothers must confront all of these barriers.

In review of the literature, Hodgson (1984) found that women are employed for financial reasons and often also for their own sense of personal satisfaction. Meaningful work tends to increase the well-being of mothers. Studies have found employed mothers are happier, more socially connected and goal-oriented, and have greater feelings of achievement and pleasure than those who are not employed. However, working mothers are challenged with job and home conflicts to resolve.

Although research suggests that men and women are changing their attitudes about gender roles and moving toward becoming increasingly egalitarian at home (Zuo and Tang, 2000), employed mothers usually continue to do the bulk of the domestic work. Most studies indicate that husbands do not do an equal share of the chores at home. Wives do twice as much housework and three times as much child care as husbands

(MacPhee, 1999). One study found that women do 77 percent of the cooking, 66 percent of the shopping, 75 percent of the cleaning, and 85 percent of the laundry (Benokratis, 1996, as cited in Hamilton, 1999). Sociologist Arlie Hochschild, a pioneer in the study of dual-earner families, estimates that women work approximately fifteen hours more per week than men. Over a year, they put in an extra month of twenty-four-hour days a year. She uses the term "second shift" to describe the work women do that is in addition to their employment. In her study of dual-earner families, Hochschild found that only 20 percent of the couples shared housework equally. Seventy percent of husbands did a substantial amount of domestic work, defined as less than 50 percent but more than one third. Ten percent of husbands did less than one third of the housework (Hochschild, 1990).

Dual-earner families devise many strategies to balance family life with employment. Recent years have seen an increase in the number of couples in which one partner works a nonstandard shift, a strategy that allows the couple to take care of their children themselves. In particular, there has been an increase in the number of families substituting fathers for paid child care. Despite this phenomenon, few fathers consistently provide more than twenty hours of care a week for newborns (Glass, 1998). When dual-earner couples "scale back" on work so that it leaves more room for family life, women do disproportionately more of the scaling back than men (Becker and Moen, 1999).

Employed mothers are torn between the demands of work and family more than their husbands, in part because women feel greater responsibility for home and children (Hochschild, 1990). Working mothers are pressed to find time for their children's needs and their own. Conflicts with their children's needs are significant stressors that may result in fatigue, emotional depletion, and guilt (Etaugh, 1984; Hochschild, 1990).

Working mothers can take comfort in knowing that most of the research on maternal employment finds no adverse effects on infants or children of any age. There are no differences in children's development from infancy through early adolescence between those who have working mothers and those who have nonworking mothers (Gottfried et al., 1988; Gottfried, Bathurst, and Gottfried, 1994). Whether mothers are employed or not, maternal role satisfaction has been found to have positive effects on children. Most research looking at the effect of a working mother on her children's educational and career aspirations shows a positive relationship. Maternal employment is linked to less stereotyped sex role concepts for school-age and adolescent boys and girls. Fathers of children with working mothers are more involved with their children (see Etaugh, 1984, and Gottfried et al., 1994, for reviews of the research).

Although studies have found few adverse effects of maternal employment, wives, husbands, and children do pay costs associated with being in a dual-earner family. Conflict may emerge as wives feel resentful of husbands who do not help enough at home or as husbands feel resentful of being asked to do more. Sacrifices may be made by wives and husbands in various arenas of their lives: work, marriage, children, and self. The many responsibilities that parents face at work, at home, and socially often lead to a dilemma known as role strain, role conflict, or role overload. Strategies to alleviate role strain include redistributing the household responsibilities among other family members, giving them to paid employees, or leaving them undone (Hammer and Turner, 1990).

In dual-earner families, women who report higher levels of marital satisfaction, less depression, and less resentment have an equitable division of labor at home (Hamilton, 1999). Equality in the division of household labor as well as in support is important for couples dealing with work and family conflict (Burley, 1995; Hochschild, 1990).

Egalitarian relationships are difficult to achieve for many reasons, including the perception that equality benefits women and costs men. Usually, wives must initiate and enforce the changes to make equality happen. But in order for that to occur, women must perceive the inequality in the marriage as unfair (Steil, 1997). Studies show that some wives do not label the so-called "second shift" unfair, often because of the value they place on domestic work and comparisons they make to their peers' situations (Gagner, 1998; Hochschild, 1990). Another obstacle to egalitarian marriages is the unwillingness of some women to relinquish responsibility or control over family matters such as domestic work. These maternal "gatekeepers" spend over five hours a week more on family work than women that are more collaborative with family members (Allen and Hawkins, 1999). Wives' views of "fairness" about family responsibilities are predicted by husbands' communicating about domestic labor, being appreciative and sympathetic, listening, and sharing in decision making (Hawkins, Marshall, and Allen, 1998). As long as husbands lend some support, especially emotional support, many women are less likely to perceive their situation as unfair. Still others choose to have a more harmonious marriage, with less conflict over household chores, over an equitable one (see Deutsch, 1999, and Hochschild, 1990, for reviews of this research).

Nevertheless, equitability and balance in wives' and husbands' roles can occur in a dual-earner family. Although the problems of such families are often characterized as issues of a working woman trying to balance work and family life, the concerns also belong to the husband and the family. Since parenting strategies change throughout a family's development, members can learn to achieve equitability and balance at any time. Patterns can change, and parenting and other roles can be renegotiated— fathers can take care of children as well as can mothers. Women can still be good mothers while sharing parenting responsibilities with fathers.

Equality can benefit a marriage and family life in many ways. As previously mentioned, research shows that men in dual-earner families are more involved with their children. Father-child relationships can deepen with this increased involvement. Shared responsibilities within the family can become a bond to intimacy instead of a source of conflict. Work and careers can also be renegotiated to accommodate shared parenting responsibilities. Mothers and fathers can remain committed to their work while limiting their hours, passing on job opportunities, adjusting career goals, and allowing family responsibilities to encroach on work responsibilities. Equality in a dual-earner family is difficult, but those who have achieved it say that the rewards gained were worth the sacrifices (Deutsch, 1999).

Response to Vignette

Clergy, like others working with dual-earner families, need to be aware of their own attitudes toward women's roles and to hold no bias against wives who want to balance work and family (Etaugh, 1984). Pastor Westfall realized that Grace, Brandon, and the children had not fully adjusted to the fact that Grace was now employed and no longer had the time she previously devoted to the house and other activities. Neither Grace nor Brandon had changed schedules or expectations to accommodate her job and the boys' activities.

One of the keys to this situation is to increase the amount of support that Brandon and the boys are willing to give Grace. Pastor Westfall explored with the couple their expectations about the role of a wife and mother and the role of a husband and father. Research has shown that couples today must renegotiate household tasks to create stronger marriages (Baker, Kiger, and Riley, 1996). Grace and Brandon were raised by mothers who were not employed, and they both believed that a woman should do traditional "woman's work" in the home. The pastor encouraged the couple to try to adopt more egalitarian attitudes and realistic standards for themselves. Grace admitted that she feels that housework is an expression of how a woman cares for her family. And she holds such high standards for how clean the home should be and what kinds of meals are acceptable, that when Brandon does help, his contributions often are not appreciated. The pastor helped them agree upon a plan that balanced work and home life for both of them. They set priorities, realizing that these may change as the children grow and careers develop. Brandon acknowledged that he needs to leave work earlier and spend more time with his boys. He resolved to start doing more domestic chores, especially those relating to him, such as washing his own clothes. The couple agreed to train the boys to do some of the chores, such as cleaning up and doing their own laundry. Grace will try to relax her high standards for the house and meals.

Brandon and Grace also decided to begin having family meetings in which every member is able to share feelings about the current home situation and have input deciding how it is run. Grace plans to use the family meetings to try to help her husband and children realize how important her job is to her and her need for their support. Pastor Westfall agreed to mediate the first family meeting at their house.

Treatment Within the Faith Community

The value of social support for people in stressful situations is well documented. For dual-earner families, in addition to the encouragement of spouses, supportive workplaces with understanding supervisors, flexible work hours, and assistance with child care are helpful (Lee and Duxbury, 1998). There is little community support for working mothers and their families, evidenced by the lack of quality affordable day care, employment practices that make it difficult for women, in particular, to take care of their children's needs without hurting their jobs, and societal expectations that women should be solely responsible for the children and the home. The faith community can provide assistance by addressing these issues. For example, church-based day care can be made more available for working families.

Religious groups can advocate changes in social policies that benefit working families, such as the Family Medical Leave Act of 1993 or government-sponsored child care. The faith community also can be supportive of nontraditional strategies that families employ to balance work and family life, such as having the husband cut back on his work hours instead of the wife.

For Grace, Brandon, and the boys, the church may be especially important at this stage of their family life. Research shows that religious involvement is positively related to marital adjustment and satisfaction (Weaver, Koenig, and Larson, 1997). In this case, Grace is active in the women's group at church. Despite her work and family commitments and press for time, she continues with the group because she feels good about the work they do and the friendship and support she finds there. Grace thinks of this activity as the only time she has for herself.

Brandon and the boys have the option of joining the Boy Scout troop that is sponsored by the church. This would enable father and sons to engage in healthy activities together, while giving Grace more personal time. The children already attend the youth group at church, so their parents were encouraged to take advantage of that time to do something together that will enhance their relationship as a couple.

Brandon and Grace also have the option of joining the parents group at the church. Doing so would give them the opportunity to hear about the lives of other dual-earner couples and how they cope. Members of the faith community can be positive role models for others in various situations.

Indications for Referral

Some of the conflicts confronted by employed parents, in particular by working mothers, can affect their mental health to the extent that they need professional help. Those feeling anxious or depressed will benefit from being referred to mental health specialists. Stress is usually experienced by both spouses in dual-earner couples, but if it cannot be managed by the individual or the couple, marital problems may result. In situations where the marriage is so conflicted that separation or divorce appears to be the only option, referral to a professional specializing in marriage and family work is strongly recommended.

Depending on therapeutic orientation, a mental health professional may assess the marital relationship, including employment, child rearing, and household tasks (Hodgson, 1984). Additionally, family and social networks may be evaluated. The specialist might first aim to help the couple renegotiate changes in their schedules in terms of work, children, and household responsibilities that would enable the couple to have more satisfaction and balance in their lives. A mental health professional can provide training in communication and problem-solving skills. Joining a dual-earner support group also may be a possible form of treatment. Sharing knowledge, experiences, and information in such a setting may improve coping skills (Hammer and Turner, 1990). There may be specialized programs available focusing on dual-earner families, such as those on parenting or on balancing work and family. Other courses and workshops that working parents may find helpful include time management, stress reduction, and relaxation techniques (Hodgson, 1984).

Treatment by Mental Health Specialist

Historically, women of color have more often been part of the workforce than have European-American women. In recent years, however, this has changed. In the 1990s, African-American women had a 57.8 percent participation rate in the labor force, European-American women were at 57.5 percent, and Latina women were at 53.0 percent (Schwartz and Scott, 1994). Immigrant families coming from traditionally patriarchal systems may experience conflict when the husband and wife both have jobs, often leading to the husband losing some of the status he is accustomed to wielding in the home.

Most of the research on dual-earner families has been conducted on European-American, middle-class families. Despite the difficulties these families have balancing family life and work, dual-earner families that are paid at rates below middle-class standards face even more challenges. Their jobs are much less likely to be flexible or stable, they usually have poorer day care options, and they are less able to afford to hire others to help them meet the demands of home and family (Hochschild, 1990).

Cross-Cultural Issues

National Resources

Resources

—American Psychological Association Help Center, www. helping.apa.org. Gives advice on when and how to access psychological services, and discusses how psychology can help with problems. The "Psychology at Work" section has articles on such topics as "Working moms: Happy or haggard?" as well as a special focus on stress. Other sections are "Family and Relationships" and "How Therapy Helps." Free brochures and information on finding a psychologist can be ordered.

—Fathers.com, www.fathers.com. Website with articles with practical tips and suggestions for fathers. Topics are organized according to the age of child, specific fathering situations, and fathering roles and responsibilities.

—Men's Issues Page, www.vix.com/men. Website providing information on various topics, including fatherhood.

—Menstuff: The National Men's Resource, www.menstuff.org. An educational, nonprofit, volunteer website developed and maintained by the National Men's Resource Center, providing information on over 100 men's issues, including fatherhood and the "daddy track."

—Mom to Mom, www.momsonline.com/momtomom. Website with information on various aspects of motherhood. Also has message boards and chat rooms so moms can network.

—National Parent Information Network, www.npin.org. This organization's mission is to provide access to research-based information about the process of parenting. Website includes a virtual library, question-answering service, and parenting electronic discussion list.

—Parents Place, www.parentsplace.com. Website covering topics of interest to families, including parenthood, family dynamics, and marriage. Also has chat rooms.

—Working Woman Network, www.workingwoman.com. On- and off-line resource for business women. The section on Work/Life Balance includes features on family issues, workplace strategies, and personal time.

Self-Help Resources

Halving It All: How Equally Shared Parenting Works (Francine M. Deutsch, Cambridge: Harvard University Press, 1999).

The Third Shift: Managing Hard Choices in Our Careers, Homes, and Lives as Women (Michele Kremen Bolton, San Francisco: Jossey-Bass Publishers, 2000).

When Mothers Work: Loving Our Children Without Sacrificing Our Selves (Joan K. Peters, Reading, MA: Perseus Books, 1997).

Working Mothers 101: How to Organize Your Life, Your Children, and Your Career to Stop Feeling Guilty and Start Enjoying It All (Katherine Wyse Goldman, New York: HarperCollins Publishers, 1998).

References   Allen, S. M., and Hawkins, A. J. (1999). Maternal gatekeeping: Mother's beliefs and behaviors that inhibit greater father involvement in family work. *Journal of Marriage and the Family, 61(19)*, 199–212.

Baker, R., Kiger, G., and Riley, P. J. (1996). Time, dirt, and money: The effects of gender, gender ideology, and type of earner marriage on time, household-task, and economic satisfaction among couples with children. *Journal of Social Behavior and Personality, 11(5)*, 161–177.

Becker, P. E., and Moen, P. (1999). Scaling back: Dual-earner couples' work-family strategies. *Journal of Marriage and the Family, 61(4)*, 995–1007.

Benokratis, N. V. (1996). *Marriages and Families: Changes, Choices, and Constraints* (2nd ed.). Upper Saddle River, NJ: Prentice Hall.

Burley, K. A. (1995). Family variables as mediators of the relationship between work-family conflict and marital adjustment among dual-career men and women. *Journal of Social Psychology, 135(4)*, 483–497.

Deutsch, F. M. (1999). *Halving It All: How Equally Shared Parenting Works*. Cambridge: Harvard University Press.

Etaugh, C. (1984). Effects of maternal employment on children: Implications for the family therapist. In J. C. Hansen and S. H. Cramer (Eds.), *Perspectives on Work and the Family* (pp.16–39). Rockville, MD: Aspen Systems Corp.

Gagner, C. (1998). The role of valued outcomes, justifications, and comparison referents in perceptions of fairness among dual-earner couples. *Journal of Family Issues, 19(5)*, 622–648.

Glass, J. (1998). Gender liberation, economic squeeze, or fear of strangers: Why fathers provide infant care in dual-earner families. *Journal of Marriage and the Family, 60(4)*, 821–834.

Gottfried, A. E., Bathurst, K., and Gottfried, A. W. (1994). Role of maternal and dual-earner employment status in children's development: A longitudinal study from infancy through early adolescence. In A. E. Gottfried and A. W. Gottfried (Eds.), *Redefining Families: Implications for Children's Development* (pp. 55–97). New York: Plenum Publishing.

Gottfried, A. E., Gottfried, A. W., and Bathurst, K. (1988). Maternal employment, family environment, and children's development: Infancy through the school years. In A. E. Gottfried and A. W. Gottfried (Eds.), Maternal Employment and Children's Development: Longitudinal Research (pp. 11–58). New York: Plenum Publishing.

Hamilton, W. (1999). Dual-earner families. In C. A. Smith (Ed.), *The Encyclopedia of Parenting Theory and Research* (pp. 142–144). Westport, CT: Greenwood Publishing.

Hammer, T. J., and Turner, P. H. (1990). *Parenting in Contemporary Society*. Englewood Cliffs, NJ: Prentice Hall.

Hawkins, A. J., Marshall, C. M., and Allen, S. A. (1998). The orientation toward domestic labor questionnaire: Exploring dual-earner wives' sense of fairness about family work. *Journal of Family Psychology, 12(2)*, 244–258.

Hochschild, A. (1990). *The Second Shift*. New York: Avon Books.

Hodgson, M. L. (1984). Working mothers: Effects on the marriage and the mother. In J. C. Hansen and S. H. Cramer (Eds.), *Perspectives on Work and the Family* (pp. 40–55). Rockville, MD: Aspen Systems Corp.

Lee, C. M., and Duxbury, L. (1998). Employed parents' support from partners, employers, and friends. *Journal of Social Psychology, 138(3),* 303–322.

MacPhee, D. (1999). Domestic labor. In C. A. Smith (Ed.), *The Encyclopedia of Parenting Theory and Research* (pp. 13–139). Westport, CT: Greenwood Publishing.

Schwartz, M. A., and Scott, B. M. (1994). *Marriages and Families: Diversity and Change.* Englewood Cliffs, NJ: Prentice Hall.

Steil, J. M. (1997). *Marital Equality: Its Relationship to the Well-being of Husbands and Wives.* Thousand Oaks, CA: Sage Press.

Weaver, A. J., Koenig, H. G., and Larson, D. B. (1997). Marriage and family therapists and the clergy: A need for clinical collaboration, training, and research. *Journal of Marital and Family Therapy, 23(1),* 1–25.

Zuo, J., and Tang, S. (2000). Breadwinner status and gender ideologies of men and women regarding family roles. *Sociological Perspective, 43(1),* 29–43.

Becoming a Parent

"I Love My Baby, but I Never Knew Being a Parent Would Be So Hard"

Virginia and Javier Alva asked to see Father McHenry about concerns they were having as parents. When they arrived at the church office with their three-month-old son, the priest could feel the tension between the couple. Virginia had bags under her eyes from lack of sleep. When the infant cried as Javier was holding him, he immediately handed the child to his wife. Virginia said that she felt as though she had to do everything for the baby. For example, Javier didn't seem to try hard enough to stop the child from crying, and he rarely changed a soiled diaper. Since Virginia was breast-feeding, there wasn't much that Javier could do in terms of helping to feed the baby, but she felt that he could help her more in other ways, such as cooking and doing laundry—especially since she was the one who had to wake up for the nighttime feedings and was sleep deprived. Since the infant demanded a lot of attention, Virginia was not able to do as much housework as she would have liked. On top of everything else, Javier wanted her to pay attention to him, too. Although she loved the child, Virginia felt exhausted and unhappy with her husband.

Javier responded that since having the baby, Virginia was either demanding that he do something, ignoring him, or crying. Since Virginia was staying home with the infant and he was employed, he believed that she should be able to do the lion's share of the child care and the housework. He was unhappy about often having to eat take-out food for dinner and having to do the laundry. He was unsure of his skills as a parent, which was why he rarely changed diapers or helped with the baby. Finally, he was unhappy with the lack of attention Virginia was paying to their marriage. They had had no sexual relations since the birth, and Virginia was unwilling to let anyone baby-sit so that they could have a night out. Both

Virginia and Javier stressed that they loved the child very much but had not realized how much a baby would change their marriage.

Pastoral Assessment

The Alvas were taking the right step in seeking help early. Marital relation is an important factor affecting parenting (Belsky, 1984). In turn, parents' stress can affect a child's behavior (Jarvis and Creasey, 1991). Becoming a father or mother can be a difficult task. In addition to adjusting emotionally and financially to having a newborn child, one's relationship with a partner is also affected. Becoming a parent used to be viewed as a psychological crisis situation. However, current research supports the thinking that becoming a parent is a manageable transition. During this period in a couple's relationship, as positive interactions decrease, conflict increases. Couples face additional household tasks, most of which fall to the women to complete. Leisure time seems to disappear. Research shows that marital satisfaction declines in as many as one third to one half of new parents. Women feel less satisfied than men, and they experience the decline earlier during the transition to parenthood (Boyd, 1999).

Relevant History

Both Javier and Virginia came from large families in which the father's and mother's roles were very traditional—the men were employed, and the women stayed home to raise the children. The couple decided that Virginia would put her career on hold and be a stay-at-home parent for a few years. She was still adjusting to the lack of social interaction and felt isolated in her new situation.

Diagnostic Criteria

Mild depression in new mothers is common, and Virginia's crying may be a symptom of such. Commonly called "baby blues," depression usually appears and disappears after a few weeks, depending on the ease or difficulty of caring for the child, the healing of birth wounds, and the hormonal shifts. This is different from postpartum depression (see Indications for Referral).

Also common are feelings of exhaustion or chronic fatigue. As one child care book describes, "There's no other job as emotionally and physically taxing as mothering in the first year. The strain and pressure are not limited to eight hours a day or five days a week, and there are no lunch hours or coffee breaks to spell relief" (Eisenberg, Murkoff, and Hathway, 1996, p. 575).

In addition to feeling unsure of his parenting skills and unhappy about the state of the marriage, Javier may be feeling left out of the relationship that Virginia and the child share. Many fathers experience such emotions.

Response to Vignette

Father McHenry gently reminded the couple of the need to slow down and adjust to the many changes that had recently taken place in their lives.

They needed to focus on the most important thing—parenting their child. The priest encouraged the Alvas to join the bimonthly support group in the parish composed of parents of children of all ages. He suggested that it might be helpful for the Alvas to interact with other parents. Virginia could meet other stay-at-home mothers, and Javier would benefit from talking with other fathers. Father McHenry also encouraged Javier to enroll in a parent training class offered by the local hospitals in order to increase his feelings of competence and reduce his stress (Pieterman, Firestone, McGrath, and Goodman, 1992).

Javier needs to understand that caring for the child takes up virtually all of Virginia's time. Immediately after having a baby, many women do not have the energy to meet the demands of the infant and the husband, choosing their role as mother over their role as wife. Some researchers believe that women are biologically programmed to choose nurturing their baby over being a mate (Sears and Sears, 1993). Javier should be sensitive to, and supportive of, the needs of both his wife and child. Although he can't help feed the infant, since Virginia is breast-feeding, he can try participating in all of the other facets of rearing the baby. Virginia must remember that a child needs both parents. She can encourage Javier to take on more parenting tasks while recognizing his insecurities and his needs.

Both of them can reach out to family members or to close friends for support, even if it is just to talk on the phone. As the baby gets older, Virginia can be encouraged to trust others to take care of the child, so that she will be able to make time for herself and for her husband. Alternatively, Father McHenry suggested that the couple try to plan leisure time activities in the form of family outings by themselves or with other parents (Roggman, Moe, Hart, and Forthun, 1991). Virginia and Javier were encouraged to reflect on all of the reasons they wanted to have a child and all of the positive aspects about being parents (LeMasters and DeFrain, 1989).

Treatment Within the Faith Community

The stress of becoming a parent has implications for the marital relationship and parents' relationship with the child, as well as for parenting in general. Such stress also may negatively affect relationships with others outside the immediate family if it is not addressed. A review of the literature shows that emotional support for a family has a positive impact on both parents and children. Social networks help parents feel competent about their skills and buffer against some stressors (Parks, Lenz, and Jenkins, 1992).

Isolation is associated with dysfunctional parenting (Webster-Stratton, 1990). The faith community can provide support to new parents in various ways, from providing formal or informal parenting support to volunteering to help with household tasks or child care.

Indications for Referral

Postpartum depression in mothers is a serious clinical condition, affecting as many as 20 percent of new mothers. It can occur soon after the birth of a child and usually lasts for several months, although it can last for up to a year. Symptoms include inability to sleep or eat, extreme anxiety, unfounded fears about the baby, and suicidal thoughts (Krueger, 1999). Depression negatively affects a mother's daily functioning, her feelings about marital harmony, and her ability to interact with, and care for, her child (Carro, Gotlib, and Compas, 1999; Gelfand, Teti, and Fox, 1992). Research indicates that postpartum depression in fathers also exists. Postpartum anxiety or panic disorder affects 5 percent of new mothers. For any of these conditions, referral for psychotherapy and/or medication is necessary (Krueger, 1999).

Marital quality declines somewhat for many couples after having a child. In some cases, this is serious enough to threaten the relationship (Boyd, 1999) and warrant referral to marriage counseling. If one or both parents experienced abuse as a child, that parent may be more psychologically vulnerable during a time of stress (Webster-Stratton, 1990). Research has linked parenting stress and the potential for abuse (Holden and Banez, 1996). If one of them has turned to abusing the other emotionally or physically, immediate referral to a mental health specialist is necessary.

Treatment by Mental Health Specialist

A mental health specialist might assess the couple's marital quality using standardized measures. Treatment could include marriage counseling and addressing intrapersonal as well as interpersonal issues and communication skills. Group therapy, in which new parents share their experiences, may also be recommended.

Cross-Cultural Issues

Some members of ethnic minority groups may avoid seeking treatment because of the shame and stigma associated with mental illness (Sue and McKinney, 1980). Turning to clergy to share the problems of becoming a new parent is one way to seek help without shame. Taking classes focused on parenting or marriage skills or joining support groups also can be acceptable ways of dealing with such issues, as opposed to seeing a mental health professional.

Resources

National Resources

—Depression After Delivery (D.A.D.), (908) 575-9121.

—Fathers.com; website containing articles with practical tips and suggestions for fathers. Topics are organized according to age of child and to specific fathering situations, roles, and responsibilities.

—*Fragile Beginnings: Postpartum Mood and Anxiety Disorders.* CO: InJoy Productions, (303) 447-2082; videotape on postpartum mental health.

—Men's Issues Page; www.vux.com/men; website providing information on various topics including fatherhood, single dads, and divorce.

—Menstuff: The National Men's Resource; www.menstuff.org; an educational, nonprofit, volunteer website maintained by the National Men's Resource Center, providing information on over 100 men's issues, including fatherhood, the "daddy track," stepfamilies, and divorce.

—Mom to Mom; www.momsonline.com/momtomom; website with information on various aspects of motherhood. Has message boards and chat rooms so moms can network.

—National Parent Information Network, www.npin.org; its mission is to provide access to research-based information about the process of parenting and about family involvement in education. Website includes a virtual library, question-answering service, and parenting electronic discussion list.

—Oxygen Newsletters, www.oxygen.com/newsletters; e-mail newsletters on different women's topics, including parenting, health, and fitness.

—Parents Anonymous of Texas, www.parentsanonymous.org; family support and education program focused on strengthening families and stopping child abuse. Provides parent education courses and parent support groups as well as a support and crisis intervention line, the Texas HEART-line; (800) 554-2323.

—Parents Place; www.parentsplace.com; website covering topics of interest to families, including parenthood, family dynamics, and marriage. Also has chat rooms.

—Postpartum Support International (P.S.I.), (805) 967-7636.

Self-Help Resources

This Isn't What I Expected: Recognizing and Recovering from Depression and Anxiety after Childbirth (Karen R. Kleiman and Valerie Davis Raskin, New York: Bantam Books, 1994).

What to Expect the First Year (Arlene Eisenberg, Heidi E. Murkoff, and Sandee Eisenberg Hathway, New York: Workman Publishing, 1996); provides information on baby care and parenting in a question and answer format.

References

Belsky, J. (1984). The determinants of parenting: A process model. *Child Development*, 55, 83–96.

Boyd, B. B. (1999). Transition to parenthood. In C. A. Smith (Ed.), *The Encyclopedia of Parenting Theory and Research* (pp. 455–456). Westport, CT: Greenwood Publishing.

Carro, M. G., Gotlib, I. H., and Compas, B. E. (1999). Postpartum depression. In C. A. Smith (Ed.), *The Encyclopedia of Parenting Theory and Research* (pp. 118–120). Westport, CT: Greenwood Publishing.

Eisenberg, A., Murkoff, H. E., and Hathway, S. E. (1996). *What to Expect the First Year*. New York: Workman Publishing.

Gelfand, D., Teti, D. M., and Fox, C. R. (1992). Sources of parenting stress for depressed and nondepressed mothers of infants. *Journal of Clinical Child Psychology, 21*, 262–272.

Holden, E. W., and Banez, G. (1996). Child abuse potential and parenting stress. *Journal of Family Violence, 11*, 1–12.

Jarvis, P. A., and Creasey, G. L. (1991). Parental stress, coping, and attachment in families with an 18-month-old infant. *Infant Behavior and Development, 14(4)*, 383–395.

Krueger, A. (with the editors of *Parenting Magazine*) (1999). *Parenting Guide to Your Baby's First Year*. New York: Ballantine Books; provides information on birth and development, baby care, and parenthood.

LeMasters, E. E., and DeFrain, J. (1989). *Parents in Contemporary America*. Belmont, CA: Wadsworth Publishing.

Parks, P., Lenz, E., and Jenkins, L. S. (1992). *Child: Care, Health, and Development, 18*, 151–171.

Pieterman, S., Firestone, P., McGrath, P., and Goodman, J. T. (1992). The effects of parent training on parenting stress and sense of competence. *Canadian Journal of Behavioural Science, 21*, 41–58.

Roggman, L. A., Moe, S. T., Hart, A. D., and Forthun, L. F. (1991). Family leisure and social support: Relations with parenting stress and psychological well-being in Head Start parents. *Early Childhood Research Quarterly, 9*, 163–180.

Sears, W., and Sears, M. (1993). *The Baby Book: Everything You Need to Know about Your Baby—from Birth to Age Two*. Boston: Little, Brown & Co.; provides information on preparing for a child, baby and toddler care, and parenting issues. This book explains attachment parenting, which is strongly supported by the authors.

Sue, S., and McKinney, H. (1980). Asian Americans in the Community Mental Health Care System. In R. Endo, S. Sue and N. Wagner (Eds.), *Asian Americans: Social and Psychological Perspectives* (Vol. 2, pp. 291–310). Palo Alto, CA: Science and Behavior Books.

Webster-Stratton, C. (1990). Stress: A potential disruptor of parent perception and family interactions. *Journal of Clinical Child Psychology, 19*, 302–312.

A Child with Special Needs: Mental Retardation

"She Was Behind Other Children Her Age"

The Cohen family had been active members of the synagogue for several generations. Rabbi Lichton had known Jason and Rachel Cohen since they were teenagers. He performed their wedding five years earlier and officiated at their Aufruf, which they celebrated in the synagogue. When their first child was born, she had been joyously welcomed by the congregation at her baby naming. Rebecca seemed normal and healthy. Her first several months were a delight and worry-free. After nine months, the Cohens began to notice that she could not crawl or sit from a lying position. It became clear over time that she was physically and developmentally behind other children her age. The family pediatrician told them that Rebecca was delayed in her motor skills and advised them to wait to see if she would grow out of her problems. When she continued to be slow in her development, the Cohens sought out a specialist to assess Rebecca further. They took her to a psychologist who specialized in evaluating children. After extensive testing, they were given the diagnosis of mental retardation in the moderate to severe range.

Both Jason and Rachel were university professors and having a child that was less than perfect was initially inconceivable. They were psychologically shattered. They felt several emotions at once—sadness, confusion, disbelief, inadequacy, guilt, and helplessness. They felt as though their life had been turned upside down and all their dreams for their beautiful child had been dashed.

In his thirty years of pastoral experience, Rabbi Lichton had counseled many families that had children with a physical or mental disability. He realized that Jason's and Rachel's reactions to the news of their child's disability were normal. He also knew that over time it would be important for

Pastoral Assessment

them to refocus their energy and emotions on Rebecca rather than on themselves. They would need to accept her for who she was rather than for who they hoped she might be.

Rabbi Lichton understood the importance of assessing and supporting family strengths as a part of a pastoral care evaluation. He knew that the Cohens had many positive attributes that would be helpful in this situation, particularly their solid marital bond and deep commitment to one another. They were good at sharing their feelings and had effective communication skills, which are particularly important in a crisis. The rabbi also had seen the couple maintain their optimism and hopefulness in the face of other difficulties. They were well-educated people who were assertive enough to seek out answers to their many questions about mental retardation and its implications for their daughter. In addition, their extended family and the congregation were very caring and supportive.

Relevant History

There was no history of mental retardation or birth defects on either side of the Cohen family.

Diagnostic Criteria

The chief features of mental retardation are below average intellectual ability along with limitations to independent functioning in areas such as communication; self-care; work; academics; and safety, social, and interpersonal skills. Intellectual ability is defined by the intelligence quotient (IQ) measured by using a standardized intelligence test (e.g., Wechsler Intelligence Scales for Children-Revised or Stanford-Binet). Intelligence is the ability to gather, make sense of, and use information gained from the environment. Learning may be slower among mentally retarded persons, but they can and do learn. Significantly below average intellectual ability is measured as an IQ of about 70 or less on a scale in which approximately 100 is average. About 1 to 2 percent of the general population is diagnosed as mentally retarded (American Psychiatric Association, 1994).

The largest group (85 percent) has mild mental retardation with an IQ of between 50 and 70. They usually develop social and communication skills during their preschool years and are frequently not distinguishable from children without mental retardation until later in their development. By their teen years, they can obtain academic skills up to the sixth grade level. With supervision and guidance, in adulthood, they usually achieve social and vocational skills sufficient to support themselves, living successfully in the community.

The moderately mentally retarded make up about 10 percent of those who are retarded. They have an IQ range from about 35 to 50. These persons can profit from vocational training and, with some supervision, can care for themselves. They benefit from training in social and occupational skills but usually do not progress beyond the second-grade level in academic achievement. During their teens, they may not recognize social rules, which can limit peer interactions. In adulthood, most are able to do unskilled or semiskilled jobs in a supervised setting in the community.

The severely mentally retarded have an IQ range from about 20 to 35 and comprise 3 to 4 percent of those who are retarded. In early childhood, they develop little or no speech. During school-age years, they may learn to talk and can be trained in basic self-care skills. Academic skills are limited to simple counting, and they may learn the alphabet and some "survival words." In adulthood, they may be able to perform simple tasks in a supervised setting. Most do best living with their families or in a group home setting.

The last group is the profoundly mentally retarded who have an IQ below 20 and comprise 1 to 2 percent of those who are retarded. Most persons in this group have a specific neurological problem that accounts for their condition. They require highly structured supervision, and some can be trained to perform simple tasks and limited self-care.

There are several factors that may cause mental retardation including heredity, early problems in embryonic development, pregnancy and perinatal difficulties, medical problems in infancy and childhood, and environmental issues (e.g., lack of nurturance or stimulation). Individuals with mental retardation are three to four times more likely to also have a mental disorder than the general population (American Psychiatric Association, 1994).

Response to Vignette

Like most parents, Jason and Rachel first reacted to the news of their daughter's mental retardation by blaming themselves. They searched their minds to find a reason for the disability. Rachel had a normal pregnancy and delivery, so what happened? Had they done something to cause the disability? Could they have done something differently? Rabbi Lichton knew it was important to address the issue of the Cohens' self-blame for their child's condition. The rabbi allowed them space to fully express their feelings in the context of their faith. Since the parents were not heavy drinkers or drug abusers, they were not responsible for their daughter's mental retardation. According to the experts, in 30 to 40 percent of cases, no clear cause for mental retardation can be found (American Psychiatric Association, 1994).

Rabbi Lichton understood the importance of the resources within the synagogue. The congregation was intergenerational with other parents, grandparents, and great-grandparents who had a physically or mentally disabled child in their families. Their experiences of caregiving for these children proved to be an invaluable source of inspiration and strength for the young couple. The compassion and guidance of other members of the congregation who had gone through similar experiences with disabled children became a key factor in the Cohen family's ability to cope and even thrive in the new situation. Over time, the young couple found that the challenges of raising a child with special needs actually brought them closer together and strengthened their marital bond (Abbott and Meredith, 1986). The young couple also had a strong faith that sustained them. It had been nurtured by years of involvement in the life of the synagogue. Researchers have found that religious involvement as well as congregational support is related to positive adjustment in caregivers of mentally retarded children in the African-American community (Rogers-Dulan, 1998) and in the Jewish community (Leyser, 1994).

Treatment Within the Faith Community

The synagogue had a history of a highly active Bikkur Cholim committee that reached out to people in health crisis whenever it was made aware of a situation. It offered concrete assistance and spiritual support. The synagogue's involvement with the Cohen family inspired the congregation to become more involved with the needs of families with mentally retarded individuals in the community. After investigating the issue, the synagogue became more aware of the practical problems that providing care for a child or youth with mental retardation and other disabilities create for families. Among the problems they face are time and physical demands, prolonged burden of care, financial burdens, lack of information and resources, and feelings of stigmatization (Leyser, 1994).

The congregation decided to become a resource for the community by addressing some of the practical needs of families with limited resources. They organized a respite care facility that could help relieve persons who became overwhelmed with the responsibilities of care, and they created a special fund to help families with limited financial resources. The synagogue also became a center that provided information and advocacy for those affected by mental retardation and served as a clearinghouse and network for parent groups. As a result of its involvement in the issue, the congregation experienced a new level of group cohesion that enriched lives and increased their compassion toward others.

About 5 percent of mental retardation is caused by inherited conditions (e.g., Down's syndrome, Fragile-X syndrome, Williams syndrome). Advances in genetic testing have made it possible to screen for several of the inherited conditions that cause mental retardation and other diseases. Clergy that are aware of how genetic testing works can educate their congregants about the subject. Such testing is a laboratory procedure that examines a specimen of genetic material, usually a blood sample, in order to detect the presence of a gene that is related to an abnormality. Such screening has become a routine part of prenatal care in families with a history of genetic diseases and in families in which a previous child has been born with abnormalities.

In a survey of 175 members of the New York Board of Rabbis, nearly 9 in 10 viewed counseling on genetic issues as a part of their pastoral role

(Steiner-Grossman and David, 1993). Unfortunately, the majority of the rabbis felt poorly prepared to counsel on genetic issues and expressed a need for additional training in seminary and post-seminary. In a similar study in Indiana, few pastors had formal training in, or saw themselves as prepared for, counseling parishioners on genetic diseases or birth defects (Mertens, Hendrix, and Mendenhall, 1986).

Indications for Referral

There are a variety of professionals that work with the mentally retarded and their families, including psychologists, special education teachers, speech/language therapists, pediatricians, occupational therapists, neurologists, physical therapists, and geneticists. The more contact and information clergy have with these specialists before a crisis, the more effective they will be when a referral is needed.

Treatment by Mental Health Specialist

The birth and continued care needs of a mentally retarded child expose a family to stress, frustration, and grief that can require major changes in family roles and relationships. The Cohen family has a very strong support system and relationship, along with good skills to adjust to the changes. When a family has fewer resources and poorer coping skills, they may need to look to a mental health specialist to help them through the crisis. A good therapist can help a couple recognize and process their emotions and communicate more effectively.

Behavioral problems such as temper tantrums, impulsiveness, repetitive behaviors (e.g., skin-picking), high rates of talking, argumentativeness, stubbornness, oppositionality, and food obsessions are sometimes developed by mentally retarded individuals. A family may need to find a psychologist trained to develop a detailed behavioral analysis and plan. Behavioral interventions are time-consuming and hard work, but they have proven to be much more effective than medications alone in such cases (Didden, Duker, and Korzilius, 1997).

Cross-Cultural Issues

Lead poisoning is an important health problem affecting an estimated 890,000 preschoolers. According to the Centers for Disease Control and Prevention, about 4.4 percent of children ages one to five have too much lead in their bodies, which may result in brain damage and mental retardation.

While lead poisoning crosses all socioeconomic and racial boundaries, the burden of this disease falls disproportionately on low-income families and those of color. In the U.S., children from poor families are eight times more likely to be poisoned than those from higher-income families. African-American children are five times more likely to experience poisoning than Caucasian children. Nationwide, about 1 in 5 African-American children living in older housing is lead poisoned.

Resources

National Resources

—Aicardi Syndrome Newsletter, Inc.; 1510 Polo Fields Court, Louisville, KY 40245; (502) 244-9152; www.aicardi.com; is an international network founded in 1983. It supports the families of females with Aicardi Syndrome (congenital disorder in which the corpus callosum has failed to develop). It offers information, referrals, resources, a phone support network, and newsletters.

—Alliance to End Childhood Lead Poisoning; 227 Massachusetts Avenue, NE, Suite 200, Washington, DC 20002; (202) 543-1147; www.aeclp.org; is a national organization created to launch a comprehensive campaign against the epidemic of childhood lead poisoning. It was formed in 1990 by national leaders in pediatrics, public health, environmental protection, affordable housing, education, civil rights, and children's welfare.

—American Association of People with Disabilities; 1819 H Street, NW, Suite 330, Washington, DC 20006; (800) 840-8844; www.aapd.com: is a group committed to furthering the productivity, independence, and full citizenship in all aspects of society of people with disabilities.

—American Association on Mental Retardation; 444 North Capitol Street, NW, Suite 846, Washington, DC 20001-1512; (800) 424-3688; www.aamr.org; promotes global development and dissemination of progressive policies, sound research, effective practices, and universal human rights for people with intellectual disabilities.

—American Council on Rural Special Education (ACRES); Kansas State University, 2323 Anderson Avenue, Suite 226, Manhattan, KS 66502; (785) 532-2737; www.ksu.edu/acres; is the only national organization devoted entirely to special education issues that affect rural America.

—Coffin-Siris Syndrome Support Group; 1524 Marshall Street, Antioch, CA 94509; (925)754-6568; www.members.aol.com/CoffinSiri; is a national network founded in 1997. It provides support and information for families of persons with Coffin-Siris Syndrome, including educational materials, referrals, phone support, and conferences.

—DeBarsy Syndrome National Network; c/o Cheryl Dinnell, Nevada Parent Network, University of Nevada—Reno, COE, REPC/285, Reno, NV 89557; (702) 784-4921 ext. 4921; www.unr.edu/repc/npn; is a national network founded in 1997. It offers support, counseling, and information sharing for parents of children with DeBarsy Syndrome.

—Easter Seals; 230 West Monroe Street, Suite 1800, Chicago, IL 60606; (312) 726-6200; www.easter-seals.org; is a nonprofit, community-based health and human services provider dedicated to helping children and adults with disabilities and special needs gain greater independence.

—FRAXA Research Foundation; P.O. Box 935, West Newbury, MA 01985-0935; (978) 462-1866; www.fraxa.org; is an international group with affiliates. It offers information and support on Fragile-X syndrome and funds medical research into the treatment of this disorder.

—Human Growth Foundation; 997 Glen Cove Avenue, Glen Head, NY 11545; (800) 451-6434; www.hgfound.org; is a national organization with forty-eight chapters that was founded in 1965. Local chapters provide members the opportunity to meet other parents of children with growth-related disorders. Mutual sharing of problems, a parent-to-parent support/networking program, conferences, research, and public education are offered.

—National Down Syndrome Congress; 7000 Peachtree-Dunwoody Road, NE, Lake Ridge 400 Office Park, Building 5, Suite 100, Atlanta, GA 30328; (800) 232-NDSC; www.ndsccenter.org; has more than 600 parent groups. It provides support, information, and advocacy for families affected by Down's syndrome and serves as a clearinghouse and network for parent groups. It has a newsletter, annual convention, phone support, and chapter development guidelines.

—National Fragile-X Foundation; P.O. Box 190488, San Francisco, CA 94119-0488; (800) 688-8765; www.NFXF.org; has eighty-one groups and was founded in 1984. It provides information to promote education and research regarding Fragile-X syndrome, a hereditary condition that is the most common familial cause of mental impairment. It offers phone support, advocacy, phone consultation, a newsletter, information, and referrals.

—National Information Center for Children and Youth with Disabilities; P.O. Box 1492, Washington, DC 20013; (800) 695-0285; www.nichcy.org; makes available a wide variety of publications, including fact sheets on specific disabilities, state resource sheets, parent guides, bibliographies, and issue papers. It also makes referrals to disability organizations, parent groups, and professional associations at the state and national level. Materials are available in Spanish.

—National Tay-Sachs & Allied Diseases Association (NTSAD); 2001 Beacon Street, Suite 204, Brighton, MA 02135; (800) 906-8723; www.ntsad.org; is dedicated to the treatment and prevention of Tay-Sachs and related diseases and to providing information and support services to individuals and families affected by these diseases. Strategies for achieving these goals include public and professional education, research, genetic screening, family services, and advocacy.

—Prader-Willi Syndrome Association (USA); 5700 Midnight Pass Road, Sarasota, FL 34242; (800) 926-4797; www.pwsausa.org; was organized in the U.S. in 1975. Its mission is to provide parents and professionals with information and support services as well as to promote research.

—Sibling Information Network; A. J. Pappanikou Center, University of Connecticut, 249 Glenbrook Road, U64, Storrs, CT 06269-2064; (860) 486-4985; is a national network, founded in 1981, as a clearinghouse of information related to the siblings and families of individuals with developmental disabilities. It offers referrals, guidelines, and resources on sibling support groups.

—Special Olympics, Inc.; 1325 G Street, NW, Suite 500, Washington, DC 20005; (202) 628-3630; www.specialolympics.org; is a nonprofit program of year-round sports training and competition for individuals with mental retardation.

—The Arc; 1010 Wayne Avenue, Suite 650, Silver Spring, MD 20910; (301) 565-3842; www.thearc.org; the national organization of and for people with mental retardation and related disabilities and their families.

—Williams Syndrome Association; P.O. Box 297, Clawson, MI 48017-0297; (248) 541-3630; www.williams-syndrome.org; exists to inform individuals with Williams Syndrome and their families and to offer them support in dealing with the disease. It also provides the most up-to-date medical and educational information available. The association is divided into eleven regions across the nation and has nearly four thousand families on its membership list.

Self-Help Resources

Children with Mental Retardation: A Parents' Guide (Romayne Smith, Bethesda, MD: Woodbine House, 1993); an exceptionally well-written book with solid information.

Pastoral Genetics: Theology and Care at the Beginning of Life (Ronald Cole-Turner and Brent Waters, Cleveland, OH: Pilgrim Press, 1996); provides helpful information about genetic testing and the pastoral role in genetic counseling.

References

Abbott, D. A., and Meredith, W. H. (1986). Strengths of parents with retarded children. *Family Relations*, 35, 371–375.

American Psychiatric Association. (1994). *Diagnostic and Statistical Manual of Mental Disorders* (4th ed.). Washington, DC: APA.

Didden, R., Duker, P. C., and Korzilius, H. (1997). Meta-analysis study on treatment effectiveness for problem behaviors with individuals who have mental retardation. *American Journal on Mental Retardation*, 101(4), 387–399.

Leyser, Y. (1994). Stress and adaptation in Orthodox Jewish families with a disabled child. *Journal of Orthopsychiatry*, 64(3), 376–385.

Mertens, T. R., Hendrix, J. R., and Mendenhall, G. L. (1986). Indiana clergy: A study of their human genetics-bioethics educational needs. *Journal of Pastoral Care*, 40, 43-50.

Rogers-Dulan, J. (1998). Religious connectedness among urban African American families who have a child with disability. *Mental Retardation*, 36(2), 91–103.

Steiner-Grossman, P., and David, K. L. (1993). Involvement of rabbis in counseling and referral for genetic conditions: Results of a survey. *American Journal of Human Genetics*, 53(6), 1359–1365.

The Troubled Teen

"They Would Be Happy If It Were Not for Him"

The Todds asked to see Father David Chun. Their thirteen-year-old nephew, Bruce, had come to stay with them for the summer, and they wanted their priest's counsel.

Bruce's parents had complained that he had become a problem, so his aunt and uncle had offered to take care of him for the vacation months. The Todds, who have two teenage boys, are a warm and stable family who are involved in the life of the parish, including serving as volunteers with the youth group. They reported that their nephew's behavior had changed markedly over the last year. Bruce now wears mostly black clothes and has become enthralled with music and video games that focus on pessimistic and morbid themes. He has a short fuse and is restless, complaining of feeling worthless and bored. Bruce's grades have dropped significantly, and he has grown increasingly distant and wary.

The Todds feel that Bruce has been blamed for all the problems in his family. He is an average student, and only the exceptional is acceptable to his high-achieving parents. The family message is, "Either you do it perfectly or you are a failure." Consequently, Bruce can do little right. His parents are overly occupied with their careers and have had serious problems in their marriage.

Pastoral Assessment

Father Chun listened carefully to their story. He realized it was important to make a careful assessment of the situation. Multiple negative changes in a young person can be a sign of problems that require serious attention.

Bruce has many of the classic signs of a depressed adolescent. Pervasive sadness may be expressed by wearing black clothing and by a preoccupation with nihilistic music and videos. His tense and restless manner may be a sign of irritability, which is not unusual among depressed teens. His boredom and drop in grades may signal decreased concentration and slowed thinking, also common in depression.

Father Chun understood that it is always important to know whether a depressed teen is using alcohol or other substances. Research indicates that about 1 in 4 depressed adolescents uses drugs or alcohol to cope with the illness (Fleming and Offord, 1990). Teens often use those substances to self-medicate the symptoms of depression, particularly adolescents who feel inadequate and have poor social skills. In addition, suicide is an increased risk when a teen is depressed, especially if there is substance abuse. The combination of depression and alcohol or drug abuse can be lethal (Burstein et al., 1993).

Relevant History

Father Chun asked if there had been recent events that may have triggered Bruce's changes in behavior. The Todds reported that his maternal grandmother, with whom he had been close, had died last year after a short illness. She had been a devout Catholic who never missed Mass and often took Bruce with her.

Bruce's mother has a history of clinical depression. Individuals with parents who have been depressed are more than three times as likely to suffer a major depression than those without that risk factor.

Diagnostic Criteria

Depression is one of the most pervasive forms of emotional problems in young people. Experts estimate that about 1 in 20 teens is depressed (Reynolds, 1995). Depression in teens has essentially the same symptoms as in adults, although adolescent symptoms can be more difficult to assess. A teen is diagnosed with a major depression when there have been two weeks or more of feeling sad, gloomy, depressed, irritable, or experiencing a loss of interest, motivation, or enjoyment in usual activities (American Psychiatric Association, 1994). Along with a depressed mood or loss of interest, an adolescent must also have experienced two or more weeks of at least four of the following eight symptoms: fatigue or loss of energy; lethargy or increased restlessness (agitation); loss of appetite and weight or excessive appetite and weight gain; difficulty sleeping or sleeping too much; loss of social or sexual interest; feelings of worthlessness or excessive guilt; difficulty concentrating; feeling that life is not worth living, wanting to die, or feeling suicidal.

A dysthymic disorder is a chronic, less severe form of depression that is diagnosed when an adolescent has had a period of at least one year in which she or he has exhibited depression or irritability. In addition, dysthymic disorder requires the presence of at least two of the following symptoms: eating problems, sleeping problems, lack of energy, low self-esteem, reduced concentration or decision-making ability, or feelings of hopelessness. Because these symptoms often become so much a part of the youth's day-to-day experience, the mood disturbance may not be easily distinguished from the person's usual functioning. A low-grade depression can be present for years. Over 75 percent of adolescents with this disorder will develop at least one major depression in their lifetime (Kovac, Akiskal, Gatsonis, and Parrone, 1994).

Father David Chun's parish was one of a group of Christian and Jewish congregations that helped sponsor a pastoral care center. Father Chun consulted with Dr. Alex Taylor, the director of the center and a family therapist, after obtaining permission from Bruce's family. Then Dr. Taylor made a full assessment of Bruce's symptoms, including psychological testing. Bruce was found to have the symptoms of a long-standing dysthymic depression that became a major depression with the loss of his grandmother. He had thoughts about suicide but no plan or means to take his life. He did not take drugs or use alcohol because his grandmother "would look down from heaven and disapprove."

Dr. Taylor advised a medical examination to rule out physical problems that could have triggered the depression. He also recommended a consultation with a child/adolescent psychiatrist to assess Bruce for antidepressant medications. The pediatrician found no underlying medical problem that would account for the negative changes in Bruce. The child psychiatrist recommended both a medication to lower the severity of depressive symptoms and individual supportive psychotherapy to help his recovery.

Dr. Taylor held a family evaluation session with Bruce's parents, who saw him as the family problem because he did not live up to their high expectations. They saw their son as the cause of all the family's difficulties. His parents said several times during the session, "We would be happy if it were not for Bruce." The couple's frustration was directed toward Bruce, allowing their anger to be turned away from each other and toward him. The parents' overt conflict over Bruce allowed them to avoid underlying marital difficulties. The marriage may be sustained because the focus is always on Bruce. This sort of scapegoating of a child creates a highly stressful and toxic environment and may account for much of Bruce's depression.

Family turmoil can trigger depression in a child who is genetically predisposed toward the illness. Some parents of youth who are depressed are rigidly controlling, overly critical, autocratic, and coercive (Kaslow, 1996). Depressed adults, recalling their early experiences, indicate that the family interactions of their youth were marked by more conflict, greater rejection, poorer communication, less expression of feelings, and more abuse than persons with nondepressive histories. Depression has also been associated with low self-esteem, high self-criticism, and perfectionistic standards (Birmaher et al., 1996).

Father Chun was skilled in working with grieving persons. He had gained specialized training in pastoral care in seminary and later in

Response to Vignette

continuing education offered by the diocese. He had a nurturing, informed pastoral counseling style. Bruce respected his role as priest because of his grandmother's Catholic faith, and this helped in building trust between them. Father Chun was a good listener who established a safe and caring relationship with Bruce. Using gentleness and support, he encouraged Bruce to grieve his loss. The priest knew that Bruce needed to mourn his grandmother according to his inner timetable and understood that he would eventually need to face the anger he felt toward his overly critical parents.

Over a period of several weeks, Bruce was able to share in detail his relationship with his beloved grandmother and his feelings of loss. She had acted as a buffer against the harsh and punitive behavior of his parents. His grandmother was the primary caregiver for most of his childhood. Father Chun encouraged him to recall the many positive memories he had of her. The priest asked Bruce to bring in photos of his grandmother and encouraged him to write a letter to her, expressing his thoughts and feelings. As the grieving process progressed, the depressive symptoms decreased in intensity. Bruce became more aware of the anger he felt toward his rejecting parents and less judgmental toward himself.

Bruce became more emotionally connected to others and less irritable and preoccupied with his morbid thoughts. He joined a parish youth softball team and made new friends. He entered longer-term supportive psychotherapy with Dr. Taylor at the pastoral counseling center. He became hopeful about his future and more accepting of his human imperfections. Bruce continued to live with the Todd family over the next school year. His grades improved, and a new self-esteem emerged. He began to enjoy his life, and he asked Father Chun to baptize him.

Treatment Within the Faith Community

Religious community is a powerful preventive and healing resource for many teens and their families. Encouraging adolescents to be active in the life of the community of faith is in itself a useful strategy when addressing depression or other teen mental health issues. Studies link religious involvement to many positive social and mental health benefits. Youth who practice their religious faith have more positive social values and more caring behaviors and their families are more stable than those who do not practice their faith. Commitment to nonpunitive, nurturing religious beliefs and activities reduces alcohol and drug abuse, antisocial behavior, suicide, and depression (Weaver, Preston, and Jerome, 1999).

Religion can protect children and their parents against depression by acting as a buffer against stressful events. According to researchers at Columbia University, children whose mothers are religiously committed are less likely to suffer depression (Miller, Warner, Wickramaratine, and Weissman, 1997). The study found that the daughters of mothers for whom religion was highly important were 60 percent less likely to have a major depression in the following ten years. A second study found that frequent church attendees in Texas with high spiritual support had lower levels of depression than had their peers without religious involvement. High school boys and girls who were infrequent church attendees with low spiritual support had the highest rates of depression, often found to be at clinically significant levels (Wright, Frost, and Wisecarver, 1993).

Although many clergy report that depression is the most common problem that they are asked to help people overcome, studies indicate that they are inadequately trained to identify depression or suicide risk (Weaver, 1995). In a national survey of clergy and pastoral care specialists, only 1 in 4 believed the church was offering helpful programs for depressed teenagers, and pastors ranked their effectiveness with teen depression as generally poor (Rowatt, 1989). The study underscores the need for clergy and other religious leaders to learn to competently recognize mental health problems in teenagers and to train members of their faith communities to provide emotional support to youths and their families. Adolescent depression is believed to be underreported and therefore undertreated.

A faith-based mentoring program for teenagers utilizing older, trusted members of the church or synagogue is a helpful way to address issues of troubled youth. Each of the mentors can be offered a congregation-sponsored initial training in basic counseling skills with information to identify distress in adolescents. Group support and continuing education can be used to help the mentors as they develop relationships with the young people, similar to the model used by the Stephen Ministries program (see Resources for more information). Positive social relationships outside one's immediate family are protective factors against developing emotional problems such as depression in at-risk youth (Huntley and Phelps, 1990).

Symptoms that mimic depression may be an indicator of a physical illness, so a referral to a medical doctor for an examination is important.

A referral to a mental health specialist is necessary any time a serious threat of suicide is present. An assessment will be based on risk factors, such as having an organized plan with access to a means, prior suicide attempts, alcohol or drug abuse, family instability, reckless behaviors, high stress, depression, and feelings of hopelessness. A referral is always appropriate when a pastor feels a problem is beyond his or her expertise. Most teens who attempt suicide do not seek professional help. A pastor can be crucial in supporting the family and adolescent through the process of seeking mental health treatment. Nine out of 10 suicidal youth are suffering from a treatable mental health disorder, which means that most teen suicides are preventable (Brent and Perper, 1995). A complete review of adolescent suicide assessment and treatment can be found in the book *Counseling Troubled Teens and Their Families: A Handbook for Pastors and Youth Workers* (Weaver, Preston, and Jerome, 1999).

Indications for Referral

85

A very small group of primarily male adolescents is at risk of being a danger to others, and sometimes this condition is precipitated by depression. However, it is important to note that danger to others occurs more often in adults than in youths (Males, 1996). A teen is at increased risk of committing homicide if he or she has one of several problems, including previous criminal violence in the family, a history of being abused, belonging to a gang, use of alcohol or illicit drugs, possession of a weapon, difficulties at school, severe learning problems, or neurological abnormalities (Zagar, Arbit, Sylvies, Busch, and Hughes, 1990). It is important for clergy to have a crisis plan to deal with dangerous youth and adults (Weaver, 1992).

Treatment by Mental Health Specialist

A combination of medication, cognitive-behavioral therapy, and family therapy is the standard treatment for adolescent depression. Given the toxic quality of Bruce's family of origin, it will be important to work with him and the family separately until Bruce is emotionally stronger and the family dynamics are less dysfunctional.

Severe depressive symptoms in teenagers can be treated with medication, which can be likened to a cast on a broken arm—a temporary support that promotes other healing activities. Any medication for minors must be carefully monitored, given the ongoing physical and psychological development of young people.

In cognitive-behavioral therapy, there is an attempt to change depression-producing beliefs and attitudes to healthier, more realistic ones. Behaviors that produce pleasure and fulfillment are also encouraged. Many depressed adolescents define their life situation in global terms such as "everything is worthless and boring," "nothing is working out," "I'm totally stupid," or "I can't do anything right." Depressed youth tend to conclude the worst, dwell on negative details, and devalue the positive, especially when they have overly critical parents. Cognitive-behavioral therapy seeks to stop or to modify these pessimistic "automatic thoughts" that people use to define themselves, their environment, and the future. If these beliefs go unrecognized and unchallenged, such distorted thinking will result in continued depression. Usually treatment involves self-monitoring of mood and activities, often in the form of keeping a daily log.

Family therapy may be useful for Bruce and his family after the toxic dynamics of blaming and scapegoating have been eliminated and after Bruce has developed more emotional strength. His parents will have to be confronted about their pattern of dysfunctional interaction and its negative impact on Bruce. They will need help to stop using him as a lightning rod for the tensions between them. "Triangulation" is the psychological term for a conflict between two people that becomes so great that a third person becomes the target of the stress. Triangulation is a way to avoid addressing problems and an indication of poor problem-solving skills in a family.

Educating Bruce's parents about the symptoms and effects of depression may be a way to begin helping them gain some empathy for their son, especially since his mother has a history of depression. Families with rigid rules and roles are likely to be resistant to change and will provide a challenge even to an experienced therapist.

When Bruce's parents have gained some insight into their role in his depression and begin to develop empathy for him, family therapy can enhance communication. It can provide a setting in which Bruce and his parents can become more aware of each other's feelings and can see the impact of their behavior on other family members. Sessions can help Bruce explore the feelings of hurt and anger that have triggered his depression and have cut off communication in the family.

Cross-Cultural Issues

Researchers have discovered differences in rates of depression in several adolescent ethnic groups. In a study of 5,423 middle school students (grades 6 through 8) in Houston, Texas, it was found that rates of depression among students ranged from a low of 1.9 percent among Chinese-Americans to a high of 6.6 percent among Mexican-Americans. The rate among Caucasians and African-Americans was 3.9 percent. These findings highlight the fact that community intervention efforts should target Mexican-American youth as a high-risk group for depression (Roberts, Roberts, and Chen, 1997).

Resources

National Resources

—Camp Fire Boys and Girls; 4601 Madison Avenue, Kansas City, MO 64112; has a suicide prevention program for adolescents in many communities in the United States. The program is cosponsored by the National Mental Health Association, 1021 Prince Street, Alexandria, VA 22314.

—Girls and Boys Town National Hotline; (800) 448-3000; 13940 Gutowski Road, Boys Town, NE 68010; www.ffbh.boystown.org; provides short-term counseling and referrals to local resources, including U.S. territories and Canada. Counsels on parent-child conflicts, suicide, depression, pregnancy, runaways, and abuse. Spanish-speaking operators are available. Operates twenty-four hours a day.

—National Depressive and Manic-Depressive Association; 730 North Franklin Street, Suite 501, Chicago, IL 60610-7204; (800) 826-3632; www.ndmda.org.

—National Foundation for Depressive Illness, Inc., P.O. Box 2257, New York, NY 10116; (800) 239-1265; www.depression.org; a twenty-four-hour recorded message describes symptoms of depression and manic depression and gives addresses for more information and physician and support group referrals by state.

—National Institute of Mental Health; 6001 Executive Boulevard,

Room 8184, MSC 9663, Bethesda, MD 20892-9663; (800) 421-4211; www.nimh.nih.gov; provides free information and literature on depressive disorders, symptoms, treatment, and sources of help. Publications are also available in Spanish.

—National Suicide Foundation; 1045 Park Avenue, New York, NY 10028; (800) ASF-4042; provides state-by-state directories of survivor support groups for families and friends of suicide victims.

—National Youth Crisis Hotline, (800) 448-4663, provides counseling and referrals to local counseling services. Responds to youth dealing with pregnancy, molestation, suicide, and child abuse. Operates twenty-four hours a day.

—Stephen Ministries; 2045 Innerbelt Business Center Drive, St. Louis, MO 63114; (314) 428-2600; www.stephenministries.org; offers training in counseling skills for local church members. Five thousand congregations worldwide offer this ministry.

Self-Help Resources

Clinical Psychopharmacology Made Ridiculously Simple (John Preston and James Johnson, Miami: MedMaster, 2000); offers the layperson a succinct, practical guide to medications used when treating mental health problems including depression.

Grief, Transition, and Loss: A Pastor's Practical Guide (Wayne E. Oates, Minneapolis: Fortress Press: 1997).

Helping the Struggling Adolescent (Les Parrot III, Grand Rapids: Zondervan, 1993).

Lost Boys: Why Our Sons Turn Violent and How We Can Save Them (James Garbarino, New York: Free Press, 1999); written by a first-rate scholar with an appreciation of the role of nonpunitive spirituality in teenage mental health.

*The Minister as Crisis Counselo*r (David K. Switzer, Nashville: Abingdon Press, 1986); offers a very informative chapter on pastoral responses to persons with normal and complicated grief reactions.

The New Handbook of Cognitive Therapy Techniques, rev. ed. (Rian E. McMullin, New York: W. W. Norton & Co., 2000); provides a theoretical and practical guide to cognitive treatment and is useful for advanced students in pastoral counseling.

Pastoral Care with Adolescents in Crisis (G. Wade Rowatt Jr., Louisville: Westminster John Knox Press, 1989).

Pastoral Counseling with Adolescents and Young Adults (Charles M. Sheldon, New York: Crossroad Publishing, 1995); a helpful book about teenagers written from a faith perspective.

Reviving Ophelia, Saving the Selves of Adolescent Girls (Mary Pipher, New York: Putnam, 1994); an important book about adolescent girls.

You Can Beat Depression: A Guide to Prevention and Recovery (John Preston, San Luis Obispo, CA: Impact Publishers, 1996); is a very helpful book written for the layperson.

American Psychiatric Association. (1994). *Diagnostic and Statistical Manual of Mental Disorders* (4th ed.). Washington, DC: APA.

Birmaher, B., Ryan, N. D., Williamson, D. E., Brent, D. A., Kaufman, J. O., Dahl, R. E., Perel, J., and Nelson, B. (1996). Childhood and adolescent depression: A review of the past 10 years: Part I. *Journal of the American Academy of Child and Adolescent Psychiatry, 35(11)*, 1427–1439.

Brent, D. A., and Perper, J. A. (1995). Research in adolescent suicide: Implications for the training, service delivery, and public policy. *Suicide and Life-Threatening Behavior, 25(2)*, 222–230.

Burstein, O. G., Brent, D. A., Perper, J. A., Moritz, G., Baugher, M., Schweers, J., Roth, C., and Balach, L. (1993). Risk factors for completed suicide among adolescents with a lifetime history of substance abuse. *Acta Psychiatrica Scandinavica, 88*, 403–408.

Fleming, J. E., and Offord, D. R. (1990). Epidemiology of childhood depressive disorders: A critical review. *Journal of the American Academy of Child and Adolescent Psychiatry, 29*, 571–580.

Huntley, D. K., and Phelps, R. E. (1990). Depression and social contacts of children from one-parent families. *Journal of Community Psychology, 18*, 66–72.

Kaslow, F. W. (1996). *Handbook of Relational Diagnosis and Dysfunctional Family Patterns*. New York: John Wiley & Sons.

Kovac, M., Akiskal, H. S., Gatsonis, C., and Parrone, P. L. (1994). Childhood-onset dysthymic disorder. *Archives of General Psychiatry, 51*, 365–374.

Males, M. A. (1996). *The Scapegoat Generation*. Monroe, ME: Common Courage Press.

Miller, L., Warner, V., Wickramaratine, P., and Weissman, M. (1997). Religiosity and depression: Ten-year follow-up of depressed mothers and offspring. *The Journal of the American Academy of Child and Adolescent Psychiatry, 36(10)*, 1416–1425.

Reynolds, W. M. (1995). Depression. In V. B. Van Hasselt and M. Hersen (Eds.). *Handbook of Adolescent Psychopathology* (pp. 297–348). New York: Lexington Books.

Roberts, E. R., Roberts, C. R., and Chen, Y. R. (1997). Ethnocultural differences in prevalence of adolescent depression. *American Journal of Community Psychology, 25(1)*, 95–110.

Rowatt, G. W. (1989). *Pastoral Care with Adolescents in Crisis*. Louisville: Westminister John Knox Press.

Weaver, A. J. (1992). Working with potentially dangerous persons: What clergy need to know. *Pastoral Psychology, 40(5)*, 313–323.

References

Weaver, A. J. (1995). Has there been a failure to prepare and support parish-based clergy in their role as front-line community mental health workers? A Review. *The Journal of Pastoral Care*, 49, 129–149.

Weaver, A. J., Preston, J. D., and Jerome, L. W. (1999). *Counseling Troubled Teens and Their Families: A Handbook for Pastors and Youth Workers*. Nashville: Abingdon Press.

Wright, L. S., Frost, C. J., and Wisecarver, S. J. (1993). Church attendance, meaningfulness of religion, and depression symptomatology among adolescents. *Journal of Youth and Adolescence*, 22, 559–568.

Zagar, R., Arbit, J., Sylvies, R., Busch, K. G., and Hughes J. R. (1990). Homicidal adolescents: A replication. *Psychological Reports*, 67, 1235–1242.

Domestic Violence

"I Thought He Was Going to Kill Me"

The story spilled out as Kay sat in the church office with bruises on her face. "Pastor," she began, "I thought he was going to kill me." The control, threats, verbal abuse, slapping, kicking, and, most recently, punching had begun nine months earlier, shortly after their wedding at the church. Pastor Sam Miller was the first person to hear her story of fear, shame, and pain.

In the beginning of their relationship, George was attentive and concerned for Kay's welfare. Their courtship had been idyllic—he brought her roses and expensive gifts. However, as the months passed after their wedding, his loving attention turned to possessiveness and jealousy. She was not as perfect as he had first thought she was. He began nagging and deriding her. He imagined that she was having sexual encounters with others. George checked on where she had been and whom she had talked to. His irrational jealousy began to isolate her. She stopped seeing friends and family, and she rarely attended church. On mornings following his assaults, George was contrite and excused his behavior because of pressure at work. He apologized and promised it would never happen again. Unfortunately, that wasn't the case; the violence continued and worsened.

She talked about her strong belief in the family and her commitment to keep the marriage together at any cost. Kay blamed herself for not being the perfect wife and felt she must be doing something wrong for George to get so angry. Kay said she knew that the Bible taught that she must forgive over and over but that it was very difficult.

Kay lived in increasing terror of his sudden mood swings and outbursts of rage. She had become emotionally numb and depressed, along with losing interest in her work. She couldn't stop thinking about George's violent outbursts, each one worse than the last. She often awoke in the middle of the night from agitated nightmares, unable to return to sleep. She had become fatigued as a result. This had been going on for a number of weeks. "Pastor, am I going crazy?" she asked in anguish.

Pastoral Assessment

The most urgent task was to ensure Kay's safety. She was in an increasingly violent situation, facing great danger. Pastor Miller listened nonjudgmentally to Kay's story, while providing her with important information. He understood that battered women often believe their abusers' negative messages and feel ashamed and afraid that they will be judged. Pastor Miller communicated his support and care, making it clear that Kay was not responsible for the violence. He told her that he was concerned about her safety and that the only person who could stop the abuse was her husband.

Physical violence and psychological abuse are never acceptable, and every human being has a right to be safe and respected. Pastor Miller made sure that Kay understood that there is never an excuse for abuse. He told her that millions of women are faced with the problem of domestic violence and that help is available. There are shelters, safe homes, and battered women's support groups ready to assist. Kay was also advised that there are legal means to help protect victims and stop abuse. He offered to introduce her to women in the congregation who work with those in her situation.

Many battered women suffer psychological trauma when they are abused. Kay was experiencing several symptoms consistent with the psychological condition called post-traumatic stress disorder (PTSD). She reported the terror of threats and physical abuse and her accompanying helpless feelings. Kay couldn't stop thinking about the beatings. That is the cardinal sign of PTSD—the intrusive reexperiencing of a trauma as if it were still happening. She became increasingly numb to her feelings, withdrawn, and depressed, losing interest in activities she used to enjoy. Kay had significant sleep disturbance, including nightmares and sleep deprivation, which resulted in daytime fatigue. When these symptoms are present for more than a month, they meet the criteria for PTSD.

Relevant History

Kay told her story to Pastor Miller after she heard him preach a sermon about domestic violence, based on the scripture "Do you not know that you are God's temple and that God's Spirit dwells in you?" (1 Cor. 3:16). Before Kay heard that sermon, she had believed it was her Christian duty to stay at home, pray, and submit to her husband.

Diagnostic Criteria

Domestic abuse is a pattern of psychological and/or physical behaviors used to establish power and control over an intimate partner, leading to the threat or use of violence. Psychological abuse may include intimidation, violent jealousy, and terrorization. Physical abuse may include pushing, slapping, kicking, and using a weapon. The primary reason that victims stay with a batterer is fear. However, other reasons such as economic and emotional dependency, family members' encouragement to stay, and religious beliefs can play a significant role.

Domestic abuse is a major social problem. It is estimated that 1.8 million women are battered each year by husbands or intimate partners (Branner, Bradshaw, Hamlin, Fogarty, and Colligan, 1999). A woman is more likely to be assaulted, injured, raped, or killed by a male partner than by any other type of assailant. Abused women comprise about 20 percent of injured women seeking help from hospital emergency services (Fortune, 1991). A National Crime Survey reveals that once a woman is battered, her risk of being a victim again is very high. In a six-month period after a domestic violence incident, about 1 in 3 women is victimized again (Langan and Innes, 1986).

Response to Vignette

After talking to Pastor Miller, Kay decided to enter a women's shelter for her safety. Volunteers from the congregation helped her gather necessary possessions from her home while her husband was at work. Kay's departure was carefully planned in order to ensure her safety. One of the most dangerous times for a victim is when the decision is made to set limits with an abuser. When the batterer perceives the loss of power and control, the risk of violence increases greatly. Most abusers will attempt to persuade the victim to come back after she leaves.

It was critical to empower Kay with knowledge about the cycle of violence often seen in domestic abuse. The cycle begins with the buildup of stress in the perpetrator. When the batterer's stress level reaches the breaking point, he strikes out in explosive anger. This is followed by a period of reality when the abuser sees such visible signs as the injuries caused by the attack, the terror of the children, and/or the destruction of property. Usually a brief "honeymoon" follows when the batterer expresses remorse and declares that it will never happen again. He may promise to be a new man and attend church, and he may beg for forgiveness. At this point the woman is often pressured to return to the abuser by well-meaning but ill-informed family members, friends, or clergy.

It is important for Kay to understand that George is choosing to use violence to control her and that the pattern will not stop until he decides to end it. Like most batterers, George is not violent at his workplace—he knows that he would be fired for hitting his boss. George chooses to attack his wife because she is not strong enough to protect herself. Victimizing another person is a choice, not a mental illness. Kay's husband is using violence because it works to control her.

Individuals who batter think that they are entitled to use force and often have learned violent behavior in their family of origin. Kay's husband saw his mother battered by his father and was occasionally physically abused as a child. George had learned from childhood that violence was an accepted means to dominate others. He must be willing to unlearn this means of dealing with stress and conflict before the cycle of violence can end.

Pastor Miller explained to Kay that beliefs about marriage and about female and male roles that arise from misinterpretations of the Bible can contribute to domestic violence. For example, premature forgiveness of George would be a way to avoid addressing the reality of the abusive situation. Her pastor affirmed that Kay's anger was appropriate and that it would help her set limits with George while he obtained treatment for his problem. Pastor Miller explained that forgiveness is a long-term process when wounds are deep and that actual forgiveness can come later, once the violence has stopped. The Bible does not condone spouse abuse.

Finally, Kay needed a response to the question, "Pastor, am I going crazy?" She was assured that "feeling crazy" or "being out of control" is a normal reaction after life-threatening assaults, especially if the perpetrator was someone she had trusted in the past. Pastor Miller helped her "normalize" her experience by explaining the pattern of PTSD symptoms and their common occurrence in the aftermath of battering. He referred her to a mental health professional for a thorough evaluation and possibly medications to help her sleep and lower her overwhelming anxiety and depressed feelings. She may need encouragement both to enter and to continue treatment.

In summary, the number one issue is Kay's protection. The second issue is stopping the abuser. The third issue is possible restoration of the relationship, but only after George's violence has completely and permanently ended.

Treatment Within the Faith Community

It is through religious faith and community that many people try to make sense out of difficult experiences and seek support in times of crisis. So it is not surprising to find that clergy are often the first professionals sought for help by abused women (Horton, Wilkins, and Wright, 1988). In a national survey of one thousand battered wives, it was found that 1 in 3 received help from clergy, and that 1 in 10 of the battering husbands was counseled by clergy (Bowker, 1988). Unfortunately, too often religious professionals are perceived to be ineffective in their efforts on behalf of battered women by groups that help victims (Gordon, 1996). Faith communities must increase their awareness of the nature and extent of domestic violence and develop cooperation with secular groups in dealing with spouse abuse.

A recent national survey of Reform, Conservative, and Orthodox rabbis provided evidence that the knowledge and attitudes of clergy about spouse abuse have begun to improve (Cwik, 1997). In the study, 80 percent of the rabbis believed that physical injury of a wife should be prosecuted as a felony. The rabbis also stated a general willingness to intervene immediately on behalf of abused wives to put a stop to maltreatment, and most advocated assertive action on the part of women. About half the rabbis had preached a sermon on domestic violence and had counseled at least one victim of abuse in the preceding year.

Most clergy feel inadequately trained in the area of spouse abuse and express a need for additional training (Cwik, 1997). They must be prepared to respond both to the personal pain it brings and to the social factors that condone and perpetuate the problem. Educational modules dealing with domestic violence and its aftermath, designed for and offered to clergy, are an effective and needed training strategy (Fortune, 1991). Working with clergy is appropriate, since almost 100 percent of them provide premarital counseling prior to performing 75 percent of all weddings in the United States, although only half of the clergy have any formal training in premarital counseling (Jones and Stahmann, 1994). Specifically, clergy must develop questions they can use in premarital counseling to screen for couples at risk for domestic violence, work on ways to help these couples understand the need for further counseling, and know how to make an effective referral.

Educating faith communities on the issue of domestic violence is crucial. Information in monthly newsletters, sermons, and classes on the topic is important, giving a victim the signal that her congregation takes abuse seriously and that she can find help among people who care. The church and synagogue should educate members that domestic violence is not a private family problem but a community concern to be addressed by all responsible people.

Research has shown that religious involvement can be a factor in reducing the risk of domestic violence. In a national survey of 4,662 Catholic and Protestant men and women in the U.S., higher levels of church attendance were predictive of lower levels of reported cases of domestic violence. The single exception to this pattern was that of Protestants who held very strong beliefs about the inerrancy of the Bible and the importance of religious authority (Ellison, Bartkowski, and Anderson, 1999).

Kay will need to see a physician to evaluate the extent of her physical injuries. She should also explore her legal options, including the possibility of seeking a temporary restraining order (TRO) against George for her safety. A TRO can help protect her by prohibiting him from contacting her in person, by phone, or by any other means. She will also need to see a mental health specialist experienced in working with victims of violence. George will need a referral to a treatment program for male batterers.

Indications for Referral

Experienced mental health specialists do not use traditional marital counseling when physical or psychological abuse is occurring in a relationship. Domestic violence creates an imbalance of power based on physical

Treatment by Mental Health Specialist

force, which undermines the openness, trust, and intimacy that are essential for helpful counseling with couples. Batterers often refuse to take responsibility for their actions, blaming them instead on a loss of control due to alcohol or drugs, frustration, stress, or the victim's behavior. Abusers frequently hold rigid views of male and female social roles and may have negative attitudes toward women in general. Batterers often believe that violence is an acceptable way to resolve marital disputes and deny that they abuse or minimize the effects on their victim.

A specialized program using a group counseling model designed for batterers is the best method of treatment. The primary goal of such programs is to eliminate all forms of abuse, focusing on the victim's safety and well-being. Batterers are held responsible for violence and for changing their behavior. The treatment challenges beliefs and attitudes used to justify violence, especially the "right" to dominate and control women. Participants are taught the effects of violence on their partners and the impact it has on children witnessing it. Abusers are taught to choose and develop non-violent attitudes and behaviors. Treatment programs teach batterers to identify the situations and feelings that trigger violence and to develop acceptable ways to express their frustration and anger. The longer-term goals will be to help George explore his underlying fears of intimacy, abandonment, and shame that are frequently the source of abuse, passed from one generation to the next.

Kay will need to work with a mental health specialist who treats victims of violence. Psychotherapists who treat PTSD seek to provide an opportunity for victims to feel safe while confronting the traumatic event and understanding its connection with their symptoms. The overall treatment strategy will be to help Kay understand and integrate the domestic violence into the ongoing context of her life so that she no longer continues to reexperience the trauma. Victims of violence need to rebuild self-esteem and self-control, as well as to develop a renewed sense of personal dignity. A knowledgeable practitioner will assess and support positive coping skills, including appropriate religious expression.

Cross-Cultural Issues

Domestic abuse affects persons of all cultures, races, ages, educational backgrounds, religions, and income levels. However, poorly educated African-American women between the ages of fifteen and thirty-four and with low incomes are at a greater risk of homicide and severe violence at the hands of an intimate partner or ex-partner than are other groups (Sullivan and Rumptz, 1994).

Many studies demonstrate the link between domestic violence and homelessness, particularly among families with children. In a national survey conducted by the U.S. Conference of Mayors, domestic violence was named the primary cause of homelessness in almost half (46 percent) of families (U.S. Conference of Mayors, 1998).

National Resources

—Battered Women's Justice Project; 125 South Ninth Street, Suite 302, Philadelphia, PA 19107; (800) 903-0111, Ext. 3; bwjp@aol.com.

—Batterers Anonymous was founded in 1980 and has twenty chapters in the U.S. It is a self-help program for men who wish to control their anger and end their abusive behavior toward women. Contact Dr. Jerry Goffman, 1850 North Riverside Avenue, Suite 220, Rialto, CA 92376; (909) 421-3092; jmgoff@genesisnetwork.net.

—Center for the Prevention of Sexual and Domestic Violence; 2400 North 45th Street #10, Seattle WA 98103; www.cpsdv.org; (206) 634-1903. The center offers training, consultation, videos, and publications to clergy, laity, seminary faculty, and students.

—Clearinghouse on Family Violence Information; P.O. Box 1182, Washington, DC 20013; (800) 233-7233.

—Family Violence Prevention Fund/Health Resource Center; 383 Rhode Island Street, Suite 304, San Francisco, CA 94103; www.fvpf.org; (800) 313-1310; is a national nonprofit organization that focuses on domestic violence education, prevention, and public policy reform.

—NARIKA; P.O. Box 14014, Berkeley, CA 94712; (800) 215-7308; is a nonprofit organization for and of women who trace their origins to South Asian nations. It provides support, information, help, and referrals to women and children in abusive situations.

—National Coalition Against Domestic Violence; P.O. Box 18749, Denver, CO 80218; (303) 839-1852. This group provides general information, resources, and materials on domestic violence.

—National Council on Child Abuse and Family Violence; 1155 Connecticut Avenue, NW, Suite 400, Washington, DC 20036; (800) 222-2000.

—National Domestic Violence Hotline; (800) 799-34224; Department of Justice, Washington, DC.

—National Network to End Domestic Violence; 701 Pennsylvania Avenue, NW, Suite 900, Washington, DC 20004; (202) 347-9520.

—National Organization for Victim Assistance (NOVA); 1757 Park Road, NW, Washington, DC 20010; (202) 232-6682; www.access.digex.net/nova. This group, founded in 1975, provides support, referrals, and advocacy for victims of violent crime and disasters. It has a newsletter and conducts conferences.

Self-Help Resources

Battered into Submission: The Tragedy of Wife Abuse in the Christian Home (James Alsdurf and Phyllis Alsdurf, Downers Grove, IL: InterVarsity Press, 1989).

Coping with Trauma: A Guide to Self-Understanding (Jon G. Allen, Washington, DC: American Psychiatric Press, 1995); explains the effects of traumatic experience on a survivor's personality and social relationships. He describes treatment approaches and self-help strategies.

Helping Traumatized Families (Charles R. Figley, San Francisco: Jossey-Bass Publishers, 1989).

Pastoral Care of Battered Women (Rita-Lou Clarke, Philadelphia: Westminster Press, 1986).

"Post-traumatic stress disorder" in *Clinical Handbook of Pastoral Counseling*, vol. 2, ed. Robert J. Wicks, Richard D. Parsons, and Donald Capps (David W. Foy and Donald Capps, New York: Paulist Press, 1993, pp. 621–637); offers a helpful chapter on PTSD from a pastoral care perspective.

Post-traumatic Therapy and Victims of Violence (Frank M. Ochberg, ed., New York: Brunner/Mazel Publishing, 1988).

Trauma and Recovery: The Aftermath of Violence—from Domestic Abuse to Political Terror (Judith Lewis Herman, New York: Basic Books, 1997).

Violence in the Family: A Workshop Curriculum for Clergy and Other Helpers (Marie M. Fortune, Cleveland, OH: Pilgrim Press, 1991); an excellent educational resource for the church

Woman-Battering (Carol J. Adams, Minneapolis: Fortress Press, 1994).

References

Bowker, L. H. (1988). Religious victims and their religious leaders: Services delivered to one thousand battered women by the clergy. In A. L. Horton and J. A. Williamson (Eds.), *Abuse and Religion: When Prayer Isn't Enough* (pp. 229–234). Lexington, MA: D.C. Health.

Branner, S. J., Bradshaw, R. D., Hamlin, E. R., Fogarty, J. P., and Colligan, T. W. (1999). Spouse abuse: physician guidelines to identification, diagnosis and management in the uniformed services. *Military Medicine, 164(1)*, 30–36.

Cwik, M. S. (1997). Peace at home? *Journal of Psychology and Judaism, 21(1)*, 7–67.

Ellison, C. G., Bartkowski, J. P., and Anderson, K. L. (1999). Are there religious variations in domestic violence? *Journal of Family Issues, 20(1)*, 87–113.

Fortune, M. M. (1991). *Violence in the Family: A Workshop Curriculum for Clergy and Other Helpers*. Cleveland, OH: Pilgrim Press.

Gordon, J. S. (1996). Community services for abused women: A review of perceived usefulness and efficacy. *Journal of Family Violence, 11(4)*, 315–329.

Horton, A. L., Wilkins, M. M., and Wright, W. (1988). Women who ended abuse: What religious leaders and religion did for these victims. In A. L. Horton and J. A. Williamson (Eds.), *Abuse and Religion: When Prayer Isn't Enough* (pp. 235–246). Lexington, MA: D.C. Health.

Jones, E. F., and Stahmann, R. F. (1994). Clergy beliefs, preparation, and practice in premarital counseling. *Journal of Pastoral Care*, 48, 181–186.

Langan, P. A., and Innes, C. A. (1986). *Preventing Domestic Violence Against Women: Bureau of Justice Statistics Special Report*. Washington, DC: U.S. Department of Justice.

Sullivan, C. M., and Rumptz, M. H. (1994). Adjustments and needs of African-American women who utilize domestic violence shelters. *Violence and Victims, 9(3)*, 275–286.

United States Conference of Mayors. (1998). *A Status Report on Hunger and Homelessness in America's Cities: 1998*. Washington, DC: U.S. Conference of Mayors.

Child Abuse

Child Abuse often occurs in homes where there is spouse abuse. In a national study, 7 in 10 men who battered their wives also abused their children (Bowker, Arbitell, and McFerron, 1988). The more severe the domestic violence, the greater the risk of harm to children in the family.

There are four types of child abuse: neglect, physical abuse, emotional abuse, and sexual abuse.

Neglect is defined as negligent treatment of a child in the form of inadequate food, clothing, shelter, medical care, or supervision.

Physical abuse is any act that results in a non-accidental physical injury. Often this occurs in the form of severe corporal punishment.

Emotional abuse is behavior on the part of a caretaker that is emotionally damaging or degrading to a child, usually in the form of severe belittling, screaming, threats, blaming, or continual family discord.

Sexual abuse is any act of sexual assault or exploitation of a minor, which includes a range of actions from rape to the handling of the genitals of a child to exposing a child to pornography. For a more detailed discussion of this subject, see *Counseling Troubled Teens and Their Families: A Handbook for Clergy and Youth Workers* (Weaver, Preston, and Jerome, 1999).

Elder Abuse

Elder Abuse is a form of domestic violence that involves the mistreatment or neglect of an older person, usually by a relative or other caregiver. It is nearly as prevalent as child abuse and may include physical violence, threats, verbal abuse, financial exploitation, neglect, or sexual abuse. Among the risk factors for suffering elder abuse are: being female, advanced age, dependency, past abuse, intergenerational conflict, lack of a support system, cognitive impairment, and shared living arrangements with the abuser.

Elder abuse is largely a hidden problem. The National Center on Elder Abuse estimates that only 1 in 14 of the between 1.5 and 2 million annual cases of abuse is actually reported. For a more detailed discussion of this subject, see *Counseling Troubled Older Adults: A Handbook for Pastors and Religious Caregivers* (Koenig and Weaver, 1997).

Bowker, L. H., Arbitell, M., and McFerron, J. R. (1988). *On the relationship between wife beating and child abuse.* In K. Yllo and M. Bogard (Eds.) *Feminist Perspectives on Wife Abuse* (pp. 158–174). Newbury Park, CA: Sage Publications.

Koenig, H. G., and Weaver, A. J. (1997). *Counseling Troubled Older Adults: A Handbook for Pastors and Religious Caregivers.* Nashville: Abingdon Press.

Weaver, A. J., Preston, J. D., and Jerome, L. W. (1999). *Counseling Troubled Teens and Their Families: A Handbook for Clergy and Youth Workers.* Nashville: Abingdon Press.

Single Parents

"Being Both Mom and Dad Does Not Leave Time for Me"

Julie Wong is a single parent. She lives with her children, eleven-year-old Eric and seven-year-old Stella. Her ex-husband, Brad, pays child support regularly but does not spend much time with his children, even though he shares custody of them with Julie. She has a full-time job at the local university. When she is not working, her time is devoted to her children—helping them with schoolwork, driving them to soccer practice and games, taking them to music lessons and play dates.

While the children were attending a church-sponsored excursion, Julie spoke to the Reverend Cheryl Ching about her situation. Julie is feeling increasingly resentful and angry with her ex-husband for not being more involved in the children's lives. Eric has been getting into trouble at school, and Brad has not attended any of the conferences with his teachers or school counselors. Julie does not know what to do about Eric's behavior. She is tired of raising the children alone.

Since the separation and divorce two years ago, Julie has worked hard at keeping the children's lives as stable as possible, but lately she does not feel that she can keep up the current schedule. Julie has thought about cutting down the children's outside activities, but then she feels guilty about depriving them. Although she has an understanding supervisor at her job, she is unable to work overtime or travel. Julie often finds herself leaving the office to take care of her children and then having to catch up with her projects late at night when they are sleeping. She believes that the quality of her work has suffered, along with her career. Julie would also like some time for herself but cannot think of a way to accomplish that.

The number of families in the United States that can be categorized as single-parent households has increased dramatically in recent decades.

Pastoral Assessment

Current statistics show single motherhood is on the rise at 12 million, up from 3.4 million in 1970 (Engber and Klungness, 2000). Experts estimate that 25 to 70 percent of American children will live with a single parent (Emery, 1994; Fine, 1999; Kinnear, 1999).

There are many different ways that single-parent families are created. Divorce, separation, death of a spouse, abandonment, unplanned pregnancies, and adoption are common ways that people become single parents (Kinnear, 1999). Other ways that are not so obvious include having one parent unavailable for a length of time, whether voluntarily or involuntarily, such as through incarceration, extended illness, military service, or other occupational responsibilities. In households where there is domestic violence, women and children often must leave their homes for safety. In less-than-amicable divorces, one parent may abduct the children. Many single women and even some men are choosing to have children, although they do not have a partner.

Most single parents (90 percent) are mothers (Fine, 1999). Research indicates that lack of involvement with children is typical of many fathers. In one study, according to mothers, one third of fathers saw their children once a year or less, while only one quarter saw them once a week or more. As length of time since the marital separation increased, father involvement decreased (Seltzer and Bianchi, 1991). However, in situations where the father is the person raising the children alone, studies show that fathers are similar to single mothers in terms of adjustment to divorce, child adjustment, and parent-child relationship (DeFrain, Fricke, and Elmen, 1987). One expert believes that the task of parenting children alone creates similar problems for both mothers and fathers (Grief, 1985). For a parent, developing appropriate and fulfilling new roles within the single parent family is a major undertaking.

The research on the adjustment of children is voluminous and often contradictory. Many studies indicate that children of divorce have more behavioral problems than those in nondivorced families (Hetherington and Clingempeel, 1992). However, after reviewing the literature, one expert concluded, "Most children cope successfully with divorce, but even successful coping takes a psychological toll" (Emery, 1994, p. 200). Sensitive parenting seems to be the key to helping children cope with divorce and all of the changes associated with this life transition.

Relevant History

One reason that Julie is reluctant to cut back on the children's activities is because she was the spouse who wanted to leave the marriage. She had been unhappy for many years prior to the actual separation and divorce. She had stayed with Brad for the children's sake, although there was frequent conflict between them. Julie is happier being divorced but misses the support of another parent. She believes that Brad is trying to hurt her by not spending time with the children. However, she admits that when he comes over to pick up the children, she and Brad start arguing. Julie feels responsible for the divorce and does not want the children to have to make any more sacrifices than they already have.

Many more women than men who are single parents report financial problems as a major concern (Kinnear, 1999). Julie is fortunate that since she is receiving child support, money problems are not the issue for her that they are with many other single mothers. Rather, Julie's feelings about her situation, coupled with Eric's problems at school, are the issues that must be addressed.

Research indicates that single parents tend to be more lenient with their children and have more difficulty controlling them than parents in two-parent families, especially in the first few years after a divorce (Hetherington, Stanley-Hagen, and Anderson, 1989). Typically, there are problems with parent-child relationships during this time (Hetherington, Cox, and Cox, 1982). During the marriage, Brad was the disciplinarian. If her lenient parenting continues, there is the possibility that the children, particularly Eric, will continue to have behavior problems.

Reverend Ching recognized the challenges that are part of single parenting. Julie has the sole responsibility of running the house and caring for the children. She is trying to be both mother and father. She is frustrated with her ex-husband and her son, as well as with the situation in general.

Reverend Ching set up an appointment to talk with Julie. She also spoke with the children and Julie together. The pastor wanted to try to understand the children's perspectives, since it is not unusual for children of divorce to have fears of abandonment by their parents or to blame themselves for the situation. This could be one of the reasons that Eric is having behavioral problems at school.

Reverend Ching encouraged Julie not to feel guilty about her current situation, but to emphasize its positive aspects: Julie is much happier as a single woman, and the children are no longer exposed to daily arguments. Reverend Ching suggested that Julie have a calm conversation with Brad about ways he could become more involved in the children's lives, especially in Eric's. She offered to mediate such a meeting, if necessary. Reverend Ching also discussed with Julie how she might let others help her. A volunteer from an organization such as Big Brothers/Big Sisters could help fill the void of a male figure in Eric's life if his father continues to be absent. Julie could trade baby-sitting duties with other parents of the play groups or soccer teams so that she could have some time to herself. Additionally, Julie might join the parents support group that meets monthly at the church or an organization such as Parents Without Partners. Julie could also explore the possibility of her parents or even Brad's parents getting more involved in the children's lives.

Treatment Within the Faith Community

Arguably, the stigma associated with being a single parent has lessened over the past couple of decades. Despite this, single parenthood has been described as a lonely situation. Some faith communities have programs focused on single parents, which are both educational and social, and many have activities for all parents and families. Single parents can be encouraged to participate in such programs to help alleviate the isolation that they may be experiencing. In addition to acting as a resource for information for single parents, clergy and church members can also act as a support network for single parents. Support networks are very significant for positive mother-child relationships after divorce.

Indications for Referral

Divorce often triggers a period of grief (Emery, 1994) or feelings of "separation distress" (Dura and Kiecolt-Glaser, 1991). Single parents who are depressed, isolated from a support network, or have financial difficulties are more likely to have problems (Emery, 1994). Parents who are depressed should seek help since their emotional well-being has implications for how the children behave; ineffective parenting can negatively affect children's behavior. Both the parent's and the child's behavior can exacerbate each other, a common situation for many mothers and sons (Hetherington, Cox, and Cox, 1978). Parents whose children are having social and emotional problems need to seek help for themselves and for the youngsters.

Treatment by Mental Health Specialist

A mental health specialist could work with Julie on parenting skills, teaching her how to be more authoritative with the children. An authoritative parent provides warmth and love but is strict and fair in disciplining the children. Youngsters raised with this parenting style are more likely to be self-confident, independent, and responsible than are children raised with other parenting styles, such as authoritarian or indulgent (Emery, 1994). Julie's guilt about getting the divorce might be an issue that she has to explore. Depressed parents may receive antidepressant medication in conjunction with other types of therapies to alleviate depression.

Cross-Cultural Issues

About two thirds of all single parents in the United States are European-American (Kinnear, 1999). Statistics from 1994 show that one quarter of all European-American families are single-parent. Among all African-American families, almost 65 percent are headed by one parent. In Hispanic families, 36 percent are headed by one parent. Overwhelmingly, for all three groups, women were most likely to be the single parent.

Resources

National Resources

—Association for Children for Enforcement of Support; 2260 Upton Avenue, Toledo, OH 43606; (800) 738-ACES; www.childsupport-aces.org. This national organization, with 350 affiliate groups, provides information and support for parents who have custody of their children and have problems obtaining child support payments.

—Beginning Experience; International Ministry Center, 1247 171st Place, Hammond, IN 46324; (219) 989-8915; www.beinfo.com. This international Christian organization, founded in 1975, provides support programs for divorced, widowed, and separated adults and for their children as they work through the grief of a marriage ending.

—Fathers.com; www.fathers.com; website of the National Center for Fathering (P.O. Box 413888, Kansas City, MO 64141; 800-593-DADS) that has articles with practical tips and suggestions for fathers. Topics are organized according to the age of the child, specific fathering situations, and fathering roles and responsibilities.

—Menstuff: The National Men's Resource; www.menstuff.org; an educational, nonprofit volunteer website developed and maintained by the National Men's Resource Center (P.O. Box 800, San Anselmo, CA 94979-0800), providing information on over 100 men's issues, including fatherhood, the "daddy track," stepfamilies, and divorce.

—Mom to Mom; www.momsonline.com/momtomom; website with information on various aspects of motherhood. Also has message boards and chat rooms so moms can network.

—National Parent Information Network; www.npin.org; this organization's mission is to provide access to research-based information about the process of parenting and family involvement in education. Website includes a virtual library, question-answering service, and parenting electronic discussion list.

—Parents Anonymous, Inc.; 675 West Foothill Boulevard, Suite 220, Claremont, CA 91711; (909) 621-6184; www.parentsanonymous-natl.org; a free family support and education program focused on strengthening families and stopping child abuse. Has parent education courses and parent support groups.

—Parents Place; www.parentsplace.com; website covering topics of interest to families, including parenthood, family dynamics, and marriage. Also has chat rooms.

—Parents Without Partners; 1650 South Dixie Highway, Suite 510, Boca Raton, FL 33432; (561) 391-8833; www.parentswithoutpartners.org; an international organization providing discussions, professional speakers, study groups, publications, and social activities for families and adults. Chapters are located throughout the United States and Canada.

—Rainbows; 2100 Golf Road #370, Rolling Meadows, IL 60008-4231; (800) 266-3206; www.rainbows.org; an international organization offering training and curricula for establishing peer support groups in churches, synagogues, schools, or social agencies for children and adults who are grieving a divorce, death, or other painful family transition. The support groups are led by trained adults. Referrals are also provided.

—Single and Custodial Fathers Network, Inc.; 608 Hastings Street, Pittsburgh, PA 15206; (412) 665-5491; www.scfn.org; an international organization dedicated to helping fathers meet the challenges of parenthood. It provides information and support to fathers and to their families through research, publications, and interactive communications.

Self-Help Resources

The Complete Single Mother: Reassuring Answers to Your Most Challenging Concerns (Andrea Engber and Leah Klungness, Holbrook, MA: Adams Media, 2000).

Divorce and New Beginnings: An Authoritative Guide to Recovery and Growth, Solo Parenting, and Stepfamilies (Genevieve Clapp, New York: John Wiley & Sons, 1992).

The Divorced Parent: Success Strategies for Raising Your Children After Separation (Stephanie Marston, New York: William Morrow & Co, 1994).

Families Apart: Ten Keys to Successful Co-parenting (Melinda Blau, New York: G. P. Putnam's Sons, 1993).

Raising Sons Without Fathers: A Woman's Guide to Parenting Strong, Successful Boys (Leif G. Terdal and Patricia Kennedy, Secaucus, NJ: Carol Publishing Group, 1996).

The Single Father: A Dad's Guide to Parenting Without a Partner (Armin A. Brott, New York: Abbeville Press, 1999).

Single Fatherhood (Chuck Gregg, New York: Sulzburger & Graham Publishing, 1995).

The Single Mother's Book: A Practical Guide to Managing Your Children, Career, Home, Finances, and Everything Else (Joan Anderson, Atlanta: Peachtree Publishers, 1990).

The Single Mother's Survival Guide (Patrice Karst, Freedom, CA: Crossing Press, 2000). The author is a single mother who shares practical advice with single moms. She covers a wide range of topics that concern parenting women struggling without a mate.

Single Mothers by Choice: A Guidebook for Single Women Who Are Considering or Have Chosen Motherhood (Janes Mattes, New York: Times Books, 1994).

Solo: A Guide for the Single Parent. Hall/Sloane Publishing, 10840 Camarillo Street #10, Tolucca Lake, CA 91602; 800-477-5877. A quarterly publication covering issues that affect single parents and their children.

Solo Parenting (Diane Chambers, Minneapolis: Fairview Press, 1997).

References

DeFrain, J., Fricke, J., and Elmen, J. (1987). *On Our Own: A Single Parent's Survival Guide.* Lexington, MA: Lexington Books.

Dura, J., and Kiecolt-Glaser, J. (1991). Family Transitions, Stress, and Health. In P. Cowan and E. M. Hetherington (Eds.), *Family Transitions* (pp. 59–76). Hillsdale, NJ: Lawrence Erlbaum Associates.

Emery R. (1994). *Renegotiating Family Relationships: Divorce, Child Custody, and Mediation*. New York: Guilford Press.

Engber, A., and Klungness, L. (2000). *The Complete Single Mother: Reassuring Answers to Your Most Challenging Concerns*. Holbrook, MA: Adams Media.

Fine, M. (1999). Single Parents. In C.A. Smith (Ed.), *The Encyclopedia of Parenting Theory and Research* (pp. 398–400). Westport, CT: Greenwood Publishing.

Grief, G. (1985). *Single Fathers*. Lexington, MA: Lexington Books.

Hetherington, E. M., and Clingempeel, W. G. (1992). Coping with marital transitions: A family systems perspective. *Monographs of the Society for Research in Child Development, 227*, Vol. 57, Nos. 2–3.

Hetherington, E. M., Cox, M., and Cox, R. (1978). The Aftermath of Divorce. In J. Stevens and M. Matthews (Eds.), *Mother-child/Father-child Relations*. Washington, DC: National Association for the Education of Young Children

Hetherington, E. M., Cox, M., and Cox, R. (1982). Effects of Divorce on Parents and Children. In M. E. Lamb (Ed.), *Nontraditional Families* (pp. 233–288). Hillsdale, NJ: Lawrence Erlbaum Associates.

Hetherington, E. M., Stanley-Hagen, M., and Anderson, E. (1989). Marital transitions: A child's perspective. *American Psychologist, 44*, 303–312.

Kinnear, K. L. (1999). *Single Parents: A Reference Handbook*. Santa Barbara: ABC-CLIO.

Seltzer, J., and Bianchi, S. (1991). Relationships between fathers and children who live apart: The father's role after separation. *Journal of Marriage and the Family, 53*, 79–101.

The Divorced Parent

"Suddenly, I Am Alone"

After fifteen years of marriage, three children, and increasing marital conflict, Craig Bethel's wife asked for a divorce. The couple have been separated for two months, and the legal details are in progress. Craig went to talk to his minister, the Reverend Richard L. W. Lee, about the situation for the first time. Although in his heart he knows that the divorce is the right thing to do, Craig confessed that he alternates between feeling angry, guilty, and depressed.

The children's grades have suffered during the separation. Six-year-old Daryl and nine-year-old Michelle have been acting out and frequently staying home from school because of headaches and other illnesses. The oldest child, thirteen-year-old Amber, is busy with her own friends and rarely has time to see Craig. Although he is close to his children, he does not visit them as often as permitted by the temporary custody agreement because he feels strange going to his former house to pick them up. When Craig returns the children to their mother, Cheryl, the younger ones cry and create a scene.

When he is with the children, Craig is sometimes at a loss as to what to do. He wants to be able to take them to amusement parks and restaurants to make up for not being with them, but he must watch his expenses because of the costs of the divorce. He considers spending even less time with his children "because it is just too painful," yet he is afraid of losing their love.

The Bethel family had been active in their church. The children attended Sunday school, and Cheryl was in the women's organization. On the surface, there didn't seem to be any marital problems, although Craig was often out of town on business. Neither Craig nor Cheryl ever spoke to their pastor about marriage difficulties. Since the separation, the family has

Pastoral Assessment

continued some church activities, but Craig has stopped attending worship services. Reverend Lee recognized that he was hearing about two different but interrelated issues—Craig's reactions to the divorce and the children's responses to it.

Relevant History

Reluctantly, Craig acknowledges that he and Cheryl had fought often in the last few years of their marriage. His way of dealing with conflict was to use work as an excuse to stay away from home. Despite this tactic, he did try to remain involved in the children's lives. When Cheryl wanted a divorce, Craig was shocked. He begged her to go with him to marriage counseling, but she refused. Cheryl had been thinking about, and planning for, a divorce for a long time.

Craig is too embarrassed to talk about his situation with friends or even to socialize with them. He has been avoiding his parents and siblings because he is the first in his extended family to get a divorce, and he worries that his relatives are judging him. Craig feels like a failure.

Diagnostic Criteria

Between 40 and 50 percent of marriages will end in divorce (Pruett, 2000). Annually, more than one million children in the United States experience divorce or separation (Hatzichristou, 1999). Divorce is now conceptualized as a long-term multistage process involving adaptation and change over a period of years (Hetherington & Clingempeel, 1992). It is one of the severest life stressors experienced. Divorce affects the whole family and the way the members function and interact with each other. Family members will experience short- and long-term outcomes that may differ from those of other members depending on their age, the presence of other stressors, available support systems, and their coping strategies (Hetherington, Cox, and Cox, 1982).

Craig is experiencing a common emotional response to divorce—his anger, grief, guilt, and self-doubt are typical (Hatzichristou, 1999). Other reactions can include shock, sadness, denial, becoming a workaholic, and acting out through substance abuse, sexual promiscuity, or eating disorders (Engel, 1994; Gold, 1992). A person's physical health may also be affected, manifested in such symptoms as abdominal pain leading to loss of appetite and weight loss, headaches, and fatigue. Depression is the single most common medical problem during a divorce (Fleming, 1994).

Some researchers think that men may be less able than women to cope with the negative emotional consequences of divorce (McKenry and Price, 1990), and it is believed that the father-child relationship is especially vulnerable to divorce (Amato, 1999). An expert states, "Divorce is the most serious threat to a child's relationship with his father and vice versa" (Pruett, 2000, pp. 112–113). One study found that all fathers who had been involved in the lives of their children prior to divorce and experienced loss of contact afterward exhibited high levels of anger and mental health problems and felt deprived and isolated (Hetherington, Cox, and Cox, 1982).

For fathers who do not live with their children following divorce, there may be increasing uncertainty about what to do with them. Craig thought that he should be a "Disneyland Dad," taking them places and buying them things (Marston, 1994), which is costly and often leads to unrealistic expectations on the part of the children (Ackerman, 1997). Many other men react by lessening contact with their offspring over the years or by not paying their child support on time or at all. One national study found that only 1 out of 6 children of divorce had weekly contact or more with the father. One third to one half had not seen their fathers in the last year (Furstenberg and Nord, 1985).

The greater the education and income levels of fathers, the more likely they are to have contact with their children after divorce. This may be because these men have good legal representation that enables them to establish better custody arrangements. A high income also enables them to afford the sometimes costly visits with children (Stephens, 1996).

Many experts emphasize that despite the pain that the parents experience with the end of a marriage, it is minor compared to the stress on their children (Gold, 1992). Most research indicates that children of divorced parents have more academic, behavioral, social, and emotional problems than those of intact families (Amato, 1999). The first two years of a family's separation are the most difficult in terms of psychological stress, economic issues, and parental conflict. After that time, families begin to adjust to their situation, and there is often a decrease in parental hostility and an increase in cooperation (Whiteside, 1998). Divorce can have negative consequences for children that persist into adulthood (Amato, 1999). However, many children are resilient and gradually adjust to their new family situation, becoming reasonably competent individuals (Hetherington, 1999).

A review of the research indicates that the quality of parents' relationships with each other, what is called the "parental alliance," affects the adjustment of both adults and children following divorce. A positive parenting alliance occurs when both father and mother respect each other, communicate about the children, and share responsibility for the child rearing. Communication includes exchanging information and solving problems together. Sharing responsibility includes day-to-day child-rearing tasks and logistical problems of moving the children between households (Whiteside, 1998).

One expert states that children need the following in order to help them adjust to the divorce: (1) children are protected from their parents' disputes, (2) children are free to love both parents, (3) parents shift their roles from intimate partners to parenting partners, (4) children have access to both parents without being placed in a loyalty conflict, and (5) parents are able to recover from the trauma of divorce and rebuild their lives (Marston, 1994, p. 15).

Response to Vignette

Reverend Lee understands his role as working with Craig individually and with his family, toward the goal of helping them adjust to the divorce and build new lives as individuals and as a family. The pastor helped develop a list of concerns that Craig needs to address to help him adjust to the divorce. Some of the items they came up with included:

- Legal issues with wife: alimony, division of property
- Legal issues with children: custody, visitation rights, child support
- Accepting the situation: guilt, anger, feelings of failure
- Handling loneliness
- Learning to be a single person again and a single father
- Learning domestic skills and parenting skills for children of various ages
- Budgeting

Reverend Lee resolved that he would help Craig in as many ways as he could, but he also encouraged Craig to seek help from a professional counselor trained in marriage and family issues.

The pastor recommended that Craig and Cheryl consider mediation as a means to resolve issues in the divorce. Mediation provides a neutral forum where a trained person helps couples decide on the terms of a divorce through equitable and workable settlements (Gold, 1992), which can help to reduce the animosity between the parties.

Another way that Reverend Lee helped Craig deal with his situation was by discussing the role of forgiveness. Since Craig believes that marriage should be forever, some of the guilt that he is experiencing is related to his feelings of failure as a man who didn't succeed in keeping his marriage and family intact. He has to learn to forgive both Cheryl and himself. The pastor and Craig explored ways to help him do this. After a lot of soul-searching, Craig concluded that becoming a competent single person and single father would help ease his feelings of failure. He needs to learn many domestic skills that he had previously left up to Cheryl to perform. He also wants to learn more about parenting in an effort to be a successful single father. Craig is determined to have a civil relationship with Cheryl in order to minimize the stress on the children and on himself. He also recognizes the support his extended family can offer him and the children, and he is beginning to reach out to them.

Craig was encouraged to talk with the children about the divorce and the reasons behind it, making sure that they understand that they are not to blame. He reminded them that even though he no longer lives with them, he is still their father and will be forever. Instead of being the "Disneyland Dad," Craig tries to incorporate the children into his new life. They now help him with chores in his new apartment and have brought over some of their things to keep at his new place, so that they feel like they have a home there. Craig also purchased some of his children's favorite toys and books so that he would be able to play games and read to them as he did when he was married.

Together, Craig and the children plan their weekend activities and have established a routine during his visitation weekends. This is especially important for the younger children, to help ease the transition back to their mother.

Craig makes time for each child individually. His teenage daughter particularly needs her father's attention at this critical stage of her life. She, like other teens in this situation, is particularly at risk for disengaging from her family and letting her peer group take priority in her life. Craig and Cheryl must be careful to keep track of who their daughter's friends are and the activities in which they are involved.

The pastor encouraged Craig to develop new traditions with his children while keeping alive some of the old ones. For example, he and the children have begun making a special pancake breakfast every Saturday morning that they are together. At Christmas, Craig plans to have a new family portrait taken. He now joins his family every Sunday at church services. Craig visited each of the schools that his children attend, gave the teachers his new address, and asked that he be kept informed of all aspects of the children's progress and all school events.

Reverend Lee also helped Craig see that the divorce can create opportunities for him. Many people have used a divorce as a reason to try new experiences, such as taking trips, enrolling in classes, and joining new organizations. The pastor reminded Craig that beyond the hurt and confusion he is experiencing, the promise of a new future and the potential for new relationships exist.

Treatment Within the Faith Community

In the past, much of the attention given to divorce within churches and synagogues emphasized the negative aspects; such families were referred to as "broken homes." Today, many faith communities offer avenues of support for divorced individuals and their families. Counseling services attached to churches exist in many locations. Educational and support groups for adults and children can also be found in religious communities.

The value of social support for persons experiencing difficult situations is well documented (Cohen and Wills, 1985). For African Americans, in particular, support from church members and religious participation has been found to buffer psychological distress (Kim and McKenry, 1998). Interestingly, some studies indicate that support from friends may be less stressful than that received from relatives. Fathers seem to rely more on friends for emotional support than mothers do (Smith, 1999).

Indications for Referral

Divorced family members are overrepresented in treatment populations for many reasons. They can have more stressors and consequently more psychological distress or disorders. A divorcing adult also may be required to be in treatment as a part of a court order.

Craig must be referred to professional help if he has increased depression or feelings of being overwhelmed. He should also seek help if he is unable to separate his emotions from the tasks that need to be resolved—for example, if his anger gets in the way of communication and cooperation with Cheryl to the detriment of the children. The youngsters should get help if their behavioral problems continue.

Treatment by Mental Health Specialist

Treatment for divorce often has the goals of improved psychological adjustment, parenting, and family relationships (Emery, Kitsman, and Waldron, 1999). A therapist can encourage and support positive behaviors and self-esteem, educating a client about the emotional process of divorce, as well as providing strategies for meeting parental responsibilities and making a new life. Communication skills and parenting skills are examples of areas that may be explored.

Family therapy is also often recommended. In that case, a family's current state can be assessed in terms of emotions, interpersonal skills and relationships, conflicts, and communication. Goals that family members might work toward, such as increasing cooperation and collaboration, would be presented and a plan for meeting the goals could be developed.

Cross-Cultural Issues

One review of the research found that 2 of 3 African-American marriages end in divorce and that divorce is a particularly stressful process for the men (Lawson and Thompson, 1996). A study of thirty divorced African-American men found that financial strain, noncustodial parenting, child support issues, and psychological distress were significant stressors for them. Most of the ex-husbands experienced financial strain, in part because they had sacrificed to their former wives all common marital assets for the benefit of their children and to prevent the women from having to seek public assistance. All of the fathers experienced emotional problems due to maternal custody and limited contact with their children. They coped by relying on family and friends for support, involving themselves in church-related activities, and increasing their social participation (Lawson and Thompson, 1996).

Resources

National Resources

—Association for Children for Enforcement of Support, 2260 Upton Avenue, Toledo, OH 43606; (800) 537-7072; nataces@aol.com. This national organization with 350 affiliate groups provides information and support for parents who have custody of their children and have problems obtaining child support payments.

—Children's Rights Council, 220 I Street, NE, Suite 140, Washington, DC 20002; (202) 547-6227. This national group is concerned with reforming the legal system regarding child custody. It offers a newsletter, information, referrals, and directory of parenting organizations, conferences, and group development guidelines.

—Divorce Care, 223 South White, P.O. Box 1739, Wake Forest, NC 27588-1739; (919) 562-2112; www.divorcecare.com. This is an evangelical Christian organization, with 2,900 affiliated groups, founded to help build networks of support groups for those recovering from separation or divorce. It provides information, referrals, support group meetings, and assistance in starting groups.

—Fathers.com; www.fathers.com; website containing articles with practical tips and suggestions for fathers. Topics are organized according to the age of the child, specific fathering situations, and fathering roles and responsibilities.

—Menstuff: The National Men's Resource; www.menstuff.com; an educational nonprofit website developed and maintained by volunteers of the National Men's Resource Center; provides information on over 100 men's issues, including fatherhood, the "daddy track," stepfamilies, and divorce.

—Mom to Mom; www.momsonline.com/momtomom; website with information on various aspects of motherhood, as well as message boards and chat rooms so moms can network.

—National Parent Information Network; www.npin.org; provides access to research-based information about the process of parenting and about family involvement in education. Website includes a virtual library, question-answering service, and a parenting electronic discussion list.

—North American Conference of Separated and Divorced Catholics, P.O. Box 1301, La Grande, OR 97850; (503) 963-8089. This is an international group, founded in 1972, to address religious, educational, and emotional aspects of separation, divorce, widowhood, and remarriage through self-help groups, conferences, and training programs. People from all faiths are welcome.

—Parents Anonymous, 675 West Foothill Boulevard, Suite 220, Claremont, CA 91711; (909) 621-6184; www.parentsanonymous-natl.org. This national organization, founded in 1970, is a professionally facilitated, peer-led group for parents who are having difficulty and would like to learn more effective ways to parent. It provides group leaders, develops chapters, and has children's groups.

—Parents Without Partners; www.parentswithoutpartners.org; an international organization providing discussions, professional speakers, study groups, publications, and social activities for families and adults. Chapters are located throughout the U.S. and Canada.

—Rainbows, 2100 Golf Road #370, Rolling Meadows, IL 60008-4231; (800) 266-3206; www.rainbows.org; an international organization with

6,300 affiliated groups. Founded in 1983, Rainbows establishes peer support groups in churches, schools, and social agencies for children and adults who are grieving a divorce, death, or other painful change in their family. The support groups are led by trained adults. Referrals are also provided.

—Single and Custodial Father's Network; 608 Hastings Street, Pittsburgh, PA 15206; (412) 665-5491; www.scfn.org; an international, member-supported, nonprofit organization dedicated to helping fathers meet the challenge of being parents. It provides informational and supportive services to fathers and their families and supports fatherhood through research, publications, and interactive communications.

—The Beginning Experience, 305 Michigan Avenue, Detroit, MI 48226; (313) 965-5110. This international Christian organization, founded in 1975, provides support programs for divorced, widowed, and separated adults and their children as they work through the grief of a marriage ending.

Self-Help Resources

"*Does Wednesday Mean Mom's House or Dad's?*": *Parenting Together While Living Apart* (Marc J. Ackerman, New York: John Wiley & Sons, 1997); a guide to the divorce and custody process. Contains practical information on custody and living arrangements, such as sleeping arrangements and sharing holidays. The author uses many actual examples of how children are affected in different divorce scenarios.

Divorce Help Sourcebook (Margorie L. Engel, Detroit: Visible Ink Press, 1994); comprehensive discussion of many divorce-related issues with listings of potential sources of help. Topics include legal, financial, parenting, and health matters. Also lists laws and resources by state.

Fatherneed: Why Father Care Is as Essential as Mother Care for Your Child (Kyle D. Pruett, New York: Free Press, 2000); discusses the importance of fathers and gives advice for fathers in specific situations, such as divorce.

Single Parents: A Reference Handbook (Karen L. Kinnear, Santa Barbara: ABC-CLIO, 1999); contains an excellent directory of organizations and a list of print, video, and Internet resources for the single parent.

References

Ackerman, M. (1997). "*Does Wednesday Mean Mom's House or Dad's?*": *Parenting Together While Living Apart*. New York: John Wiley & Sons.

Amato, R. (1999). Children of divorced parents as young adults. In E. M. Hetherington (Ed.), *Coping with Divorce, Single Parenting, and Remarriage* (pp. 147–163). Mahwah, NJ: Lawrence Erlbaum Associates.

Cohen, S., and Wills, T. A. (1985). Stress, social support, and the buffering hypothesis. *Psychological Bulletin*, 98, 310–357.

Emery, R., Kitsman, K. M., and Waldron, M. (1999). Psychological interventions for separated and divorced families. In E. M. Hetherington (Ed.), *Coping with Divorce, Single Parenting, and Remarriage* (pp. 323–344). Mahwah, NJ: Lawrence Erlbaum Associates.

Engel, M. L. (1994). The importance of family health and medical care during divorce. In M. L. Engel (Ed.), *Divorce Help Sourcebook* (pp. 3–16). Detroit: Visible Ink Press.

Fleming, M. O. (1994). The importance of family health and medical care during divorce. In M. L. Engel (Ed.), *Divorce Help Sourcebook* (pp. 231–235). Detroit: Visible Ink Press.

Furstenberg, F. F., and Nord, C. W. (1985). Parenting apart: Patterns of childrearing after marital disruption. *Journal of Marriage and the Family, 47,* 893–904.

Gold, L. (1992). *Between Love and Hate: A Guide to Civilized Divorce.* New York: Plenum Publishing.

Hatzichristou, C. (1999). Divorced families. In C. A. Smith (Ed.), *The Encyclopedia of Parenting Theory and Research* (pp. 135–137). Westport, CT: Greenwood Publishing.

Hetherington, E. M. (1999). Should we stay together for the sake of the children? In E. M. Hetherington (Ed.), *Coping with Divorce, Single Parenting, and Remarriage* (pp. 93–116). Mahwah, NJ: Lawrence Erlbaum Associates.

Hetherington, E. M., and Clingempeel, W. G. (1992). Coping with marital transitions: A family systems perspective. *Monographs of the Society for Research in Child Development, 227(57),* Nos. 2–3.

Hetherington, E. M., Cox, M., and Cox, R. (1982). Effects of divorce on parents and children. In M. E. Lamb (Ed.), *Nontraditional Families* (pp. 233–288). Hillsdale, NJ: Lawrence Erlbaum Associates.

Kim, H., and McKenry, P. C. (1998). Social networks and support: A comparison of African Americans, Asian Americans, Caucasians, and Hispanics. *Journal of Comparative Family Studies, 29(2),* 313–334.

Lawson, E. J., and Thompson, A. (1996). Black men's perceptions of divorce-related stressors and strategies for coping with divorce. *Journal of Family Issues, 17(20),* 249–273.

Marston, S. (1994). *The Divorced Parent.* New York: William Morrow & Co.

McKenry, P. C., and Price, S. J. (1990). Divorce: Are men at risk? In D. Moore and F. Leafgren (Eds.), *Problem Solving Strategies and Interventions for Men in Conflict* (pp.110–125). Alexandria, VA: American Association for Counseling and Development.

Pruett, K. D. (2000). *Fatherneed: Why Father Care Is as Essential as Mother Care for Your Child.* New York: Free Press.

Smith, C. A. (1999). Social support, informal. In C. A. Smith (Ed.), *The*

Encyclopedia of Parenting Theory and Research (pp. 407–409). Westport, CT: Greenwood Publishing.

Stephens, L. S. (1996). Will Johnny see Daddy this week? *Journal of Family Issues, 17(4)*, 466–494.

Whiteside, M. F. (1998). The parental alliance following divorce: An overview. *Journal of Marital and Family Therapy, 24(1)*, 3–24.

Stepparenting

"Fairy Tales Have Wicked Stepmothers, but No One Ever Talks About Stepfathers"

Tony Shimakawa recently married Darlene Marumoto—the second marriage for each. He moved in with his new wife and her two children, thirteen-year-old Portia and eight-year-old Vickie. Darlene's daughters were ambivalent about their mother remarrying. Portia, particularly, does not like her stepfather and resents his moving into their house. Tony also has a daughter, Tasha, who is six years old and lives with her mother. Tasha spends every other weekend with her father, Darlene, and the girls. Darlene's daughters spend occasional weekends and holidays with their father and his new family. The children do not get along. Portia and Vickie compete with Tony for their mother's attention. When Tasha visits, she is very needy and cries when she has to leave. She does not understand why she cannot live with her father or why he has another little girl to take her place. Tony would like to have a child with Darlene, but she is hesitant to do so until their children get along better. They spoke with the Reverend Bill Chung together about the conflicts in their household.

This situation illustrates the complexity of many of today's families. Reverend Chung had counseled Darlene and her daughters during her divorce three years ago. Now their family situation has changed again. Darlene and her children had to adjust to the dynamics of divorce and single parenthood. Only a few years later, they have a new man in their lives and a new stepdaughter and stepsister. Likewise, Tony and Tasha first had to cope with a divorce and Tony moving out of the home. Now they have to adjust to his remarriage and a stepfamily. Although Darlene and Tony are deeply in love and happy in their marriage, the conflicts related to the children are proving stressful.

Pastoral Assessment

Relevant History

Darlene's daughters never wanted her to date, keeping alive the dream that their parents would reconcile. They finally abandoned that hope when their father remarried one year ago and started a new family. Their father has minimized contact with his children, saying that he does not have time for two families. Nevertheless, Darlene's daughters resent Tony's presence in their lives. Since Darlene did not want to upset her children, she was content to have a relationship with Tony in which both of them maintained separate residences until Portia left for college. However, once they decided to marry, Darlene asked Tony to move into her house so her children would not have to relocate. Now married, Darlene feels torn between her children's and her new husband's needs. She also feels the stress of trying to make Tasha's visits pleasant for the whole household. Although she would love to have a baby with Tony, Darlene fears another child will increase the stress and conflict for everyone.

Tony describes feeling uncomfortable in his new home, although he was the one who pushed the relationship toward marriage. Despite the problems with the children, Tony wants Darlene to become pregnant as soon as possible. He is at a loss as to what to do about his stepdaughters. He copes with the situation by reminding himself that in a few years, Portia will be going to college.

Tony feels guilty about Tasha's emotional state when she visits him and his new family. Tony would like to have his daughter live with them, but his ex-wife refuses even to entertain that idea. He thought about going to court to press the issue but decided against it because of the potential emotional cost to Tasha, not to mention the negative effect it could have on the fragile civility that he and his ex-wife maintain. For now, he does not know what to do when Tasha cries about his new family, except to hope that she will eventually adjust to the situation.

Diagnostic Criteria

Stepfamilies are defined as families with at least one child under age eighteen living with a biological parent and a stepparent married to the child's biological parent (Fine, 1999). Other labels for stepfamilies are: reconstituted, blended, reconstructed, reorganized, reformed, recycled, and remarried families (Ganong and Coleman, 1997). According to the 1990 census, 5.3 million married-couple households (20.8 percent) were stepfamilies (Hughes and Schroeder, 1997). There are more stepfathers than stepmothers, since mothers are more likely to be awarded custody of the children after divorce (Fine, 1999), although fathers more frequently have custody of their children now than in previous years (Eggebeen, Snyder, and Manning, 1996). Fairy tales and popular culture abound with stories of wicked stepparents, particularly stepmothers. Historically, stepfamilies have had negative connotations (Phillips, 1997). Societies usually compare stepfamilies to nuclear families and find stepfamilies lacking in virtually all categories of comparison (Ganong and Coleman, 1997). The same approach characterizes most stepfamily research (Gamache, 1997), some of which is discussed here.

Stepparents face a challenge in developing positive relationships with their stepchildren while simultaneously establishing a solid marriage with the new spouse. Many newly remarried couples never enjoy a "honeymoon" period because there are children and stepchildren requiring care. These demands may make it difficult for the newly married couple to find the time or means to invest in each other (Sholevar, 1985). Second and later marriages have a higher divorce rate than first marriages have—a contributing factor is the presence of children from previous marriages. The presence of an adolescent stepchild is particularly associated with increased family problems (Bray, 1999).

Stepparents may also be required to deal with family members other than children, including ex-spouses and their new partners, current and ex-in-laws, and various sets of current and ex-grandparents, uncles, aunts, and cousins (Blau, 1993; Hetherington and Clingempeel, 1992). There are no labels for some of these relationships (Ganong and Coleman, 1997)—for example, the one between Darlene and Tony's former wife.

Stepparents often enter a marriage with unrealistic expectations that they and the stepchildren will immediately adjust and love each other, which are likely to lead to disappointment (Visher and Visher, 1996, as cited in Fine, 1999). Another difficulty is that stepparents and their spouses are sometimes confused or conflicted about the role of the new stepparent (Fine, 1999). Should the new partner be a "parent" or a "friend" to the stepchildren or have nothing to do with them? A stepparent is often in the role of an outsider entering a single-parent family that has a previously existing history and established routines. Children may see stepparents as competition or a threat to the relationship with their biological parent (Bray, 1999; Hetherington and Clingempeel, 1992).

Children from remarried and divorced families show more behavioral, social, emotional, and learning problems than children from nondivorced families. The research is mixed with regard to how marital transitions, such as remarriage, affect boys and girls of various ages and different stages of development. One result that seems consistent is that early adolescents have the greatest difficulty adjusting to a parent's remarriage (Hetherington and Clingempeel, 1992). Similarly, teens in stepfamilies have more problems coping with adolescent development issues than teens in nuclear families. Some stepparents react to behavior problems by disengaging from the stepchild, which actually may increase the difficulties (Bray, 1999). The stepparent-child relationship is affected by both the stepparent's predisposition and effort and the child's developmental status and readiness for it. In general, stepparent-child relationships are more distant, more conflicted, and have more negative interactions than parent-child relationships in intact families (Bray, 1999). Stepmothers report more difficulty in raising stepchildren than do stepfathers (Ihinger-Tallman and Pasley, 1997; MacDonald and DeMaris, 1996), perhaps because they are more involved in their care, leading to potentially more occasions for conflict (Ihinger-Tallman and Pasley, 1997). In blended families where there were children from the stepfather, parents indicated high rates of marital, child-rearing, and parental role conflict. They also reported treating natural children and stepchildren differently (Hetherington, Cox, and Cox, 1982).

There are conflicting conclusions with regard to the addition of new biological children to a blended family. Some studies indicate that a new baby adds to the attachment of the stepfather to the stepfamily while it detracts from the attachment of the stepmother (Ambert, 1986); other research shows that a new child has no effect on the stepparents with regard to raising stepchildren (MacDonald and DeMaris, 1996) unless the baby is a firstborn biological child. One study found that the birth of a new child in a remarriage was related to increased marital satisfaction (Hetherington, Cox, and Cox, 1982).

Research shows that remarried parents reported being happier and less lonely and anxious than divorced parents. Families with stepparents who were warm, set consistent limits, and communicated well with stepchildren produced children who functioned better than children in divorced or nondivorced families with a lot of conflict (Hetherington, Cox, and Cox, 1982). Although there are many indications that children in blended families are at risk for developing mental health problems and having adjustment issues during a remarriage transition or during adolescence, the majority of them function within a normal range (Bray, 1999).

Response to Vignette

Reverend Chung talked to Tony and Darlene individually and as a couple and to Darlene's daughters together. He is also willing to talk to all four of them at once, when everyone is ready. Since the pastor did not feel adequately trained to counsel young children, he advised Tony to seek other help for Tasha, perhaps from her school counselor. One recommendation that Reverend Chung made to the couple was that they learn more about their roles by talking to others in similar situations, joining a support group, or getting stepfamily counseling. In this case, Tony and Darlene joined the parents group at their church where they got many suggestions from other stepparents. The first pieces of advice they heard were to be patient and to be flexible. It can take two to five years for stepfamily members to adjust to each other and develop cohesion (Bray, 1999; Ihinger-Tallman and Pasley, 1997).

Both Tony and Darlene must define their roles as stepparents, including agreeing to communicate to each other their feelings about the marriage, the children, and their respective relationships with each child. Tony was encouraged not to be a "father" to Portia and Vickie, but initially to have less involvement with the girls (Ihinger-Tallman and Pasley, 1997). He can act like a supportive friend, and as the relationship grows, perhaps he will be able to play an increasing role in their lives (Fine, 1999). Trying to become involved too quickly, especially with regard to discipline of the girls, is likely to be met with hostility or withdrawal. Despite this, Tony should be aware and supportive of the children's behavior and activities (Bray, 1999).

Darlene and Tony were encouraged to learn to accept and assert their place and right to authority within the household and with each other's children. This was especially important for Tony, since he had been uncomfortable in his new home. He felt that he was expected to follow the rules that Darlene and her daughters had traditionally operated under and that he had no say in changing them. He realized that he might never be comfortable in that house for a variety of reasons, some of them having to do with Portia and Vickie seeing him and his daughter as unwanted and uninvited. The pastor discussed some solutions, including the possibilities of the family someday moving into a new home, which would be "neutral territory," and of slowly developing new routines and traditions.

In terms of "blending" the family, Tony and Darlene were advised not to force their children on one another. On Tasha's visitation weekends, in addition to having some activities with the family as a whole, Tony needs to spend time with her alone, and Darlene needs to spend time with just her daughters to help reassure the children of their place in their parent's heart and life. Initially, Darlene should not try to "mother" Tasha, instead she should simply be a supportive adult. As the relationship develops, perhaps Darlene can become more involved in Tasha's life.

Treatment Within the Faith Community

The prevalence of divorce and remarriage means that stepfamilies are no longer uncommon. The faith community can be supportive by ignoring the negative stereotypes (Ganong and Coleman, 1997) and helping to normalize stepfamilies. Darlene and Tony joined the parents group at their church, which became an effective support group for them. Portia could join the youth group, which would offer her a healthy, supportive environment to air her issues. Despite their difficulties, Darlene and Tony plan to continue attending worship as a family. In general, being a part of a faith community offers benefits to families of all kinds. In addition to organized groups, the informal social interaction and camaraderie of a congregation are healthy avenues for interaction.

Indications for Referral

Among couples with stepfamilies, the most common area of stress that interferes with marital satisfaction is parent-child relationships (Hetherington and Clingempeel, 1992). In one study, some stepmothers sought divorces because of issues related to their stepchildren. Some youngsters never adjust to having a stepparent and deliberately try to sabotage the marriage (Jones and Schiller, 1992).

In stepfamilies, the formation of a coalition between the biological parent and child against the stepparent is extremely dysfunctional. Other problems that may warrant referral to a mental health professional include increased conflict, communication problems, decreased problem-solving ability, poor marital adjustment, and increasingly negative parent-child interactions.

Treatment by Mental Health Specialist

A mental health specialist can assess the marriage, identifying its strengths and weaknesses. The purpose of an evaluation is to decide on the most appropriate method of treatment. Depending on the theoretical orientation of the professional, different aspects of the marriage may be examined, such as the history of the relationship, personality traits of the partners, and relationships with family of origin. An assessment also enables the couple to objectively understand their issues and work with the specialist to develop plans to address them.

One mental health professional has created the following approach to working with remarried couples: (1) eliminate chaos and confusion and establish order in the family, (2) build trust in the marriage, (3) extend this trust to the entire remarried family, (4) resolve past allegiances and ties, (5) revise unrealistic expectations, and (6) develop ways and means for the family relationship to meet the needs of all the members (Goldberg, 1985). In this approach and in many others, one of the first tasks of the specialist would be to assess the communication patterns of the couple. Clear and effective communication is the cornerstone of a healthy marriage (Sholevar, 1985) and is essential in stepfamilies, in which there are often many complex relationships (Ganong and Coleman, 1997). To this end, couples often are trained to communicate with each other more effectively.

Most stepparents' disagreements are related to the children. Like other couples, stepparents often seek professional help because of child-rearing difficulties. These conflicts can be intensified with stepparents because of the looser definition of roles in the family (Goldberg, 1985). In such situations, one solution may be to develop a parenting plan that is agreeable to both partners. Specific training in parenting skills may also be included in the treatment plan.

Related to conflicts about children and child rearing are issues about pregnancy. These difficulties are often due to the partners being at different points in their lives, depending on their ages or other issues. Because Darlene is primarily responsible for raising her daughters, she feels that her child-rearing plate is full and that the addition of a baby will only increase her burden. Tony, on the other hand, does not have primary responsibility for the raising of his child and does not feel responsible for Darlene's daughters. Thus, he is willing and eager to have a baby in order to feel like a family with Darlene. A mental health specialist could help Tony and

Darlene understand each other's viewpoint about this issue as a first step to its resolution.

Despite an increase in research on stepfamilies, studies on ethnic minority stepfamilies are almost nonexistent. Interestingly, one set of researchers found that minority stepparents experience less relative difficulty finding parental satisfaction with stepchildren versus biological children than do European-Americans (MacDonald and DeMaris, 1996). This finding is not unexpected in regard to African-American families, which often have extended-family networks that offer resources and support for parents. African-American families tend to have egalitarian and flexible male-female roles in which financial, household, and child care decisions are shared. Parenting responsibilities may also involve other adults in the extended family and fictive kin (Kane, 2000). All of these family dynamics may make stepparenting less of a burden for African-Americans than for other ethnic groups.

In this case, Tony and Darlene are Japanese-American. Although there is variation among Asian-American groups, most of them exhibit more family cohesion than do European-Americans (Uba, 1994). Asian-Americans use the family and extended family as the principal means of support (Fong, 1994).

Cross-Cultural Issues

National Resources

Resources

—American Psychological Association Help Center; a website with information on different topics related to mental health, including "Interventions that Help Stepfamilies"; www.helping.apa.org. Also provides referrals for psychologists and free brochures.

—Fathers.com, www.fathers.com, is the website of the National Center for Fathering (P.O. Box 413888, Kansas City, MO 64141; 800-593-DADS) that has articles with practical tips and suggestions for fathers. Topics are organized according to age of child, specific fathering situations, and fathering roles and responsibilities.

—Menstuff: The National Men's Resource; www.menstuff.org; an educational, nonprofit volunteer website developed and maintained by the National Men's Resource Center (P.O. Box 800, San Anselmo, CA 94979-0800), providing information on over 100 men's issues, including fatherhood, the "daddy track," stepfamilies, and divorce.

—Mom to Mom; www.momsonline.com/momtomom; a website with information on various aspects of motherhood. Also has message boards and chat rooms so moms can network.

—National Parent Information Network; www.npin.org; this organization's mission is to provide access to research-based information about the process of parenting and about family involvement in education. Website includes a virtual library, question-answering service, and parenting electronic discussion list.

—Rainbows; 2100 Golf Road #370, Rolling Meadows, IL 60008-4231; (800) 266-3206; www.rainbows.org; an international organization offering training and curricula for establishing peer support groups in churches, synagogues, schools, or social agencies for children and adults who are grieving a death, divorce, or any other painful family transition. The support groups are led by trained adults. Referrals are also provided.

—Stepfamily Association of America; 650 J Street, Suite 205, Lincoln, NE 68508; 800-735-0329; www.stepfam.org; a national organization with chapters across the U.S. and in Canada. Founded in 1977 by researchers Drs. John and Emily Visher, it provides networking, information, education, support, and advocacy for stepfamilies and those who work with them. Members receive the book *Stepfamilies Stepping Ahead* published by the association, a newsletter, access to resources, and referrals to professionals and support groups.

—Stepfamily Foundation, Inc.; 333 West End Avenue, New York, NY 10023; 24-hour information line: (212) 877-3244; www.stepfamily.org; founded by Jeanette Lofas, Ph.D., CSW, an authority on step-relationships, it provides in-person and telephone counseling, seminars and lectures for professionals, research, and programs for corporations.

Self-Help Resources

Families Apart: Ten Keys to Successful Co-Parenting (Melinda Blau, New York: G. P. Putnam's Sons, 1993); in addition to discussing the ten keys, this book contains a sample parenting agreement and a directory of resources, including books for children of different ages.

Stepmothers: Keeping It Together with Your Husband and His Kids (Merry Bloch Jones and Jo Ann Schiller, New York: Carol Publishing Group, 1992); contains accounts of experiences and advice based on interviews with 52 stepmothers. Topics include expectations, legal and material issues, the ex-wife, and the marriage.

References

Ambert, A. M. (1986). Being a stepparent: Live-in and visiting stepchildren. *Journal of Marriage and the Family, 48,* 795–804.

Blau, M. (1993). *Families Apart: Ten Keys to Successful Co-Parenting.* New York: G. P. Putnam's Sons.

Bray, J. (1999). From marriage to remarriage and beyond: Findings from the developmental issues in Step Families Research Project. In E. M. Hetherington (Ed.), *Coping with Divorce, Single Parenting, and Remarriage* (pp. 253–271). Mahwah, NJ: Lawrence Erlbaum Associates.

Eggebeen, D. J., Synder, A. R., and Manning, W. D. (1996). Children in single-father families in demographic perspective. *Journal of Family Issues, 17(4),* 441–465.

Fine, M. (1999). Stepparents. In C. A. Smith (Ed.), *The Encyclopedia of Parenting Theory and Research* (pp. 420–422). Westport, CT: Greenwood Publishing.

Fong, R. (1994). Family preservation: Making it work for Asians. *Child Welfare, 73(4)*, 331–341.

Gamache, S. (1997). Confronting nuclear family bias in stepfamily research. In I. Levin and M. Sussman (Eds.), *Stepfamilies: History, Research, and Policy* (pp. 41–69). Binghamton, NY: Haworth Press.

Ganong, G., and Coleman, M. (1997). How society views stepfamilies. In I. Levin and M. Sussman (Eds.), *Stepfamilies: History, Research, and Policy* (pp. 85–106). Binghamton, NY: Haworth Press.

Goldberg, M. (1985). Remarriage: Repetition versus new beginnings. In D. C. Goldberg (Ed.), *Contemporary Marriage: Special Issues in Couples Therapy* (pp. 524–544). Homewood, IL: Dorsey Press.

Hetherington, E. M., and Clingempeel, W. G. (1992). Coping with marital transitions: A family systems perspective. *Monographs of the Society for Research in Child Development, 227*, Vol. 57, Nos. 2–3.

Hetherington, E. M., Cox, M., and Cox, R. (1982). Effects of divorce on parents and children. In M. E. Lamb (Ed.), *Nontraditional Families: Parenting and Child Development* (pp. 233–288). Hillsdale, NJ: Lawrence Erlbaum Associates.

Hughes, R., and Schroeder, J. (1997). Family life education programs for stepfamilies. In I. Levin and M. Sussman (Eds.), *Stepfamilies: History, Research, and Policy* (pp. 281–300). Binghamton, NY: Haworth Press.

Ihinger-Tallman, M., and Pasley, K. (1997). Stepfamilies in 1984 and today: A scholarly perspective. In I. Levin and M. Sussman (Eds.), *Stepfamilies: History, Research, and Policy* (pp. 19–40). Binghamton, NY: Haworth Press.

Jones, M. B., and Schiller, J. (1992). *Stepmothers: Keeping It Together with Your Husband and His Kids*. New York: Carol Publishing Group.

Kane, C. (2000). African American family dynamics as perceived by family members. *Journal of Black Studies, 30(5)*, 691–702.

MacDonald, W., and DeMaris, A. (1996). Parenting stepchildren and biological children. *Journal of Family Issues, 17(1)*, 5–25.

Phillips, R. (1997). Stepfamilies from a historical perspective. In I. Levin and M. Sussman (Eds.), *Stepfamilies: History, Research, and Policy* (pp. 5–18). Binghamton, NY: Haworth Press.

Sholevar, G. P. (1985). Assessment of marital disorders. In D. C. Goldberg (Ed.), *Contemporary Marriage: Special Issues in Couples Therapy* (pp. 290–311). Homewood, IL: Dorsey Press.

Uba, L. (1994). *Asian Americans: Personality Patterns, Identity, and Mental Health*. New York: Guilford Press.

Visher, E. B., and Visher, J. S. (1996). *Therapy with Stepfamilies*. New York: Brunner/Mazel Publishing.

Sudden Job Loss

"The Terminations Were Sudden and Unexpected"

Mark and Pam Collins were devout Presbyterians in their early fifties with two daughters in college. The Reverend Hal Walker was close to the family, and he had talked with Mark several times about his high level of stress at work.

For over twenty years, Mark had been a manager in a company that had recently merged with a giant impersonal corporation concerned only about the bottom line. The downsizing of the company began a few weeks after the corporation took control. Terminations were sudden and unexpected; often it was learned only by rumor that a trusted colleague had been laid off. The dysfunctional process used to terminate employees added to the destructive effect on the confidence of those dismissed, creating a widespread and deep lack of trust among those remaining.

The downsizing became particularly impersonal, without care for the well-being of faithful and dedicated workers. The anger, anguish, and despair among employees became palpable. When Mark repeatedly complained to the new management about the negative impact of the process on morale, he received a termination slip.

Mark had looked for a new job for several months, but in spite of being a highly qualified manager, he had had no success. The financial disruption from losing his job was beginning to be felt by the family. He feared that being an older worker was making it hard for him to find employment. Pam and their daughters were concerned about Mark's mounting self-doubts and lowered sense of self-worth, as well as the loss of contact with his former colleagues at work. Mark was beginning to isolate himself from old friends because he felt embarrassed that he did not have a job. Pam was also concerned about the increased tensions in the family and the irritability between her and her husband.

Pastoral Assessment

No one can take a major blow, such as that caused by an unexpected loss of employment, without having self-doubts and sustaining damage to one's self-esteem. The results of unemployment cannot be fully understood outside of the context of the family, since major changes in the life of one member reverberate through the whole family and affect everyone. Although families vary greatly in their structures and dynamics, the negative effects of unemployment can be felt keenly by all members. For many people, particularly men, the stigma of being unemployed and the desire to avoid the embarrassment of having to answer questions about one's job can trigger avoidance of social relationships.

Early in his ministry, Reverend Walker had had several unemployed members who came to him for counseling, and he had felt inadequate in his efforts to help them. After searching for resources, he found a book written by Richard Bolles, an Episcopal priest, that has become for many the standard manual for job-hunters and a guide for career changers titled *What Color Is Your Parachute?* At the heart of Bolles's practical formula for finding the right job are two questions: What do you want to do? and Where do you want to do it? Reverend Walker now keeps several copies in his library to lend to people. He highlighted the major points of the book and referred Mark to a career counselor for more specialized help.

Relevant History

After their daughters went off to college, Pam became interested in the Internet and began to develop a business idea on-line with a friend. She and her partner joined the 23.8 million Americans working at least part-time from their home (Bolles, 1999).

Diagnostic Criteria

The industrial revolution that began in the early nineteenth century changed the social organization of work. Prior to that time, most people farmed as a family unit. Then the industrial economy separated the location of production from the family, making the workplace the sphere of males. We have now entered what some call the "post-industrial economy" or "information society," which is causing as much social upheaval as the industrial revolution did. Computers are the most visible sign of the new information technologies that are changing the nature of work. Information and services are replacing manufacturing as employment's focus, and this is profoundly impacting families.

Work provides more than just an income; it also offers a means to find fulfillment and to experience the satisfaction of achievement and creativity. Research has found that the experience of unemployment is a highly stressful life event (Dohrenwend, Krasnoff, Askenasy, and Dohrenwend, 1978) that can lead to psychological distress, drinking problems, family conflict, depression, and anxiety (Hamilton, Hoffman, Broman, and Rauma, 1993). When a person or family becomes highly distressed by unemployment, a referral to a mental health specialist is well advised.

On the advice of Reverend Walker, Mark went to see a career counselor, which proved to be a life-changing experience. With the guidance of the counselor, he began to think very differently about his job search. Instead of asking where he could find a way to earn a living as an "over-the-hill" worker in his fifties, Mark began to ask what he would like to do if he had his ideal job, what he felt passionate about doing, and what work energized him. He began to identify his favorite talents and skills and looked for places he could use them. This was a liberating and creative experience.

The church provided space to Mark and a faith-based support group of unemployed persons from the community that met each weekday morning to develop job-hunting skills and to offer one another understanding and encouragement. They worked on their résumés and interviewing skills and helped one another network in the job market. Group members no longer viewed themselves as out-of-work—their jobs now were to work full-time on their career changes. From this experience, Mark began to see that he had skills and enjoyed helping others find employment. After researching the career counseling field and talking to several professionals, he found a position in a Christian career counseling group. His new job gave him a chance to combine his work interests with his deeply felt faith.

The nuclear family is part of a larger social network, which includes extended family, neighborhood, and community. Research indicates that unemployed workers cope best when they have a strong social support system (Linn et al., 1985). A caring, supportive community of faith can be an important factor in coping with stressful life situations.

Couples who have high levels of trust and communication cope better and are less anxious and depressed during periods of unemployment than couples with less trust and poorer communication skills (Gore, 1978). Faith-based programs that are targeted at strengthening marital bonds and increasing family communication can serve a preventive function when a family faces a high-stress situation, such as unemployment.

Work provides more than just an income—it also offers a means to find fulfillment and to experience the satisfaction of achievement and creativity. Research has found that the experience of unemployment is a highly stressful life event (Dohrenwend et al., 1978) that can lead to psychological distress, drinking problems, family conflict, depression, and anxiety (Hamilton et al., 1993). When a person or a family becomes too highly distressed by unemployment, a referral to a mental health specialist is well advised.

A combination of psychotherapy (cognitive and behavioral) and medication has become the standard for successful treatment of depression and anxiety disorders. A detailed look at recommended forms of treatment for

Response to Vignette

Treatment Within the Faith Community

Indications for Referral

Treatment by Mental Health Specialist

several types of depression, anxiety disorders, and substance abuse can be found in both *Counseling Troubled Older Adults: A Handbook for Pastors and Religious Caregivers* (Koenig and Weaver, 1997) and *Counseling Troubled Teens and Their Families: A Handbook for Pastors and Youth Workers* (Weaver, Preston, and Jerome, 1999).

Long-term unemployment can negatively affect family stability, marital adjustment, couple communication, and harmony in family relations (Voydanoff and Donnelly, 1988). Families that are good at sharing their feelings and have effective communication skills are best at problem solving, which is particularly important in a crisis. An effective mental health specialist can help a couple identify dysfunctional patterns of coping and develop more functional ones, as well as help spouses process hidden feelings.

Cross-Cultural Issues

British researchers found that religious involvement among Muslim Asians of Bangladeshi and Pakistani origin predicted psychological well-being and was a helpful buffer against the impact of long-term unemployment (Shams and Jackson, 1993). These scientific findings support other studies that have found that severe stressors, such as long-term unemployment, are moderated by religious beliefs and practices (Pargament, 1997). Faith can help a person maintain a sense of personal identity and resilience in the midst of a crisis.

Resources

National Resources

—ACCESS: Networking in the Public Interest; 1001 Connecticut Avenue, NW, Suite 838, Washington, DC 20036; (800) 417-6351; www.communityjobs.org; is a nationwide resource on employment, internships, and career development for nonprofit organizations.

—Employment Resources for People with Disabilities; www.disserv.stu.umn.edu/TC/Grants/COL/listing/disemp.

—Intercristo; P.O. Box 33487, Seattle, WA 98133; (800) 251-7740; www.jobleads.org; is a job referral service matching Christians with service opportunities in the United States and overseas. It works with more than ten thousand individuals and at least three thousand Christian organizations providing customized and up-to-date job leads to individuals and candidate information to hiring managers.

—International Employment Hotline; 1088 Middle River Road, Stanardsville, VA 22973; (800) 291-4618; cc@internationaljobs.org; offers a monthly newsletter that lists international employment opportunities.

—Job Hunters Bible, www.jobhuntersbible.com/intro, is the website for Richard Bolles, author of *What Color Is Your Parachute?* It has many helpful Internet links.

—Minorities' Job Bank, www.minorities-jb.com, has as its primary mission to help minorities find good jobs.

—The Monster Board, www.monster.com, (800) MONSTER, is one of several on-line websites that posts résumés for those seeking jobs.

Self-Help Resources

America's Fastest Growing Employers: The Complete Guide to Finding Jobs with over 275 of America's Hottest Companies (Carter Smith and Peter Hale, Holbrook, MA: Adams Media, 1999).

The Best Home Businesses for the 21st Century: The Inside Information You Need to Know to Select a Home-Based Business That's Right for You (Paul Edwards and Sarah Edwards, New York: J. P. Tarcher/Putnam, 1999).

Finding Your Perfect Work: The New Career Guide to Making a Living, Creating a Life (Paul Edwards and Sarah Edwards, New York: J. P. Tarcher/Putnam, 1996).

I Could Do Anything If I Only Knew What It Was: How to Discover What You Really Want and How to Get It (Barbara Sher and Barbara Smith, New York: Delacorte Press, 1994).

Job-Hunting on the Internet (Richard Nelson Bolles, Berkeley, CA: Ten Speed Press, 1997).

Losing Your Job, Reclaiming Your Soul: Stories of Resilience, Renewal, and Hope (Mary Lynn Pulley, San Francisco: Jossey-Bass Publishers, 1997).

Making Money with Your Computer at Home: The Inside Information You Need to Know to Select and Operate a Full-Time, Part-Time, or Add-On Business That's Right for You (Paul Edwards and Sarah Edwards, New York: J. P. Tarcher/Putnam, 1997).

Occupational Outlook Handbook (Department of Labor, Lincolnwood, IL: NTC Publishing Group, 1999).

The Pathfinder: How to Choose or Change Your Career for a Lifetime of Satisfaction and Success (Nicholas Lore, New York: Simon & Schuster, 1998).

What Color Is Your Parachute? 2000 (Richard Nelson Bolles, Berkeley, CA: Ten Speed Press, 1999).

References

Bolles, R. N. (1999). *What Color Is Your Parachute? 2000*. Berkeley, CA: Ten Speed Press.

Dohrenwend, B. S., Krasnoff, L., Askenasy, A. R., and Dohrenwend, B. P. (1978). Exemplification of a method for scaling life events: The PERI life events scale. *Journal of Health and Social Behavior, 19*, 205–229.

Gore, S. (1978). The effects of social support in moderating the health consequences of unemployment. *Journal of Health and Social Behavior, 19*, 157–165.

Hamilton, V. L., Hoffman, W. S., Broman, C. L., and Rauma, D. (1993). Unemployment, distress and coping: A panel study of autoworkers. *Journal of Personality and Social Psychology, 65(2)*, 234–247.

Linn, M. W., Sandifer, R., and Stein, S. (1985). Effects of unemployment on mental and physical health. *American Journal of Public Health,* *75(5),* 502–506.

Pargament, K. I. (1997). *The Psychology of Religion and Coping: Theory, Research, Practice.* New York: Guilford Press.

Shams, M., and Jackson, P. R. (1993). Religiosity as a predictor of well-being and moderator of the psychological impact of unemployment. *British Journal of Medical Psychology, 66,* 341–352.

Voydanoff, P., and Donnelly, B. W. (1988). Economic distress, family coping and quality of family life. In P. Voydanoff and L. C. Majka (Eds.), *Families and Economic Distress.* Newbury Park, CA: Sage Publications.

Grandparents Parenting Grandchildren

"A Major Disruption to Her Life"

New pastor Nathan Taylor was making his first calls among the members of his urban church. He visited with fifty-eight-year-old Vera Young, a widow and longtime member of the church, who had become less active after recently becoming the primary caregiver to her five-year-old grandson, Wesley. Vera's daughter had died tragically from a drug overdose, and Wesley's father had disappeared before the baby was born. The child had ongoing medical problems caused by exposure to illegal drugs in the womb. Vera had tried for years to help her daughter stop using drugs and had even paid for expensive private inpatient drug treatment when no public facility was available. Vera had recently taken early retirement from the high school teaching that she enjoyed because of the huge demands of raising Wesley. His medical expenses were draining her savings. Taking full responsibility for her grandson was a major disruption to Vera's life. She said to Reverend Taylor, "I feel like my life has been on hold since Wesley came. I love him, but I had looked forward to leisure in retirement."

Vera is experiencing several major stressors. She is the caregiver for a youngster with serious medical problems and special needs. She is grieving the death of her daughter, after years of trying to help her recover from drug addiction, and the loss of her vocation as a teacher with its income. Vera is also faced with the loss of the expectation of having leisure in her retirement years, which has been replaced with the problems of increasing financial burdens and little free time. She is isolated with no child care available and few family resources. Grandparents without spouses who are primary caregivers for their grandchildren report having poorer health and less emotional support than those whose spouses live in the home (Dowdell, 1995).

Pastoral Assessment

135

Grandparents stepping in to raise grandchildren or other relatives is not a new concept. Families, particularly in minority communities, have depended upon extended, multigenerational family arrangements for child rearing and economic survival for decades. However, the recent and unprecedented increase of grandparents that are involved in child rearing requires the faith community to become aware of the issue and to begin helping these families.

Relevant History

Researchers have documented high rates of asthma, weakened immune systems, poor eating and sleeping patterns, physical disabilities, and hyper-activity among children being raised by their grandparents (Dowdell, 1995; Minkler and Roe, 1993). Grandparents raising their grandchildren also appear to be in poorer health than their counterparts. Studies have noted high rates of depression, poor self-rated health, and multiple chronic health problems among adults raising their grandchildren (Dowdell, 1995; Minkler and Roe,1993).

Diagnostic Criteria

In the U.S., the number of children who live with grandparents and other relatives has increased 76 percent since 1970 from 2.2 million (3.2 percent of all children) to 3.9 million (5.5 percent of all children) in 1997 (Lugaila, 1998). The greatest increase in the 1990s was among children living in grandparent-headed households with neither parent present. Those numbers rose almost 300 percent, from .5 million to 1.5 million households, between 1990 and 1997 (Casper and Bryson, 1998). If not for the unselfish contributions that these grandparents make on a daily basis to keep their families together, millions of children would be denied the opportunity to grow up in stable homes and communities among their relatives and friends.

In a national study of 3,477 grandparents, 10.9 percent reported having primary responsibility for raising a grandchild for a period of six months or more at some point in their lives (Fuller-Thomson, Minkler, and Driver, 1997). More than 4 in 10 of these grandparents became primary caregivers for an infant, and nearly three quarters began caregiving before a child turned five. In over half the cases, the role of grandparent as primary caregiver lasted for a period of at least three years. Twenty percent of the time the grandparents raised a grandchild for ten years or more. About half the caregivers were married, and almost 8 out of 10 were women. The average age of the surveyed caregiving grandparents was sixty, and nearly 75 percent lived in an urban area. Twenty-three percent of the grandparents reported living on an income below the poverty line. African-Americans had an 83 percent greater chance of being grandparent caregivers than members of other ethnic groups. The unprecedented number of grandparents who are rearing children in the U.S. is due to the steep rise in parental substance abuse; child abuse, neglect, or abandonment; parental incarceration; emotional problems; teen pregnancy; divorce; HIV/AIDS; and the death of a parent. Approximately two thirds of the 90,000 women in prisons and jails in the United States have children under the age of eighteen, and about half of those children stay with grandparents during their mother's absence (Dressel and Barnhill, 1994).

Vera Young was not the only adult in the church that Pastor Taylor found to be raising grandchildren. During the first months in his new parish, he discovered several others. When he talked with fellow clergy, they reported that relatives caring for children is common; in some cases, they even found members raising great-grandchildren. The clergy knew that these older persons raising children often faced multiple challenges, such as their own declining health and the desire to provide support to the absent parent of the grandchild. Additional stressors included lack of support and respite services, unavailability of affordable housing, poor access to medical care, and other physical, emotional, and family strains. In some cases, relatives lacked the financial resources to raise another family or exhausted their savings or depleted their retirement funds in order to do so.

Response to Vignette

After recognizing the compelling needs of these caregivers, Pastor Taylor decided to provide leadership in his church and ministerial association to help these grandparents with their burden. He recognized that faith communities touch the lives of a large percentage of community residents who need assistance and that they can help in creating a natural supportive network that is easily accessible and trustworthy. After researching how to help, Reverend Taylor found that there are hundreds of grandparent groups across the U.S. Support groups that provide grandparents with practical information and emotional support are highly valued by those who have used them (Minkler and Roe, 1993). Having other persons who understand, with whom to share painful feelings, and who are willing to help carry the burden can greatly increase the ability of an individual to cope with stressful situations. Grandparents working together, learning from each other, and becoming advocates for their own concerns, can be empowered to enhance the quality of life for their grandchildren and themselves.

The church began a weekly group led by a parish social worker knowledgeable in gerontology. Because many grandparents could not afford babysitters and had no one else to watch their grandchildren, the church provided child care. After the group met for a few months and became cohesive, the grandparents decided to invite experts such as attorneys, pediatricians, and representatives from the welfare office to address them and give advice. Recognizing that much had changed since they raised their first set of children, they also invited mental health specialists to conduct a series of parenting classes.

Once a month, the church sponsors a weekend activity that involves both grandparents and grandchildren. The events give the children space to run and play together and provide the adults a chance to relax and socialize. Since the grandparent group is composed of people with diverse skills, the group developed an exchange program. One man volunteers his carpentry skills for respite care for his grandson, while a women cuts hair to get her appliances repaired. The ministerial association set up a fund to help provide financial assistance for the families and has a community fund-raiser twice a year to buy clothing and toys.

Treatment Within the Faith Community

The important role of the church in the lives of older adults, particularly in those of ethnic minorities, has been well documented (Koenig and Weaver, 1997). Studies show that persons with a strong faith who pray frequently and find comfort in religion survive the rigors of caregiving better than those without such resources, and this is particularly true for African-American women (Picot, Dehanne, Namazi, and Wykle, 1997). The black church is a place of affirmation and celebration, providing members with recognition, respect, and emotional and material support. In one survey, almost 80 percent of older African-Americans reported receiving emotional and/or financial support from fellow church members in times of need. In fact, during times of sickness or when needing advice and encouragement, they were more likely to find help from their church than from family members (Taylor and Chatters, 1986).

In a comprehensive study of seventy-one African-American grandmothers and great-grandmothers who were primary caregivers of children, all but one described themselves as religious (Minkler and Roe, 1993). More than three quarters were church attendees, and many reported that they would like to be more active in the church were it not for their many responsibilities. The caregiving grandmothers indicated that prayer, reading the Bible, and turning to God were by far the most frequently used means of coping with the stress of caregiving.

A separate study of seventy-four Puerto Rican and Dominican women rearing their grandchildren in New York City documented the important role of informal support from friends, family, church groups, and neighbors for meeting the emotional and social needs of daily life (Burnette, 1999). The researcher found that 40 of the 74 women indicated that church was a part of their support system. And more women found help from their church than from any of the other five sources of support named, including senior centers and grandparent support groups.

Indications for Referral

Given the multiple stressors with which caregiver grandparents are confronted, it is not surprising that a national survey found that grandparents raising their grandchildren were twice as likely to be clinically depressed compared to those grandparents who play more traditional roles (Minkler, Fuller-Thomson, Miller, and Driver, 1997). Pastors need the skills to screen for depression in older adults, since it is the most common and treatable mental health problem among the elderly, affecting 15 percent of those age sixty-five and older. A serious risk in a major depression is suicide, with 15 percent of depressed persons taking their lives. Unfortunately, most depressed older adults never receive professional mental health treatment, contributing to chronic mental health deterioration and the risk of suicide (Weaver and Koenig, 1996).

Several indicators of a serious depression will require referral to a mental health specialist for a complete evaluation. They include: persistent sadness and the inability to experience pleasure with no signs of improvement after several weeks of pastoral counseling; a significant weight loss or weight gain; serious problems with sleep; severe fatigue or complaint of slowed movement (psychomotor retardation); intense helpless or hopeless feelings and pessimistic thinking; trouble concentrating, remembering, or making decisions; marked irritability, agitation, restlessness, or suicidal thoughts; and bizarre nonreality-based thinking (delusions) or paranoid thinking. If at any point a person's difficulties are beyond a pastor's level of training or experience, a referral should be made.

Treatment by Mental Health Specialist

Treatment for depression is one of the genuine success stories in mental health. It can be improved in almost all individuals by one of three types of treatment: psychotherapy, antidepressant medication, or electroshock therapy (ECT). Mild forms of depression respond to supportive, insight-oriented forms of psychotherapy. More severe depressions respond to a combination of medication and psychotherapy and, in some cases, ECT.

Many depressed persons describe their life situations with global statements such as "Everything is hopeless," "Nothing is working in my life," "I'm old and useless," or "I can't ever get anything right." Depressed individuals tend to conclude the worst about themselves, their life situation, and their future. If these beliefs go unrecognized and unchallenged, such distortions in thinking will continue to intensify the emotional pain of depression. An effective therapist will encourage activities that give pleasure and fulfillment to a person and that may decrease the emotional pain of depression, such as religious activities. Usually these interventions, called cognitive-behavioral therapy, involve self-monitoring of mood and activities, often in the form of keeping a daily log (Preston, 1997).

Antidepressant medications are effective in the treatment of depression in 70 to 80 percent of cases. Their beneficial effects are achieved by restoring the levels of brain chemicals that are depleted when an individual is depressed (Preston, 1997). These drugs are not addictive, and they are not tranquilizers or "uppers." Unfortunately, the effects of antidepressants are not immediate, and many people stop taking them before normal brain cell functioning is restored. In most cases, an individual will experience improvement within ten days to three weeks. The type of medication that is most effective depends on the side effects and on the symptoms an individual has. Sometimes several drugs will be tried before an effective one is found.

Among some severely depressed persons, for whom medication has not worked, the only remaining treatment is ECT. It has proven to be particularly effective for dangerously suicidal and psychotic depressed older adults who do not respond to any other form of therapy. ECT is administered as a controlled electrical current passed through electrodes attached to the head, creating a seizure that lasts about one minute. ECT is used only under medical supervision after an anesthetic and muscle relaxants have been administered.

A complete review of depression assessment and treatment for the elderly can be found in *Counseling Troubled Older Adults: A Handbook for Pastors and Religious Caregivers* (Koenig and Weaver, 1997).

Cross-Cultural Issues

In a national survey, grandparent caregivers tended to be women in their middle to late fifties. About two thirds of them were Caucasian, 29 percent were African-American, 10 percent were Hispanic, 2 percent were Asian/Pacific Islander, and 1 percent were American Indian. African-Americans are three times and Hispanics are twice as likely as Caucasian grandparents to be the primary caregiver of a grandchild (Fuller-Thomson, Minkler, and Driver, 1997).

Church involvement is a significant predictor of positive feelings about being a grandparent. In a study of 883 primarily Caucasian grandparents in the primarily rural state of Iowa, researchers discovered that those who felt most effective and confident in their role as grandparent were more often church attendees than not (King and Elder, 1998). The churchgoing grandparents tended to be active in the lives of their grandchildren, reporting more frequent contact and a higher quality of relationship than non-attendees.

Resources

National Resources

—Administration on Aging (AoA), U.S. Department of Health and Human Services, 330 Independence Avenue, SW, Washington, DC 20201; (202) 619-7501; www.aoa.dhhs.gov; has many resources that can be accessed through the national aging network. These resources are available to support older persons who are serving as primary caregivers to their grandchildren or to other young family members. The network includes regional offices; 57 state units on aging; more than 661 area agencies on aging; 222 tribal organizations, representing 300 tribes; and thousands of service providers, senior centers, caregivers, and volunteers. Working in close partnership, the members of the aging network plan, coordinate, and develop community-level systems of services designed to meet the unique needs of older persons. In addition, the Eldercare Locator, a nationwide toll-free information and assistance directory for older people and care-givers of all ages, can provide the name and phone number of the agency nearest to the person needing assistance. The Eldercare Locator can be reached at (800) 677-1116.

—Brookdale Foundation; 126 East Fifty-sixth Street, New York, NY 10022; www.ewol.com/brookdale; began a grandparents raising grandchil-dren initiative in 1991. A current effort is the Relatives as Parents Program (RAPP), designed to establish community-based services for grandparent caregiving. There are currently forty-three state and local programs oper-ating around the country.

—Child Welfare League of America (CWLA); 440 First Street, NW, Washington, DC 20001-2085; (202) 638-2952; www.cwla.org; began advancing a national initiative on kinship care in 1993. CWLA can pro-vide information on grandparent caregiving and is currently developing a training curriculum for kinship care service workers.

—Creative Grandparenting; 100 West Tenth Street, Suite 1007, Wilmington, DE 19801; (302) 656-2122; provides education to enable and empower grandparents and older adults to value and encourage the natural development of children as unique individuals. Its goal is to help persons become better grandparents. Newsletters, conferences, and help in starting new groups are provided.

—Foundation for Grandparenting; 180 Farnham Road, Ojai, CA 93023; www.grandparenting.org; is dedicated to the betterment of society through intergenerational involvement. It sponsors a weeklong Grandparent-Grand-child summer camp.

—GAP (Grandparents As Parents); P.O. Box 964, Lakewood, CA 90714; (562) 924-3996; linstead@oxy.edu; is a support network designed for the sharing of experiences and feelings among grandparents who are raising their grandchildren for various reasons. Information and referrals, a phone support network, group member listings, and assistance in starting groups are available.

—Generations United; 122 C Street, NW, Suite 820, Washington, DC 20001; (202)638-1263; www.gu.org; is a national coalition dedicated to intergenerational policies, programs, and issues. It can provide general information on grandparent caregiving.

—GRAM (Grandparent's Rights Advocacy Movement); P.O. Box 523, Tarpon Springs, FL 34688-0523; (727) 789-1176; gramps@cftnet.com; is a national network, founded in 1989, to assist grandparents whose grand-children are forced to live in problematic situations because of chemical dependency, loss of parents, divorce, abuse, or neglect. Information, refer-rals, group meetings, and literature are available.

—Grandparents Information Center; AARP, 601 E Street, SW, Washington, DC 20049; (202) 434-2296; Spanish: (202) 434-2281;

www.aarp.org; is a national bilingual group sponsored by the American Association of Retired Persons. It provides information for grandparents raising their grandchildren. Referrals to support groups are nationwide. Free publications on a variety of issues related to raising grandchildren, financial assistance, and advocacy are available.

—GrandsPlace, www.grandsplace.com, is an Internet website devoted to grandparents raising grandchildren. It provides useful links to a wide array of resources.

—National Coalition of Grandparents, 137 Larkin Street, Madison, WI 53705; (608) 238-8751; is a national coalition of grandparent caregivers working for legislation and other policy changes in support of relative caregivers.

—National Family Caregivers Association; 10400 Connecticut Avenue, Suite 500, Kensington, MD 20895-3944; (800) 896-3650; www. nfcacares.org; is a national network, founded in 1992, dedicated to improving the quality of life for family caregivers. It provides network members with phone support, information, referrals, resources, and literature.

—National Foster Parent Association; 7512 Stanich Avenue #6, Gig Harbor, WA 98335; (800) 557-5238; www.nfpainc.org; publishes a booklet entitled, "Grandparents Raising Grandchildren: A Guide to Finding Help and Hope." It discusses the needs of grandchildren, the problems of the parents, and the legal and social issues confronting the grandparents and provides sources to turn to for help and support. It is available for a nominal fee.

—R.O.C.K.I.N.G., Inc. (Raising Our Children's Kids: an Intergenerational Network of Grandparenting, Inc.); P.O. Box 96, Niles, MI 49102; (616) 683-9038; is a national organization that helps relative caregivers access support groups and other resources in their areas.

—Young Grandparents' Club; 5217 Somerset Drive, Prairie Village, KS 66207; (913) 642-8296; sunielevin@worldnet.att.net; is a national group, founded in 1989, to promote the understanding and education of grandparents to develop close relations among generations. Referrals to local groups, advocacy on grandparents' rights, and information are provided. It offers workshops, classes, seminars, conferences, networking, and assistance in starting informal neighborhood groups.

Self-Help Resources

The Essential Grandparent: A Guide to Making a Difference (Lillian Carson, Deerfield Beach, FL: Health Communications, 1996).

Going It Alone: A Closer Look at Grandparents Parenting Grandchildren (D. Chalfie, Washington, DC: American Association of Retired Persons, 1994).

Grandparents as Parents: A Survival Guide for Raising a Second Family

(Sylvie De Toledo and Deborah Edler Brown, New York: Guilford Press, 1995); a very helpful and informative book.

Grandparents Raising Grandchildren: A Guide to Finding Help and Hope (Marianne Takas, Crystal Lake, IL: National Foster Parents Association, 1995).

Kinship Care: A Natural Bridge (Child Welfare League of America, Washington, DC: Child Welfare League, 1994).

Raising Our Children's Children (Deborah Doucette-Dudman and Jeffrey R. LaCure, Minneapolis: Fairview Press, 1996).

References

Burnette, D. (1999). Social relationships of Latino grandparent caregivers: A role theory perspective. *Gerontologist, 39(1),* 49–58.

Casper, L. M., and Bryson, K. R. (1998). *Coresident grandparents and their grandchildren: Grandparent maintained families.* U.S. Bureau of the Census, Population Division Working Paper No. 26. Washington, DC: U.S. Bureau of the Census.

Dowdell, E. B. (1995). Caregiver burden: Grandparents raising their high risk children. *Journal of Psychosocial Nursing, 33(3),* 27–30.

Dressel, P. L., and Barnhill, S. K. (1994). Reframing gerontological thought and practice: The case of grandmothers with daughters in prison. *The Gerontologist, 34(5),* 685–691.

Fuller-Thomson, E., Minkler, M., and Driver, D. (1997). A profile of grandparents raising grandchildren in the United States. *The Gerontologist, 37(3),* 406–411.

King, V., and Elder, G. H. (1998). Perceived self-efficacy and grandparenting. *Journal of Gerontology, 53B(5),* S249–S257.

Koenig, H. G., and Weaver, A. J. (1997). *Counseling Troubled Older Adults: A Handbook for Clergy and Religious Caregivers.* Nashville: Abingdon Press.

Lugaila, T. (1998). *Marital status and living arrangements:* March, 1997 U. S. Bureau of the Census, Current Population Reports, Series p29-56. Washington, DC: U.S. Government Printing Office.

Minkler, M., Fuller-Thompson, E., Miller, D., and Driver, D. (1997). Depression in grandparents raising grandchildren: Results of a national longitudinal study. *Archives of Family Medicine, 6(5),* 445–452.

Minkler, M., and Roe, K. M. (1993). *Grandmothers as Caregivers: Raising Children of the Crack Cocaine Epidemic.* Newbury Park, CA: Sage Publications.

Picot, S. J., Dehanne, S. M., Namazi, K. H., and Wykle, M. L. (1997). Religiosity and perceived rewards of black and white caregivers. *The Gerontologist, 37(1),* 89–101.

Preston, J. D. (1997). *You Can Beat Depression.* San Luis Obispo, CA: Impact Publishers.

Taylor R. J., and Chatters, L. M. (1986). Patterns of informal support to elderly Black Americans: family, friends, and church members. *Social Work, 31,* 431–438.

   Weaver, A. J., and Koenig, H. G. (1996). Elderly suicide, mental health professionals and the clergy: A need for collaboration, training and research. *Death Studies, 20(5),* 495–508.

Retirement

"They Decided to Sell the Farm and Retire"

The Preston family had been Midwestern farmers for three generations. Jim Preston had hoped his only son would follow him on the farm. However, David had given up on farming and had taken a job in Chicago. David had watched his parents work very hard to survive on the family farm for years, and he did not want that struggle for his family. Jim did not blame David for moving on and doing what he thought was important for himself and for his family. Jim understood that even with its rewards, family farming has become very difficult in the United States. In fact, a few years after David left, Jim and Pearl Preston decided to sell their farm to a neighbor, retire, and move to the closest small town.

Pearl sought out the Reverend Davis for counseling a few months after their retirement. She explained that she was enjoying the increased free time, but Jim was becoming irritable and difficult to live with. He found the adjustment to retirement much harder than he had imagined. Jim had moved suddenly from a very active life with many responsibilities to a sedentary one with lots of time on his hands. After several weeks of keeping himself busy making improvements on their new home, he became restless and tried to take up golf. He became bored fast. Pearl was concerned that Jim was getting depressed. Reverend Davis said he would make a pastoral visit and talk with Jim.

Pastoral Assessment

Retirement is a developmental transition that affects retirees and their families and calls for a life reevaluation. It requires changes in family and personal goals, roles, and values. Suddenly the forty or more hours a week one spent in work are now free for other things; retirement requires different ways of using one's time. Leisure activities do not necessarily increase one's sense of self-worth or help a person feel needed.

One expert suggests that 30 percent of individuals have significant difficulties with actual retirement (Atchley, 1976). Some retirees feel useless and unneeded by a society that places great value on youth and productivity. One day an individual is seen as productive, but the next day, he or she is over the hill. Persons no longer have their work to talk about with family or friends. Following retirement, former colleagues no longer have the same interests, and work friendships based upon years of mutual goals, concerns, and interests come to an end. The self-esteem and satisfaction that come with knowing that one is doing a good job and making a contribution to society may stop. A person can feel isolated and alone.

Relevant History

The Prestons sold the farm for a good price that gave them reasonable financial security. However, the sale occurred quickly and somewhat unexpectedly, which left little time for them to think through their retirement plans.

Diagnostic Criteria

The population of the United States and Canada is aging rapidly, and there are large numbers of persons entering retirement. About 1 in 8 Americans is now sixty-five years of age or over—a figure that will increase to about 1 in 5 by 2030. The membership of mainline Protestant churches is aging even more rapidly than the general population. In the year 2000, about half of church members were over age sixty, and the percentage is growing (Custer, 1991). In a recent Gallup poll, 80 percent of older adults claimed membership in a church or synagogue, and 52 percent of seniors attended worship services weekly (Gallup, 1994). As a result, the pastoral care of older adults, most of whom are retired, has become a central concern for pastors. This is particularly so for clergy who serve in rural and small community settings where mental health services are sparse and churches often function as the chief community counseling resource (Rowles, 1986).

Response to Vignette

Reverend Davis had known the solid, hardworking Preston family for many years. They were regular worship attendees who became less involved in church activities when the demands of the farm increased after their son and his family moved away.

When the reverend visited Jim, he listened to him talk about the farming life he had left with obvious sadness and regret. Jim was beginning to recognize that retirement had brought him many losses: meaningful work, contact with fellow working farmers, role identity, and a sense of purpose and fulfillment. Reverend Davis knew that it was important to listen to his story and give him a chance to grieve. The pastor also knew that this life transition crisis provided an opportunity to get Jim involved in activities that would give him a renewed sense of purpose and fulfillment. He suggested that Jim join a group of men in the church who were involved in

Habitat for Humanity, building housing for low-income people in the county. Some of the houses they had built were for widows of farmers who had lost family farms in the farm crisis. Jim was willing to go with Reverend Davis to a meeting.

Jim was a natural for Habitat for Humanity. He had building and organizational skills that were useful, and he found that he was working with other people he enjoyed, some of whom were retired farmers like himself. The faith-based group gave him a chance for fellowship with others and to reflect on his spiritual journey. Jim gained a new sense of direction as he became more and more involved in Habitat for Humanity. He experienced renewed enthusiasm in his Christian commitment to serve, along with fulfillment in doing meaningful work that made a difference.

Studies indicate that pastors in rural America spend more of their time in counseling than their urban counterparts, and they are likely to counsel persons outside their local church (Orthner, 1986). This is understandable because of the importance of the church in the fabric of rural life for seniors. In a study of Midwestern older adults who attended church regularly, the majority reported that 80 percent or more of their closest friends came from their congregation (Koenig, Moberg, and Kvale, 1988). The importance of religious life for rural seniors is also illustrated by the remarkable number of elderly who stay active in the church, despite increased medical problems that restrict daily life. Researchers found that 67 percent of elderly men and 79 percent of elderly women living in rural Iowa reported attending church once a month or more, despite limitations of mobility due to health (Cerhan and Wallace, 1993).

According to a comprehensive study of Catholic, Lutheran, and Methodist pastors in North Dakota (Samuel and Sanders, 1991), almost 100 percent made regular home visits to the elderly, 87 percent indicated they had weekly or monthly services at local nursing homes, 72 percent made transportation available to seniors, 70 percent worked with hospice programs, and 44 percent were involved in Meals on Wheels. The older members in these churches were also involved in voluntary activities. Eighty-three percent assisted in worship services, 74 percent taught in the educational program, 81 percent served in a telephone ministry, 70 percent volunteered in a hospice, 51 percent volunteered in assisted refugee resettlement, and 38 percent delivered meals. These high rates of involvement are consistent with other research showing that retirees who are the most active volunteers in the community also attend church more frequently than less active volunteers (Okun, 1993). Clearly, for many older adults and retirees in rural America, there is little separation between church, community, and family.

A key reason for clergy being widely accepted and effective as pastoral counselors to seniors is their positive attitude toward the elderly when

Treatment Within the Faith Community

147

compared to other professionals. Research shows that when compared to others working with seniors (e.g., registered nurses, agency administrators), pastors score high in their acceptance and approval of the aging (Gulledge, 1992). Given the tendency in our society to devalue, stereotype, and marginalize the elderly, these affirming attitudes are an important positive mental health factor that clergy bring to pastoral care. Supportive attitudes toward aging can help people move from seeing it as slow decay and reason for despair to experiencing aging as a gradual unfolding and maturing to be embraced.

Indications for Referral

Individuals who are at greatest risk of depression or anxiety are those who feel that they are unable to deal with the changes involved in retirement, those with little prior planning for it, and those with financial and health difficulties (Fretz, Kluge, Ossana, Jones, and Merikangas, 1989). When a person or family becomes highly distressed by the changes brought by retirement, a referral to a mental health specialist is advised.

Treatment by Mental Health Specialist

When persons are in psychological distress and cannot address their problems with supportive pastoral care, there are very effective treatments for both depression and anxiety disorders that usually involve a combination of psychotherapy (cognitive and behavioral) and medications. A detailed look at the recommended forms of treatment for several types of depression, anxiety disorders, and substance abuse in seniors can be found in *Counseling Troubled Older Adults: A Handbook for Pastors and Religious Caregivers* (Koenig and Weaver, 1997).

Couples who are good at sharing their feelings and have effective communication skills are better at problem solving, which is particularly important in stressful times. An effective mental health specialist can help a couple identify dysfunctional patterns of coping and work on more functional patterns, as well as help process hidden feelings.

Cross-Cultural Issues

Often those who could benefit the most from retirement planning are the least likely to do so. It has been found in several studies that ethnic minorities and the less educated are not as active in retirement preparation as the majority population and the more educated (Ferraro, 1990). In a separate study of older African-American men and women in rural Missouri, it was found that after retirement, the family and church had increased importance (Farakahan and O'Connor, 1984).

Resources

National Resources

—American Association of Retired Persons; 601 E Street, NW, Washington, DC 20049; (800) 424-3410; www.aarp.org; is an organization for people age fifty and older. It seeks to serve the needs and interests of older adults through information, education, advocacy, and community services provided by a network of local chapters and experienced volunteers throughout the country. It has information on retirement planning.

—Habitat for Humanity International; 121 Habitat Street, Americus, GA 31709; (229) 924-6935; www.habitat.org; is a nonprofit ecumenical Christian organization dedicated to eliminating substandard housing and homelessness worldwide. It is founded on the conviction that every person should have a simple, decent, affordable place to live in dignity and safety. It invites people of all backgrounds, races, and religions to build houses together in partnership with families in need. Habitat has built more than 80,000 houses around the world, providing more than 400,000 people in more than 2,000 communities with needed shelter.

Self-Help Resources

Adventures in Senior Living: Learning How to Make Retirement Meaningful and Enjoyable (J. Lawrence Driskill, New York: Haworth Press, 1997).

Counseling Troubled Older Adults: A Handbook for Pastors and Religious Caregivers (Harold G. Koenig and Andrew J. Weaver, Nashville: Abingdon Press, 1997).

Creating a Successful Retirement: Finding Peace and Purpose (Richard P. Johnson, Liguori, MO: Liguori Publications, 1999).

From Work to Retirement (Marion E. Haynes, New York: Crisp Publications, 1993).

The Healing Journey Through Retirement: Your Journal of Transition and Transformation (Phil Rich, Dorothy Madway Sampson, and Dale S. Fetherling, New York: John Wiley & Sons, 2000).

How to Enjoy Your Retirement: Activities from A to Z (Tricia Wagner and Barbara Day, Acton, MA: VanderWyk & Burnham, 1998).

Life Begins at 50: A Handbook for Creative Retirement Planning (Leonard J. Hansen, Hauppauge, NY: Barron's Educational Series, 1989).

The Retirement Sourcebook (Mary Helen Smith and Shuford Smith, Los Angeles: Roxbury Publishing, 1999).

References

Atchley, R. (1976). *The Sociology of Retirement.* New York: John Wiley & Sons.

Cerhan J. R., and Wallace, R. B. (1993). Predictors of decline in social relationships in the rural elderly. *American Journal of Epidemiology, 137,* 870–880.

Custer, C. C. (1991, September). The church's ministry and the coming of the aged. *Circuit Rider,* 9–10.

Farakahan, A., and O'Connor, W. A. (1984). Life satisfaction and depression among retired Black persons. *Psychological Reports, 55,* 452–454.

Ferraro, K. F. (1990). Cohort analysis of retirement preparation: 1974–1981. *Journal of Gerontology: Social Sciences, 45(1)*, S21–S31.

Fretz, B. R., Kluge, N. A., Ossana, S. M., Jones, S. M., and Merikangas, M. W. (1989). Intervention targets for reducing preretirement anxiety and depression. *Journal of Counseling Psychology, 36(3)*, 301–307.

Gallup, G. H. (1994). *Religion in America: 1994, Supplement*. Princeton, NJ: Gallup Poll.

Gulledge, J. K. (1992). Influences on clergy attitudes toward aging. *Journal of Religious Gerontology, 8(2)*, 63–77.

Koenig, H. G., Moberg, D. O., and Kvale, J. N. (1988). Religious activities and attitudes of older adults in a geriatric assessment clinic. *Journal of the American Geriatrics Society, 36*, 362–374.

Koenig, H. G., and Weaver, A. J. (1997). *Counseling Troubled Older Adults: A Handbook for Pastors and Religious Caregivers*. Nashville: Abingdon Press.

Murray, J. D., and Keller, P. A. (1991). Psychology and rural America: Current status and future direction. *American Psychologist, 46(3)*, 220–231.

Okun, M. A. (1993). Predictors of volunteer status in a retirement community. *International Journal of Aging and Human Development, 36(1)*, 57–74.

Orthner, D. K. (1986). *Pastoral Counseling: Caring and Caregivers in The United Methodist Church*. Nashville: The General Board of Higher Education and Ministry of The United Methodist Church.

Rowles, G. D. (1986). The rural elderly and the church. *Journal of Religion and Aging 2(1-2)*, 79–98.

Samuel, M., and Sanders, G. F. (1991). The role of churches in the supports and contributions of elderly persons. *Activities, Adaptation and Aging, 16(2)*, 67–79.

Caring for a Family Member After a Stroke

"He Became Dizzy and Slumped Over"

Bill and Eve Samuels had worked hard for many years on their small farm. They were about to retire and begin traveling, but just as they were starting to free themselves from responsibilities on the farm, it happened. Suddenly while working in the yard, seventy-eight-year-old Bill became dizzy, slumped over, and slid slowly to the ground. Eve saw him collapse and ran to him.

She rushed him to the emergency room where the doctor explained that Bill had experienced a stroke. He would be in the hospital for at least a week and then would need rehabilitation to try to regain normal functioning. While in the hospital, Bill began having difficulty swallowing. A feeding tube was placed directly into his stomach to ensure that Bill would get sufficient nutrition and hydration, even if he couldn't swallow.

A speech therapist began helping Bill learn to speak again. It was difficult, though, because he had lost control of the muscles necessary to form words. Soon he gave up trying. He had been an independent and active man all of his life, and now he was completely helpless. Bill had to be propped up in bed with pillows so he would not fall to one side, unable to straighten himself out. He was also incontinent and had to be cleaned several times a day. Because he could not move on his own, he had to be turned every two hours to prevent bedsores.

After ten days, Bill was taken to a rehabilitation center to help him regain physical functioning. He desperately wanted to go home, but the doctors were not sure that Eve could handle him alone unless he improved considerably. Bill was nearly dead weight and needed to be fully supported even when moving from his bed to a waiting wheelchair. He sometimes would try to get out of bed by himself and would fall to the floor. So he had to be watched or physically restrained in bed.

It was hard to tell what was going on in Bill's mind. He had difficulty communicating his needs, which was terribly frustrating for him. The stroke had also lessened his ability to control his temper. When Eve tried to help him, he would occasionally strike out at her and then begin to cry. This was not what either of them had envisioned for their retirement years.

Eve was fiercely loyal, however, and was determined to help Bill get better so he could go home. Every day she was at the hospital, sitting with him for hours. Their son arrived from across the country for a short stay but soon had to return to his job. So it was all left up to Eve. Bill's siblings came for visits, but they lived about fifty miles away, and their visits became less and less frequent.

After several weeks of rehabilitation, the physical therapist indicated that Bill had improved as much as was likely, and he was moved to a nursing facility. Eve wanted to take him home, but she was advised against this. Bill was unhappy at the nursing facility. So against everyone's advice, Eve checked him out and took him home. Luckily, even though Eve was eighty-one years old, she was strong and had no major medical problems. The doctor recommended home health care services and arranged for a nurse and physical therapist to visit weekly. A home health aide came for several hours daily to bathe and walk Bill. Soon, however, the home health services were discontinued because insurance would no longer pay for them, and the couple decided they could not afford them.

It was a full-time job caring for Bill. Eve had to learn how to give the tube feedings, to move him from the bed to the wheelchair, to change his soiled sheets, and to continue to do all the chores in the house and yard. There was no one to help. This schedule began to take its toll on Eve, and it was during these long nights and exhausting days that she depended on her faith in God to sustain her. She was committed to both God and her husband, and she served them both with a tenacious persistence and unyielding spirit.

Over time, Bill's condition worsened. He no longer took an interest in things, spent most of his days sleeping, and was irritable and demanding when awake. The doctor diagnosed Bill with depression and placed him on an antidepressant. Initially, he seemed to brighten up, become more alert, and take an interest in his surroundings. Then he had a small stroke, which made it impossible for him to walk, and he slowly slipped back into a state of despair. When his son telephoned, Eve would have to force Bill to make a grunt of acknowledgment—otherwise he would simply sit there silently and breathe heavily. The same was true when Bill's siblings visited. They soon stopped coming altogether; it was just too painful to watch him suffer and see how much he had changed from his former self.

Eve needed assistance. With no family in the area who would help, it was entirely up to her. The couple had always been somewhat reclusive and had few relationships outside of their family and a few church friends. Eve's only contacts now were a few women at church. They were faithful, however, visiting her and calling on the telephone. Some men from the church helped out by doing chores in the yard, making house repairs, and keeping her car running. Sometimes a woman would stay with Bill so that Eve could go to church, get groceries, or run errands. The couple had been devout churchgoers all of their lives, but when she attended worship now, she felt guilty for leaving Bill at home So Eve seldom went. She was wearing out, but she felt helpless to do anything about it.

Eve's pastor could see the haggard look in her eyes. Reverend Thomas had been their minister for over ten years, and the couple had come to trust him. He regularly visited, praying with both Bill and Eve, bringing them communion, and reading scriptures that comforted them both. Reverend Thomas spent time listening as Eve described her frustrations with other family members, the pain she felt for Bill, and her lost dreams of their retirement. The pastor also helped mobilize church members to provide support to the couple. He could see, however, that Eve needed more help than the church could provide. The time came to put Bill in a nursing facility or to hire someone to help Eve at home on a regular basis. Eve was initially opposed to both alternatives, but Reverend Thomas urged her to consider those options.

Eve finally decided to seek help. She would hire someone to come for four hours daily to provide personal care for Bill and to clean the house. This would give Eve some time to rest and regain her strength. Her pastor explained that taking care of herself was an important way that Eve could take care of Bill. If she became sick, Bill would have to be placed in a nursing facility. At Reverend Thomas's urging, she saw a doctor who prescribed an antidepressant that helped increase her energy and relieve her exhaustion after the many sleepless nights and physically strenuous days. He also encouraged her to have a geriatric psychiatrist evaluate Bill to see if there was anything that could be done about his withdrawn state.

Pastoral Assessment

Because a pastor cannot meet every emotional and health need in the church, he or she must prioritize, identifying those at highest risk for serious problems. There were several aspects of the couple's situation that put them at high risk for a poor outcome, suggesting a need for attention. One was the suddenness and severity of Bill's health condition. Prior to this, Bill was active, independently caring for himself and his family. The stroke changed him, bringing into question many of the things that gave his life meaning and purpose. Bill needed help adjusting to his new situation, as did Eve. They had to reorganize their lives and priorities around Bill's extraordinary needs. Because both were independent and previously self-sufficient, they found it difficult to accept help from others.

The couple were also strong-willed and resistant to advice. Eve was determined to bring Bill home and care for him herself. She did not follow the advice to place her husband in a nursing facility or to get in-home help. Reverend Thomas saw that the burden of care was taking a toll on Eve and that she was becoming physically and emotionally exhausted. She needed someone to whom she could ventilate her concerns and frustrations and who could help her reach the decision to obtain further help.

The pastor recognized that the couple needed professional help to cope with the problems they were facing. Bill was withdrawn; had lost interest in usual activities; was irritable, demanding, and impatient; and spent much of his time sleeping. He was emotionally overwhelmed with his new life, and Eve had allowed herself to become psychologically and physically worn out. She was tired, not sleeping well, and losing weight. They were both experiencing symptoms of depression that needed professional attention. Although Bill was taking an antidepressant, that did not mean that everything necessary had been done to treat his condition. Since he was not responding to the treatment, the dosage of medication had to be increased, the drug switched to a different antidepressant, or consideration given to electroshock therapy (ECT). These options were not within Reverend Thomas's expertise, and he recognized that referral was necessary.

Relevant History

The couple were somewhat socially isolated, and no other support systems were in place. They had only a few church friends who volunteered to provide assistance. The few family members in the area were not committed to helping. Their only child lived very far away, and his work prevented him from providing the kind of assistance they needed. Thus, once the health care system removed its support, there were few natural support systems to take its place.

Diagnostic Criteria

The number of persons over age sixty-five with a severe disability is expected to reach twelve to fourteen million in the decades ahead (Kunkel and Applebaum, 1992). Nearly 4.5 million Americans (2 percent of the population) who are alive today have had a stroke (American Heart Association, 1999). After heart disease and cancer, stroke is the third leading cause of death in the U.S. With 600,000 strokes occurring each year, someone in the U.S. suffers a stroke every 53 seconds. The vast majority of persons who have a stroke are over age sixty-five (72 percent), and this illness is about 20 percent more likely to affect men than women. Of particular importance is that strokes are the leading cause of long-term disability in this country. Among survivors alive today, about one million have significant disability resulting from their stroke (American Heart Association, 1999). Three quarters of stroke survivors cannot work, nearly one third need help caring for themselves, and over 15 percent require institutionalization. Studies indicate that one third of survivors die within a year of their first stroke, and two thirds die within twelve years of the event.

Physical disability caused by stroke or other chronic health conditions has an enormous impact on a person's self-esteem and sense of purpose in life. Bill could see that he was a tremendous burden on his wife, whom he loved dearly. He could see no meaningful end to this horrifying journey that he had unwillingly embarked upon. It is difficult to understand why such events happen, unless one believes that something good can come out of even the worst situation. If a disabling stroke can rally a religious community to support and care for one of its members, then a greater good may indeed result.

Bill was experiencing a depressive disorder related to the major life changes he had experienced and to the alterations in his brain related to the stroke. Eve was experiencing caregiver burden and the loss of her once active husband and partner, which also led to depression.

Depressive disorder is extremely common following a stroke, and when it occurs, it substantially increases the mortality rate (Morris, Robinson, Andrzejewski, Samuels, and Price, 1993). Robinson and Price (1982) found that nearly one third of post-stroke patients experienced a significant depression in the month following the event, and two thirds of these persons continued to be depressed for the next seven to eight months. Bill exhibited many of the symptoms of depression, including irritability, loss of interest, and withdrawal from others. Because he could not verbalize his feelings, it was difficult to make the diagnosis. Reverend Thomas had to rely on Bill's behavior, which indicated that he had given up hope and lost the will to live.

He had the classic symptoms of depression, including depressed mood (or irritability), loss of interest (or social withdrawal), difficulty sleeping (or excessive sleeping), loss of energy, difficulty concentrating, restlessness (or slowing of movements), weight loss (or loss of appetite), feelings of guilt or worthlessness, and a desire to die (or loss of the will to live) (APA, 1994). If four or more of these symptoms are present for two weeks or longer, a person is suffering from major depression. In Bill's case, his symptoms were irritability, social withdrawal, excessive sleeping, and the apparent loss of the will to live.

Eve was experiencing an extremely common type of depression related to her caregiver role. Between one third and one half of all long-term family caregivers suffer significant depressive symptoms (Gallagher, Rose, and Rivera, 1989). These persons not only have the burden of assisting a loved one, but also often have to manage the house, do the laundry, care for a yard, maintain a car, do the dishes, cook the meals, and perform many other tasks. Caregivers become socially isolated since most of their time is spent performing tasks, rather than developing and maintaining relationships. When the person being looked after has heavy care demands and does not sleep through the night, this quickly leads to physical and emotional exhaustion, which often becomes a depressive disorder. Eve's fatigue,

155

sense of frustration, difficulty making decisions, and lack of flexibility point to excessive caregiver burden.

Response to Vignette

Reverend Thomas was in a unique position to be able to help the couple. Having been their pastor for many years, he knew them, and they trusted him. The doctors did not spend much time with either spouse, and once medical treatment had been completed, they urged Eve to place Bill in a nursing facility and then withdrew their support. It was then that Reverend Thomas did several things that were key in helping this family:

- He visited them regularly, so he was able to assess the situation and see what had to be done.
- He mobilized church members to provide assistance. Because Eve trusted their pastor and realized that she could not make it on her own, she was willing to accept the help that he and others offered.
- He used the powerful spiritual tools that he had at his disposal—prayer and scripture—to support Bill's and Eve's often-strained faith.
- He recognized when the couple needed professional help. He knew when he had done all he could and then made appropriate referrals.

Treatment Within the Faith Community

The religious faith that the couple had shared during nearly fifty years of marriage became extremely important during this time of crisis. Bill was comforted after the stroke by having scripture read to him. Eve's faith was crucial to her as she struggled with the burden of caregiving.

Religion is a common way of coping with illness, particularly when it involves a significant life change. In a study of hospitalized, seriously ill patients, Koenig (1998) discovered that religious coping (prayer, depending on God for support and comfort, reading scriptures, and so forth) was the most important factor that kept many of these persons going; nearly 90 percent indicated that religion was used at least moderately to facilitate coping. Other studies demonstrate that these religious beliefs and practices help to prevent the onset of depression (Koenig et al., 1992), and if depression develops, help to resolve it quickly (Koenig, George, and Peterson, 1998). Having a deep religious faith can provide a sense of control over situations or illnesses that otherwise seem out of control. By praying to God, chronically ill persons feel that they are doing something to help their situation. Prayer can provide hope, meaning, and strength to endure, relieving the sense of isolation so common with chronic illness.

Reverend Thomas took time to pray with the couple, to read them comforting scripture, and to bring communion. This reinforced their faith and hope that God would help them. The pastor listened when Eve expressed her frustrations with God and struggled to understand why God had allowed this to happen. He also assisted them in working through their guilt. When people become sick or experience a severe traumatic loss, they often question what they did wrong to deserve this seeming punishment. Reverend Thomas explained that sometimes bad things happen to good people for no reason other than that we live in an imperfect world where there is pain and suffering. He knew that if people were allowed to work through their guilt and anger at God, they may embrace their faith again and receive the great comfort and strength it can offer.

As the number of older persons increases and health care resources are stretched for those with chronic illness and disability, the faith community will be increasingly called upon to provide support and assistance. While the church may have limited financial assets, it does have significant people resources. It is essential that church members are motivated and inspired to reach out to those within their congregation who need assistance. That assistance includes emotional support, companionship, and spiritual support, as well as practical assistance.

Reverend Thomas was able to mobilize members of the church to provide assistance to the couple. If faith communities are alert to the needs of those in their congregation, they can volunteer their time, talents, and financial resources to assist. This will only happen, however, if members are regularly reminded of their responsibilities to others.

Indications for Referral

When a stroke survivor or the caregiver develops a major depression, he or she will need a referral for specialized treatment. Indications of a major depression that require a referral include: physical symptoms such as weight loss, insomnia, or fatigue that cause excessive social difficulties; suicidal thoughts; psychotic symptoms, such as auditory or visual hallucinations; and paranoid delusions (fixed, false beliefs from which a person cannot be dissuaded) with no improvement for three to four weeks.

Treatment by Mental Health Specialist

Bill's symptoms indicated the presence of a depressive disorder that responds to biological treatments (i.e., antidepressant medication or ECT). The same drug will not work for every person, and several kinds may need to be tried—each at a sufficient dose and duration to ensure that an adequate trial of the medication is given—before concluding treatment failure. In Bill's case, either the dose of the antidepressant was too low or he was receiving the wrong medication.

Counseling Troubled Older Adults: A Handbook for Pastors and Religious Caregivers (Koenig and Weaver, 1997) and *Pastoral Care of Older Adults* (Koenig and Weaver, 1998) can be helpful to pastors and caregivers who need more information about the physical and psychiatric disorders experienced by older persons. These books provide further information about diagnosing and treating depression in persons with chronic illness, the medical needs of the chronically ill or disabled, and the community resources that can be utilized to help meet those needs.

Cross-Cultural Issues

Deaths by stroke are higher for African-Americans and Hispanic-Americans than for European-Americans. In a study conducted in New York City by Columbia University, it was found that the average annual age-adjusted stroke rate per 100,000 persons was 223 for blacks, 196 for Hispanics, and 93 for whites. Blacks had a 2.4-fold and Hispanics a twofold increase in stroke incidence compared to whites (Sacco et al., 1998).

Resources

National Resources

—National Stroke Association; 9707 East Easter Lane, Englewood, CO 80112; 800-STROKES; www.stroke.org; is dedicated to reducing the incidence and impact of stroke through prevention, treatment, rehabilitation, family support, and research. It provides a newsletter, publications, information, referrals, and guidance for starting stroke clubs and groups.

—Rosalynn Carter Institute; Georgia Southwestern College, 600 Simmons Street, Americus, GA 31709; provides information on caregiving. Reading lists, video products, and other caregiver resources are available by mail.

—Stroke Clubs International; 805 Twelfth Street, Galveston, TX 77550; (409) 762-1022; was founded in 1968 and has more than 900 groups. It is an organization of persons who have experienced strokes and their families and friends with the purpose of mutual support, education, and social and recreational activities. It provides information and assistance to Stroke Clubs (usually sponsored by local organizations) and has a newsletter, videotapes, and group development guidelines.

—Stroke Connection of the American Heart Association; 7272 Greenville Avenue, Dallas, TX 75231; (800) 553-6321; www.amhrt.org; is a national organization of twelve hundred groups that was founded in 1979. It maintains a listing of support groups for stroke survivors, their families, friends, and interested professionals. It publishes *Stroke Connection* magazine, a forum for survivors and their families to share information about coping with strokes; provides information and referrals; and has stroke-related books, videos, and literature available for purchase.

—The Well Spouse Foundation; P.O. Box 501, New York, NY 10023; (800) 838-0879; provides support for the husbands, wives, and partners of people who are chronically ill or disabled.

Self-Help Resources

After Stroke: Enhancing Quality of Life. (Wallace Sife, New York: Haworth Press, 1998).

American Heart Association Family Guide to Stroke Treatment, Recovery, and Prevention (Louis R. Caplan, Mark L. Dyken, and J. Donald Easton, New York: Times Books, 1996).

The Stroke Recovery Book: A Guide for Patients and Families (Kip Burkman, Omaha: Addicus Books, 1998).

Strokes: What Families Should Know (Elaine Fantle Shimberg, New York: Ballantine Books, 1990).

When Someone You Love Has a Stroke (Marilynn Larkin and Lynn Sonberg, New York: Dell Publishing, 1995).

References

American Heart Association. (1999). Stroke statistics; stroke risk factors. *1999 Heart and Stroke Statistical Update*. Dallas: American Heart Association (www.americanheart.org).

American Psychiatric Association. (1994). *The Diagnostic and Statistical Manual of Mental Disorders* (4th ed.). Washington, DC: APA.

Gallagher, D., Rose, J., and Rivera, P. (1989). Prevalence of depression in family caregivers. *Gerontologist, 29,* 449–456.

Koenig, H. G. (1998). Religious beliefs and practices of hospitalized medically ill older adults. *International Journal of Geriatric Psychiatry, 13,* 213–224.

Koenig, H. G., and Weaver, A. J. (1997). *Counseling Troubled Older Adults: A Handbook for Pastors and Religious Caregivers*. Nashville: Abingdon Press.

Koenig, H. G., and Weaver, A. J. (1998). *Pastoral Care of Older Adults*. Minneapolis: Fortress Press.

Koenig, H. G., Cohen, H. J., Blazer, D. G., Pieper, C., Meador, K. G., Shelp, F., Goli, V., and DiPasquale, R. (1992). Religious coping and depression in elderly hospitalized medically ill men. *American Journal of Psychiatry, 149,* 1693–1700.

Koenig, H. G., George, L. K., and Peterson, B. L. (1998). Religiosity and remission from depression in medically ill older patients. *American Journal of Psychiatry, 155,* 536–542.

Kunkel, S. R., and Applebaum, R. A. (1992). Estimating the prevalence of long-term disability for an aging society. *Journal of Gerontology (Social Sciences), 47,* S253–S260.

Morris, P. L., Robinson, R. G., Andrzejewski, P., Samuels, J., and Price, T. R. (1993). Association of depression with 10-year post-stroke mortality. *American Journal of Psychiatry, 150,* 124–129.

Robinson, R. G., and Price, T. R. (1982). Post-stroke depressive disorders: a follow-up study of 103 patients. *Stroke, 13,* 635–640.

Sacco, R. L., Boden-Albala, B., Gan, R., Chen, X., Kargman, D. E., Shea, S., Paik, M. C., and Hauser, W. A. (1998). Stroke incidence among white, black, and Hispanic residents of an urban community: the Northern Manhattan Stroke Study. *American Journal of Epidemiology, 147(3),* 259–268.

Caring for a Family Member with Alzheimer's Disease

"She Often Asked the Same Question Over and Over Again"

It was an autumn day when seventy-year-old Michael brought his sixty-nine-year-old wife, Susan, to the geriatric assessment clinic. It was an appointment they had been looking forward to yet at the same time dreading. For the past year, Susan had had problems remembering names and misplacing items and had difficulty setting the table. Her memory problems seemed to progress very slowly, and until recent months, she and her husband had attributed these minor difficulties to growing older. Over the years, Susan occasionally forgot people's names, wandered into the kitchen and forgot why, or misplaced her purse. These episodes of forgetting, however, had increased in frequency over the past three months. Michael reported that his wife often asked him the same question over and over again. These symptoms were particularly worrisome because Susan's mother had experienced memory problems in her mid-seventies, which eventually led to her placement in a nursing home. Susan had become so preoccupied with her memory problems (fearful of having the same fate as her mother) that she was having difficulty sleeping, was losing weight, and feeling overwhelmed with even the smallest challenges of day-to-day life.

As they walked into the physician's office, questions were whirling about in their minds. Were these memory problems just related to growing older? Was Susan simply depressed and having difficulty concentrating? Was she overreacting to minor memory lapses due to fear of having the same condition as her mother? Or did she have that disease that Susan and Michael would not talk about to each other—Alzheimer's disease (AD)?

The doctor introduced himself and began questioning Susan and her husband about the kinds of symptoms she was having. He then did a thorough physical and neurological examination and tested her memory. Susan was a well-educated woman with a master's degree in education. After graduation, she began teaching high school social studies, a position she held for nearly thirty years. Michael was a retired United Methodist minister who recently had become preoccupied with church affairs. Despite some recent squabbles over her memory, Susan and Michael were a close couple married for over forty years and the parents of three adult children who were successfully involved in their own careers.

After the evaluation, the physician informed the couple that Susan was having memory problems that were slightly outside the normal range for her age and education level. He suggested a reevaluation in six months to see if significant changes occurred during that time. In addition, he encouraged Susan to begin taking vitamins E and C and gingko biloba daily.

When they returned in six months, Susan's memory problems had progressively worsened. She was now having difficulty remembering even the names of close friends, occasionally became disoriented in the grocery store, and had some trouble preparing meals without incident. This time, the doctor expressed more concern and told the couple that there was a distinct possibility that Susan had AD. This news came as a shock to both of them, since they had slowly accommodated to Susan's difficulties. Michael had taken over the checkbook, was helping with meal preparation, and drove the car wherever they needed to travel. How certain was the diagnosis? What did this mean for their future? How much time did they have? Was there any treatment available?

The physician explained that the diagnosis of AD is based on symptoms and their course over time, and, consequently, the diagnosis is subject to error in about 25 percent of cases. The only way to be certain is to have a brain biopsy. He advised against this, however, and suggested another evaluation in three to six months. In case this was early AD (in light of her mother's history), the doctor suggested she start taking a low dosage of donepezil hydrochloride (Aricept).

Six months later, they returned for a follow-up evaluation. Michael was now having to do most of the work around the house, including meal preparation and all the shopping, and was afraid to leave his wife at home alone. She had attempted to press a shirt when he was out and left the iron on facedown, starting a small fire. She was now unable to set the table or make the bed and even had some trouble putting on her clothes. While most of her social graces were preserved, she easily became disoriented in unfamiliar settings and preferred not to leave the home. The doctor increased the dose of her medication and confirmed the diagnosis of probable AD. He gave Michael a copy of *The 36-Hour Day* (Mace and Rabins, 1999) and suggested he carefully read it and seriously consider joining an Alzheimer's support group.

Susan, once she realized what was happening to her, became despondent, irritable, and tearful. Her physician started her on an antidepressant, which promptly decreased her crying and increased her mood and energy.

The antidepressant also made her less irritable, which made life easier for Michael, too. He was holding his own and was a wonderful caregiver, attentive to his wife's every need. Susan's personality hadn't changed much, and she was still pretty much her old self as far as Michael was concerned. That was also to change.

When they saw the doctor six months after the last evaluation, Susan could no longer dress or bathe herself or be left unsupervised for even a moment. At times, she didn't recognize where she was and tried to leave the house to go "home." She was convinced that her neighbors were coming into the house and stealing things from her. On more than one occasion, she confronted the neighbors about this, requiring apologies from Michael. Caring for Susan was becoming difficult. She was combative when Michael tried to bathe her and at times did not even recognize him, telling him to get out of her home and go back to his own house. Susan's sleep cycle also became disrupted, and she was up most of the night wandering around looking in closets and drawers in a confused state. Sometimes she spoke with relatives who were long deceased, and at other times she herded up her small children for imagined family outings. These activities disrupted Michael's sleep and made it difficult for him to function during the day. In fact, he stopped all volunteer work at the church and began focusing on his caregiver duties full-time.

The physician suggested that Susan take a low dose of antipsychotic medication to help with the paranoia and delusions and to enable her to sleep better at night. She had also lost weight, and he hoped that this medicine would help stimulate her appetite. The doctor prescribed olanzepine (Zyprexa) at bedtime. After a week, her sleep pattern improved, and the paranoia lessened. The physician also suggested that Michael hire someone to help with Susan's care and to perform some of the chores around the house, since he was having health problems resulting from his poorly controlled diabetes.

Michael began to realize that he had lost Susan. Although she was physically there, the person he knew and had loved for over forty years was gone. Michael's distress was funneled into an obsession with his wife's care. He frequently criticized the nursing aides who attended to her needs. The helpers were fired, and new ones were hired to replace them; no one seemed to be able to provide the kind of care Michael wanted for his wife. Finally, a close friend and current pastor of the church Michael attended had a talk with him. Michael appeared tired and angry. He asked his pastor where God was in all this mess. He had served God his entire life in the ministry and was this how God had rewarded him? Michael frankly admitted that his faith was at an all-time low, and he was fearful that he might lose it altogether. His friend listened and made a point to visit Michael every week, allowing him to talk about whatever he wanted. The pastor seldom provided advice or direction but simply spent time with

Michael and tried to listen and understand. Slowly, Michael's spirits improved, and his faith grew stronger.

Six months later, Susan was nearly bed-bound. She was incontinent, had to be fed, and required full-weight assistance when walking. Michael now had nursing aides in the home around the clock to care for his wife and perform the household chores, since he had recently experienced a heart attack and a mild stroke and was now a semi-invalid. Their three children were very supportive and took turns staying with their parents. It became evident, however, that the current situation could not continue forever. The cost of twenty-four-hour nursing care was consuming the couple's savings. So arrangements were made to admit Susan to a local nursing home. Michael visited her faithfully, even though she no longer recognized him. She lived another five months and then died of pneumonia, surrounded by family members and friends.

Pastoral Assessment

Pastors and caregivers need to recognize problems with memory and cognitive functioning that indicate early signs of AD or other dementia. Prompt diagnosis and early treatment may slow the progression of memory loss. Referral to a specialist initially will be for diagnostic purposes. Once a diagnosis has been made, particularly in the early stage of the illness, support is best directed at the person with AD. Coping with the diagnosis and what it means for one's future can be difficult, and most people need assistance and support.

During the intermediate stage of the illness, the caregiver has to deal with several issues that require both emotional and physical assistance. The "loss" of the loved one must be grieved as the caregiver discovers the personality of the family member changing. This usually occurs as the physical burden of caregiving is also increasing. Family caregivers often have to assume not only the tasks of caring for another person's basic needs, but also the chores that that person did, while continuing to carry out their own responsibilities. Thus, two additional jobs must be assumed. In addition to emotional support, the family caregiver at this stage usually needs respite—someone to help perform the many tasks needed and give the caregiver a break.

Clergy can offer counseling to the caregiver at this stage, as Michael's pastor did. If the minister or another trained religious leader cannot do this, referral for professional counseling may be indicated. In order to provide a caregiver with respite, the pastor may want to both mobilize members of the church to provide such assistance and encourage the caregiver to accept it, which is often a problem. Alternatively, the minister may want to encourage the caregiver to hire someone to provide assistance at home on a regular basis. If the church has funds to pay for such services and the caregiver does not, the pastor may decide to provide at least partial financial support.

As the disease worsens and caregiver burden increases, a pastor should be alert for signs of exhaustion or burnout in the caregiver. If not relieved, it will quickly progress to depression, which will likely require professional treatment. Without assistance at this stage, the caregiver is usually forced to place the loved one in a nursing home. This is not the best solution for either the person with AD or the caregiver, but it is sometimes unavoidable. If this is necessary, the pastor may need to help the caregiver work through the guilt over placing the loved one in a nursing home. Guilt may prevent the caregiver from visiting the loved one, which is a real tragedy. While the caregiver may not be able to provide the care, he or she can be of enormous assistance by visiting the loved one regularly in the nursing home. If guilt remains despite regular visits, professional help may need to be sought.

Relevant History

Church members had long suspected that something was wrong with Susan. They had gone out of their way to be helpful, offering to spend time with her while Michael was away doing church business. He seldom left her with others, however, and frequently took her with him on trips. This changed, however, when Susan became reluctant to leave the house because of her increasing disorientation. Since her social graces were preserved, social events—especially if held in her house—continued much as usual. Their friends and family simply avoided asking Susan new or difficult questions.

Diagnostic Criteria

Making a diagnosis of AD is difficult, particularly in its early stages. Family members may be confused by what the physician says, and the doctor may not be very clear in what he or she says to the family. AD is a clinical diagnosis—meaning that there is no test to definitively confirm it other than a brain biopsy, which is usually not recommended. Thus, in about 20 percent of early cases (even those of geriatric psychiatrists or neurologists), the diagnosis is not correct. Only careful follow-up can increase accuracy.

Accurate diagnosis is important because there are many conditions other than AD that cause dementia (memory loss and impairment of other cognitive processes that impair ability to function). AD accounts for about 50 to 60 percent of irreversible dementias, while multiple strokes or vascular dementia account for 10 to 20 percent of cases and chronic alcohol abuse for about 6 to 11 percent. Vascular dementia and alcoholic dementia may not continue to worsen if the cause is removed (i.e., strokes are prevented or alcohol is stopped). There are also some dementias that, if treated, will completely reverse the memory problems. These include B_{12} deficiency, hypothyroidism or hyperthyroidism, neurosyphilis, normal pressure hydrocephalus, brain tumors, and perhaps most common, medication-induced or illness-induced cognitive impairment (delirium). For this reason, a complete evaluation by a physician—usually a geriatric medicine specialist, geriatric psychiatrist, or neurologist—is necessary.

Susan progressed steadily through the four stages of AD during the course of her illness. The early phase is characterized by loss of recent memory (ability to learn new information), minor language problems (difficulty with word finding), and minor personality changes. Remote memory remains largely intact. The intermediate stage is characterized by nearly complete loss of ability to learn and recall new information. The person may require some assistance with bathing, eating, dressing, or toileting, and there may be some problems with wandering, agitation, and getting lost. The severe phase occurs when the person is no longer able to walk and is usually incontinent. They may have difficulty swallowing and eating and are at high risk for developing pressure sores because of the large amount of time spent in bed. In the end stage, there may be seizures or other neurological problems; the person may go into a coma and will usually die of infection (Merck Manual, 1995). The course of the illness may range from two to fifteen years. Susan's disease course was fairly rapid.

Response to Vignette

The initial symptoms were a slow, progressive loss of memory and a decline in Susan's ability to perform activities of daily living. Michael gradually took over her responsibilities. Her symptoms progressed so slowly that only a trained outside observer evaluating her at six-month intervals could detect the relentless march of decline that is characteristic of AD. The fact that Susan's mother also experienced significant memory problems requiring nursing home placement in her mid-seventies was important information, since the risk of developing AD increases if there is a family history of the disease. Approximately 20 percent of AD cases are genetic, and 80 percent are unrelated to family history (Merck Manual, 1995).

Even before making the diagnosis, the doctor suggested that Susan take vitamins E and C and gingko biloba. These are relatively harmless preparations that have been shown to slow the memory loss in AD. Once the diagnosis has been established, treatment with prescription medication during the early or intermediate phase of the disease is appropriate. The goal of this treatment is not to cure the disease but to slow the decline of memory.

Depression is commonly encountered in the early stages of AD. Sometimes it is difficult to distinguish whether depression is the primary diagnosis with memory complaints or whether the primary diagnosis is AD with depression as secondary to the disturbing awareness of memory decline. Susan's depression was a reaction over having the same condition as her mother, and after the diagnosis of AD was confirmed, a response to the diagnosis itself. When the depression was treated, however, her quality of life significantly increased. Her irritability lessened, enhancing the relationship with her husband during those final months when she was nearly her usual self. Once her condition progressed to a certain point, however, she lost all insight to her condition, and her depression actually disappeared.

The most difficult stage of the illness for Michael, as for most caregivers, was when Susan's personality began to change and when she lost the ability to recognize family members. This is when a spouse caregiver frequently begins to mourn the death of the loved one. The spouse begins to sense that the person he or she knows is no longer there. What is difficult for caregivers, however, is the fluctuating nature of this condition. At times, the person with AD—who for months may not remember anything or recognize anyone—suddenly appears to remember and behave just like normal. This typically lasts only a short time before he or she plunges back into a state of confusion.

It is during the stage when the caregiver may begin to mourn the loss of the loved one that support is needed. Michael's pastor recognized this and responded appropriately. He allowed Michael to talk about his losses, to express his doubts and fears, and to ventilate his pain and anger. This is part of the normal grieving process and is best dealt with as the pastor did. This is an important time to provide the caregiver with emotional support and human contact. Treatment with antidepressants at this time is probably counterproductive, unless bereavement deepens into a depressive disorder.

After working through bereavement issues, the next challenge (although not necessarily in this order) involves the physical burden of caregiving. This is the time when the caregiver needs help to provide physical care for the loved one. Safety issues are also crucial, since persons with AD usually require nearly constant monitoring to prevent them from harming themselves or wandering off and getting lost. This is a key time to mobilize resources from within the family, the community, and the church to provide respite for the caregiver.

During this stage of AD, paranoia and/or delusional thinking occurs in about 40 percent of persons. Medications can be prescribed that help reduce the symptoms and may help regulate sleep patterns. A new group of antipsychotics that are much safer and more effective than earlier drugs is now available. The newer medications such as olanzapine (Zyprexa) or risperidone (Risperdal) cause less stiffness, fewer problems with movement, and less-impaired functioning than the older antipsychotics cause. If agitation, paranoia, or other psychotic symptoms are present, these symptoms will impair quality of life and increase the burden of caregiving. Thus, if disturbing to the patient or disrupting care, they should always be treated.

Michael was fortunate in that he had relatively good health for most of Susan's illness, good friends, a supportive family and religious community, and sufficient financial resources to provide care at home throughout most of her illness. Many persons are not as fortunate and must rely on either the health care system or the religious community for such support. The alternative is to admit a person to a nursing home, which becomes necessary when resources to provide home care are no longer sufficient. Even in

Susan's case, where resources were not a big problem, nursing home place-ment was eventually required.

Treatment Within the Faith Community

Family caregivers of persons with AD often rely heavily upon their reli-gious faith to cope with the burden of caregiving. Rabins, Fitting, Eastham, and Fetting (1990a) at Johns Hopkins University surveyed caregivers of persons with AD and of those with end-stage cancer. They revealed that successful coping was associated with only two variables: number of social contacts and support received from religious faith. When these persons were followed over two years to determine what characteristics predicted faster adaptation to the caregiver role, again, only the number of social contacts and support received from personal faith predicted better adapta-tion over time (Rabins, Fitting, Eastham, and Zabora, 1990b). Thus, hav-ing support from one's religious community appears to be one of the most important factors responsible for successful adaptation to the caregiver role.

Why is this so? Religious faith gives the caregiver role meaning. Victor Frankl (1959) said that the search for meaning is the primary motivator in life. Involvement in a burdensome task that has no meaning or purpose quickly becomes intolerable. If the caregiver can see his or her efforts as serving God and furthering God's purpose, then almost anything can be endured. Religious faith also provides tools for coping with hardship. Prayer for strength, prayer for endurance, prayer for hope are all grounded in religious faith.

There are many ways that the faith community can help a family care-giver deal with the stress of caring for a loved one with AD. In studies (Rabins et al., 1990a; Rabins et al., 1990b), the number of social contacts was the only more powerful predictor of caregiver adaptation than religious faith. Support by the faith community includes both of these—social con-tacts and religious faith. Because of the social isolation inherited in the caregiver role, the church can play a unique role in supporting families car-ing for Alzheimer's patients. First, members can call a caregiver on a regu-lar basis, checking to see if there is anything that can be done to help or simply listening to him or her talk about frustrations, fears, or pain. Second, they can visit and spend time with caregivers, keeping them com-pany and providing friendship. Third, members can provide respite to fam-ily caregivers by offering to sit with the patient to ensure that the person does not harm himself or herself or wander off. This provides the caregiv-er with needed time off from the twenty-four-hour-a-day job, permitting refreshment that is essential for continued functioning. Fourth, they can give assistance to caregivers, such as grocery shopping, house cleaning, lawn mowing, car repair, and so forth. Such tangible acts send a powerful message to caregivers that they are not alone and that the religious com-munity is behind them in this effort. Finally, members can donate money to a special church fund to pay for home care services for families who cannot afford them. Caregiving in the religious community should be a community effort.

If a person with a chronic illness or a caregiver develops a major depression, he or she will need a referral for specialized treatment. Indications of a major depression may include physical symptoms, such as weight loss, insomnia, or fatigue; suicidal thoughts; psychotic symptoms, such as auditory or visual hallucinations; or paranoid delusions (fixed, false beliefs from which a person cannot be dissuaded) with no improvement for three to four weeks.

Susan needed treatment by a mental health specialist. The treatment of choice for moderately and severely depressed persons is a combination of antidepressive medications and psychotherapy (Conte, Plutchik, Wild, and Karasu, 1986). Treatment for depression is effective in up to 80 percent of cases—even in cases of severe depression (Preston, O'Neal, and Talaga, 1994). A therapist may also work with the couple to seek improved communication and help them manage conflict more effectively.

Counseling Troubled Older Adults: A Handbook for Pastors and Religious Caregivers (Koenig and Weaver, 1997) and *Pastoral Care of Older Adults* (Koenig and Weaver, 1998) can be helpful to pastors and caregivers who need more information about the medical and psychiatric disorders experienced by older persons. These sources provide further information about diagnosing and treating depression in persons with chronic illness, about the medical needs of the chronically ill or disabled, and about community resources that can be utilized to help meet those needs.

In a study of patterns of coping with caregiving strain among African-American and European-American women who were primary caregivers to relatives with Alzheimer's, researchers found that the idea of a personal God was particularly valued among African-Americans. God was perceived as very personal and as much a part of their support system as a family member or a friend (Wood and Parham, 1990).

National Resources

—Alzheimer's Disease and Related Disorders Association; 919 North Michigan Avenue, Suite 1100, Chicago, IL 60611-1676; (800) 272-3900; www.alz.org; is a national organization with 220 chapters and 1,600 support groups that was founded in 1980. It provides information and assistance for caregivers of Alzheimer's patients, a newsletter, literature, and a chapter development kit.

—Alzheimer's Disease Education and Referral (ADEAR); P.O. Box

8250, Silver Spring, MD 20907-8250; (800) 438-4380; www.alzheimers.org; is a service of the National Institute on Aging (NIA), one of the National Institutes of Health under the U.S. Department of Health and Human Services. It provides information about Alzheimer's disease and related disorders.

—Alzheimer's Disease International (ADI); 45/46 Lower Marsh, London, SE1 7RG, United Kingdom; (44) 20-7620-3011; www.alz.co.uk; is an umbrella organization of fifty Alzheimer's associations around the world whose main purpose is to improve the quality of life of people with dementia and their caregivers and to raise awareness of the disease. It was registered in 1984 in Illinois as a nonprofit group and is in official relations with the World Health Organization.

—Alzheimer Society of Canada; 20 Eglinton Avenue, West, Suite 1200, Toronto, Ontario M4R 1K8, Canada; (416) 488-8772 or (800) 616-8816 (valid only in Canada); info@alzheimer.ca; is a nonprofit Canadian health organization founded in 1978. It works to provide a network of services to help Canadians affected by this disease. Its mission is to alleviate its personal and social consequences and to promote the search for a cause and cure.

Self-Help Resources

Alzheimer's: Caring for Your Loved Ones, Caring for Yourself (Sharon Fish, Wheaton, IL: Harold Shaw Publishers, 1996).

Alzheimer's: The Complete Guide for Families and Loved Ones (Howard Greutzner, New York: John Wiley & Sons, 1997).

Alzheimer's and Dementia: Questions You Have . . . Answers You Need (Jennifer Hay, Allentown, PA: People's Medical Society, 1996).

The Alzheimer's Sourcebook for Caregivers: A Practical Guide for Getting Through the Day, 3rd ed. (Frena Gray-Davidson, Los Angeles: Lowell House, 1999).

Forgetting Whose We Are: Alzheimer's Disease and the Love of God (David Keck, Nashville: Abingdon Press, 1996).

My Journey into Alzheimer's Disease (Robert Davis, Wheaton, IL: Tyndale House Publishers, 1989).

The 36-Hour Day: A Family Guide to Caring for Persons with Alzheimer Disease, Related Dementing Illnesses, and Memory Loss in Later Life, 3rd ed. (Nancy L. Mace, Peter V. Rabins, and Paul R. McHugh, Baltimore: Johns Hopkins University Press, 1999). Highly recommended.

References

Conte, H. R., Plutchik, R., Wild, K. V., and Karasu, T. B. (1986). Combined psychotherapy and pharmacotherapy for depression. *Archives of General Psychiatry, 43,* 471–479.

Frankl, V. (1959). *Man's Search for Meaning.* New York: Simon and Schuster.

Koenig, H. G., and Weaver, A. J. (1997). *Counseling Troubled Older Adults: A Handbook for Pastors and Religious Caregivers*. Nashville: Abingdon Press.

Koenig, H. G., and Weaver, A. J. (1998). *Pastoral Care of Older Adults*. Minneapolis: Fortress Press.

Mace, N. L., and Rabins, P. V. (1999). *The 36-Hour Day: A Family Guide to Caring for Persons with Alzheimer Disease, Related Dementing Illnesses, and Memory Loss in Later Life* (3rd ed.). Baltimore: Johns Hopkins University Press.

Merck Manual. (1995). *Merck Manual of Geriatrics* (2nd ed.). Whitehouse Station, NJ: Merck Research Laboratories, p. 1148.

Preston, J., O'Neal, J. H., and Talaga, M. C. (1994). *Handbook of Clinical Psychopharmacology for Therapists*. Oakland, CA: New Harbinger Publications.

Rabins, P. V., Fitting, M. D., Eastham, J., and Fetting, J. (1990a). The emotional impact of caring for the chronically ill. *Psychosomatics, 31*, 331–336.

Rabins, P. V., Fitting, M. D., Eastham, J., and Zabora, J. (1990b). Emotional adaptation over time in caregivers for chronically ill elderly people. *Age and Aging, 19*, 185–190.

Wood, J. B., and Parham, I. A. (1990). Coping with perceived burden: Ethnic and cultural issues in Alzheimer's family caregiving. *Journal of Applied Gerontology, 9*, 325–539.

Placing a Family Member in a Nursing Home

"He Became Completely House-bound and Needed Total Care"

A small creek ran into a pond behind Janet and Robert's dream house. Their entire savings was invested in this home that they had built for their retirement. The pond was important to seventy-eight-year-old Robert, who loved to fish. He had health problems caused by advancing Parkinson's disease, and he wanted to have a ready access to a small body of water where he could throw in a hook. A cement walkway led directly to the pond, enabling Robert to roll his wheelchair down to the shore.

Over the past year, Robert's illness worsened. Soon, he became unable to wheel his chair down to the pond by himself. He would often ask Janet to assist him in getting to his fishing spot and back. She, however, preferred socializing with friends to sitting with Robert while he fished, since she was more outgoing and extroverted than he. Janet's health at age seventy-five was not the best, and she frequently used it as an excuse not to help Robert to the pond. Her doctor had warned her against overexertion because of her heart condition. She and Robert argued over how they should spend their time—whether to invite people over to the house or to spend evenings down at the pond.

By spring, the Parkinson's disease had progressed to the point that Robert could not cast his line into the water. With Robert's increasing disability, Janet had to assume most of the responsibilities around the home, and she resented it. Robert also began refusing to attend church with his wife. He said he was too self-conscious there and had difficulty hearing the sermon, and the bathroom was inaccessible.

After not seeing him in church for several Sundays, Pastor Ron stopped Janet after the service and asked about Robert. She reported that he was doing poorly, that nothing interested him, and that she was worried that he might have given up hope. The pastor decided to pay him a visit. When he arrived at their home, Pastor Ron asked Robert how he was doing and told him that he had been missed at church the past several Sundays. Robert admitted that he had neither the interest nor the energy to do anything in recent weeks and was beginning to feel like a burden on Janet. After finding out what was bothering Robert, the pastor encouraged him to see his doctor.

At the physician's office, Robert learned that he was depressed, would benefit from counseling, and needed to take an antidepressant medication. Robert reluctantly agreed, and both therapies were initiated. His attitude improved significantly, and Janet noted that he was more like his old self. He started going to church again. Things continued to go well through the summer and fall, but then Robert's health gradually worsened. Janet's heart condition was progressing, and she experienced chest pain more frequently and with little exertion.

Robert became completely housebound and needed total care, including help with dressing and bathing. His depression slowly returned, and he had some cognitive impairment due to the Parkinson's disease, which made him increasingly impatient and demanding. Janet felt overwhelmed by the requirements of keeping up the house and providing personal care to Robert. What helped her were the many church members who called and visited, who told her that they were praying for her and for Robert, and who assisted when either of them had to go to medical or other appointments.

Pastor Ron and Robert's doctor urged Janet to hire in-home help to relieve her of some caregiving responsibilities. She was slow to agree due to the expense involved and because Robert did not want anyone but her giving him personal care. Janet put off her coronary artery bypass surgery because there would be no one at home to take care of Robert. Her doctors suggested she place him in a nursing home temporarily. She was reluctant, and Robert was adamantly opposed.

The couple finally decided to hire a home health aide for two to four hours a day to assist with Robert's care and to do some of the heavier chores around the house. Even with this help, however, Janet was exhausted and fell into a deep depression.

Her friends at church brought this to Pastor Ron's attention. When he arrived at the couple's house, it was evident that the situation was not good. Robert was yelling from his bedroom for Janet, who was lying on the couch, holding her chest. She had been having chest pains for several hours and was unable to do anything. The pastor dialed 911, and paramedics took Janet to the emergency room, from which she was admitted to the hospital. Pastor Ron asked a church leader to go to the house and stay with Robert until arrangements could be made to admit him temporarily to a nursing home. Janet required emergency open-heart surgery, and she remained in the hospital for one week. When the time for discharge was near, the doctors advised that she leave Robert in the nursing home for several weeks while she recovered. Reluctantly, she agreed.

When Janet visited Robert in the nursing home one week after her hospitalization, she found him sitting in a wheelchair in his room, sleeping with his head slumped forward on his chest. Awakening slowly, he seemed not to recognize her. After awhile, some hint of recognition crossed his face. He began to cry, begging her to take him home. This was too much for Janet, and she had to leave. When she returned to the empty house, she felt lonely, and a deep sense of despair engulfed her. She drove to a church friend's home.

Janet broke down in tears. Her friend offered to pray with her, but Janet declined, saying that she felt too guilty to pray. She and Robert had promised that neither one would ever put the other in a nursing home, and now she had broken that promise. Janet talked about her relationship with Robert. While it had been a difficult marriage, each was devoted to the other. Janet confessed that, at some level, she had hoped she would die during her open-heart surgery, rather than come back to face this. She did not feel that she could either emotionally or physically care for Robert in the way she had been doing. At the same time, she didn't feel that she could leave Robert in the nursing home. When she left her friend that day, she had resolved to remove him from the institution.

In one week, Robert was home, despite the strenuous objection of both his and Janet's doctors. When Pastor Ron visited, she confided in him that she simply had to try one more time. The women at church set up a schedule so that someone either phoned or visited the couple daily. These calls and visits were of enormous help to Janet in those difficult days.

Robert's cognitive impairment worsened, and he began to lose all control over his physical functioning. Often, he would not even recognize Janet, at whom he sometimes yelled and cursed. The doctors unsuccessfully tried both antidepressant and antipsychotic medications to help control Robert's agitation and to enable him to sleep at night so that Janet could get rest. The only time she could sleep, however, was when the aide was there each morning.

Janet began to have chest pain again, but medical evaluation revealed that her heart was functioning well. Her doctor sent her to a psychiatrist, who started her on medication to calm her nerves and help with sleep. Pastor Ron visited weekly to check on the couple. It was clear that the current situation was not working.

One day, the pastor had a long talk with Janet. He pointed out to her that she was worn out and soon could not provide the kind of care that her husband needed. He discussed her pact with Robert. Pastor Ron helped Janet understand that the most Christian action was to place Robert in a nursing home. This was consistent with Jesus' commandment to love your neighbor as yourself. What she was doing—keeping Robert at home to assuage her guilt—was not loving Robert or herself, nor did it demonstrate concern for his highest welfare.

Finally, Janet made arrangements for Robert to be moved to the nursing home, and within the week, he was there. Janet still struggled with her guilt, however. She felt no joy in visiting Robert, and after each trip, she became despondent. Soon she stopped seeing Robert altogether. She quit going to church and answering her telephone. Janet's church friends caught Pastor Ron after the Sunday service and encouraged him to visit her.

She admitted to the pastor that putting Robert in the nursing home was necessary—the only thing she could do. But she still had an awful feeling that would not go away. After several visits with Janet at her house, Pastor Ron suggested that they meet at the nursing home, hoping to restore contact between Janet and her husband. Reluctantly, she agreed. The pastor met Janet at the facility each week, and they visited Robert together. After a month, she was able to see Robert alone again. At Pastor Ron's suggestion, Janet made each visit as an intentional expression of love to Robert and as service to God. Robert's condition continued to advance so that he seldom recognized her. Yet Janet knew that, at some level, he sensed her presence, and it comforted him. Over time, Janet was able to increase her visits to three times a week, and, occasionally, she even participated in his care at the nursing home.

Pastoral Assessment

The decision to put a loved one in a nursing home can be one of the most difficult decisions made by family members in their entire lives. It is almost never easy, and families typically put it off until long past the time when placement should ideally be made. For a person with a progressive condition like Robert's, the best time for nursing home placement to occur is when the burden of caregiving threatens the health of either the patient or the caregiver. Placement becomes necessary in order to avoid further deterioration of health.

Even then, as in Janet's case, the caregiver is likely to feel guilty—particularly if he or she has been caring for the person for a long time or if there is conflict in the relationship. The healthier the relationship between patient and caregiver, the less likely that guilt will persist if the patient is admitted to a nursing home. In that situation, both partners usually recognize that placement is the best option. Because of the ongoing conflict between Janet and Robert, there was ambivalence in their relationship. Robert was focused on his needs, neglecting his wife's. Janet, in turn, knew that placing her husband in a nursing home would relieve her of tremendous responsibility and allow her to pursue the social relationships that were an important part of her life.

Relevant History

Both Robert and Janet had been married before and had children from those relationships. It had been an effort to blend the two families together. Consequently, the marriage had been a difficult one from the start, often characterized by conflict. The relationship improved after the children left home. However, they were two very different people, and their interests did not match well, which became particularly obvious after Robert retired and began spending more time at home. Both Robert and Janet had hoped that building their new house and separating from the children would improve their marriage.

As Robert's disease progressed, he became discouraged, losing interest in his usual activities. Persons with a chronic illness impairing their ability to do the things that give meaning and pleasure to their lives are at risk for the development of emotional disorders—especially depression. There may be a loss of hope, increasing irritability, decreasing sociability, loss of energy, and a sense of being a burden on others. Robert needed professional help for his depression. As the burden of caregiving increased, Janet plunged into a depression, which may have affected her physical health. The counseling with Pastor Ron was helpful, particularly in assisting to resolve her ambivalence and guilt, which can be associated with depression.

Janet experienced excessive guilt, manifested by her extreme ambivalence toward placing Robert in a nursing home. It was excessive because it interfered with her ability to recognize when the placement was necessary. Her guilt was so severe that it threatened her own life. Janet indicated that, at some level, she wished to die rather than recover from surgery to resume the increasingly heavy burden of caring for Robert.

Summing up, the following is a list of signs that nursing home placement is indicated:

Diagnostic Criteria

- Family member's health is deteriorating, and caregiver cannot keep up with the demands.
- Caregiver's health (mental or physical) is worsening, and continuing to provide care is exacerbating the condition.
- Resources are not sufficient at home to provide optimal care for the ill family member.
- Others are not available or willing to provide for the sick family member, and the ill person cannot afford in-home care.
- Family member wishes to be placed in a nursing home, rather than to burden other family members with care.

When a family is no longer able to care for a sick family member at home, the following living arrangements are possible, depending on how much care and supervision is needed:

- Continuing care community—Affluent persons planning to retire and not to move again may decide to enter one of these communities when they are still healthy. They offer different levels of care ranging from independent living to assisted living to skilled nursing care with twenty-four-hour-a-day supervision.

- Assisted living facility—Offers meals, recreation, and assistance with basic activities of daily living. Residents have a room, which may be shared with another person. Medications and assistance with personal care are provided.
- Adult foster care facility—Provides twenty-four-hour-a-day personal care for a small number of chronically ill or disabled adults. These typically are not licensed by the state, do not have nursing or medical personnel on premises, and usually cost less than rest homes.
- Rest home (domiciliary care home)—Provides personal care twenty-four hours a day for persons not able to live independently. These facilities are licensed by the state and provide meals, transportation, housekeeping, and social and recreational programs. Medications are administered by a licensed practical nurse typically on duty twenty-four hours a day, but specialized nursing or medical care is limited.
- Intermediate care facility (sometimes called a convalescent or extended care home)—Provides twenty-four-hour personal care for persons with occasional but not continuous skilled nursing needs. Social activities and rehabilitation also are available if needed. Medicaid will pay for this level of care if patient is indigent.
- Skilled nursing facility—Provides twenty-four-hour-a-day skilled nursing care for persons confined to bed with physical problems. Patients may stay in such a facility for short periods after hospitalization for intensive physical and occupational therapy prior to returning home. Medicaid will pay for this level of care if patient is indigent.
- Special care unit—Usually associated with a skilled nursing facility but may be found in other settings. These typically provide specialized care for persons with Alzheimer's disease. They are generally more expensive than other nursing homes because more nurses are needed to staff these units.

Factors to consider when choosing a nursing home include the following:

- Cost of the facility. The average nursing home costs significantly more than Medicaid will pay annually.
- Reputation of the nursing home. It is essential to talk with relatives of persons in the facility to determine how satisfied they are. Ensure that the home is Medicaid-certified, which guarantees a minimum quality of care; furthermore, when the person can no longer afford to pay the costs, Medicaid will take over.
- Location of the facility. It is important that it is located near family

members' homes. The type of care patients receive is strongly influenced by frequency of visits from family members. Establishing relationships with staff helps to ensure that loved ones will get the best possible care.
- Staffing of the nursing home. Is there an adequate number of nurses and nursing aides? This can be determined best by making unannounced visits to the facility on holidays or on weekends.
- Nature of the contract. It is important to have a lawyer review the contract, paying special attention to what is not provided.

Pastors and other religious leaders must be alert to situations of one person having a progressive or chronic illness that is taxing the emotional or physical health of the family (Rolland, 1987). Periodic home visits or telephone calls are important to monitor how both the patient and the caregiver are coping. Counseling may help relieve the burden of caregiving. When chronically ill persons are assisted in coping better with their illnesses, they may be less irritable, less demanding, and easier to care for. Counseling caregivers may help them better tolerate the demands and better perform the job with less emotional turmoil. This, in turn, can benefit patients, who will feel like less of a burden on caregivers.

A pastor can play a role in helping a caregiver recognize when nursing home placement is necessary. Given his or her role as a religious leader, the clergyperson can help relieve guilt by pointing out that it is acceptable and appropriate to make this decision. The caregiver may have known his or her pastor for many years, so trust is more likely to be present in this relationship than in relationships with other professionals, including physicians. A clergyperson's ability to influence important decisions should be carefully utilized. However, a pastor should attempt to affect decisions only if he or she is fully informed about the situation, never trying to force family members to take actions against their will. It is best to help a caregiver weigh the pros and cons of various options, never insisting on a choice that the caregiver is not ready to make. Some families, however, need only a small nudge to make the right choice, and the pastor can provide encouragement in that direction.

Once a loved one has been placed in a nursing home, it is essential to encourage family members to visit. The pastor or a religious leader may accompany family members on such trips if necessary.

After placement—particularly if the loved one is still cognitively aware of the situation—persons may be angry and disappointed and feel rejected. They may ignore visiting family members or refuse to see them. This will make it more difficult for family members to visit, which adds to their own guilt about the placement. Pastoral interventions may help to facilitate the patient's adjustment to the home and assist the rest of the family in

Response to Vignette

179

overcoming their guilt so that they will visit. It is important to bring families back into loving relationships with each other. Failure to do so may result in unresolved pain and unhappiness that can last for years.

Treatment Within the Faith Community

A person's religious faith will play an important role in helping a patient adjust to being placed in a nursing home (Koenig, Weiner, Peterson, Meador, and Keefe, 1997b). This is a huge life transition, and there is little doubt that deep religious faith provides an anchor of stability during this time. Praying and reading scriptures and inspirational literature may go on largely unchanged both before and after nursing home placement. Realizing that one's usefulness to God in ministering to others is not finished upon arrival at the nursing facility may provide a continued (or even renewed) sense of purpose and meaning in life. Given the spiritual needs in such places, there will be plenty of work for those residents who are called. And as long as there is any degree of consciousness remaining, these persons are equipped for the task.

Because of the important role of religious faith in helping people cope with the stress of nursing home placement, pastoral counseling may assist persons in resolving their questions for, and anger toward, God for allowing this to happen. Once such issues are addressed, patients need an opportunity to develop and strengthen their religious faith by participating in religious services (at the nursing home), reading religious literature, talking with chaplains or visiting pastors, and having an opportunity to pray with others. Listening to religious tapes or music may also nurture one's faith.

The potential of faith communities in ministering to family caregivers, chronically ill persons, and patients in nursing homes is enormous. Members can visit and support caregivers, providing friendship and companionship. They can provide practical services around the home and respite care by sitting with a chronically ill person, giving caregivers a reprieve to refresh themselves. Church members can visit and call, bring gifts, send cards, and provide friendship to the sick person. They may listen, encourage, support, and help nurture the religious faith of chronically ill persons by praying with them, praying for them (and letting them know about this), reading scriptures to them, providing transportation to religious services, and otherwise supporting their faith. Church members can help sick persons realize that they are not alone and are still part of their faith community. They can also provide opportunities for chronically ill persons to use their own gifts and talents to help others and serve God (Koenig, Lamar, and Lamar, 1997a).

All of this applies to nursing home patients, as well. Many of those in such facilities have no one to visit them, are lonely and unhappy, and feel outside the mainstream of life. Regular visits from members of the religious community, who are willing to make the time and effort to develop relationships with them, can be a significant ministry. Mentally alert nursing home patients receive great delight from visits by children and teenagers. Pastoral care visits from clergy in the community are also very important and yet seldom occur—except to hold an occasional religious service.

When a person with a chronic illness or that person's caregiver develops a major depression, he or she will need a referral for specialized treatment. Indications of a major depression that require a referral include physical symptoms, such as weight loss, insomnia, or fatigue; suicidal thoughts; psychotic symptoms, such as auditory or visual hallucinations; and paranoid delusions (fixed, false beliefs from which a person cannot be dissuaded) with no improvement for three to four weeks.

Indications for Referral

Robert and Janet needed treatment by mental health specialists. The treatment of choice for moderately and severely depressed persons is a combination of antidepressive medications and psychotherapy (Conte, Plutchik, Wild, and Karasu, 1986). Treatment is effective in up to 80 percent of cases of depressed persons—even in severe cases (Preston, O'Neal, and Talaga, 1994). The therapist may also work with a couple to seek improved communication and to help the partners manage conflict more effectively.

Counseling Troubled Older Adults: A Handbook for Pastors and Religious Caregivers (Koenig and Weaver, 1997) and *Pastoral Care of Older Adults* (Koenig and Weaver, 1998) can be helpful to pastors and caregivers who need to know more about the medical and psychiatric disorders experienced by older persons. These books provide further information about diagnosing and treating depression in persons with chronic illness and about the medical needs of the chronically ill or disabled, and community resources that can be utilized to help meet those needs.

Treatment by Mental Health Specialist

In a study of elderly women in Finland living in long-term institutional care in which 1 in 4 was bedridden, it was found that 88 percent believed in God and 75 percent prayed every day (Nores, 1997). The elderly women, who were primarily Christian, indicated that prayers were a valued resource in helping them face their difficulties and cope with chronic illness.

Cross-Cultural Issues

National Resources

Resources

—Family Caregiver Alliance; 690 Market Street, Suite 600, San Francisco, CA 94104; (415) 434-3388; www.caregiver.org; is an organization addressing the needs of families and friends providing long-term care at home. Founded in 1977, it serves as a public voice for caregivers, illuminating the daily challenges they face, offering them the assistance they need, and championing their cause through education, services, research, and advocacy.

—Information about choosing a nursing home can be obtained by writing to the U.S. Department of Health and Human Services and asking for the pamphlet "Guide to Choosing a Nursing Home" (publication number HCFA-02174, 1993).

—National Family Caregivers Association; 10400 Connecticut Avenue, #500, Kensington, MD 20895-3944; (800) 896-3650; www.nfcacares.org; is a national network, founded in 1992, dedicated to improving the quality of life for family caregivers. It provides members with phone support, information, referrals, resources, and literature.

—National Parkinson Foundation; 1501 NW Ninth Avenue, Miami, FL 33136; (800) 327-4545; www.parkinson.org is dedicated to finding the cause and cure for Parkinson's disease and related neurodegenerative disorders through research. It works to educate patients, their caregivers, and the general public about the disease and to improve the quality of life for both patients and their caregivers.

—Rosalynn Carter Institute; Georgia Southwestern College, 600 Simmons Street, Americus, GA 31709; provides information on caregiving. Reading lists, video products, and other caregiver resources are available by mail.

—The Well Spouse Foundation; P.O. Box 501, New York, NY 10023; (800) 838-0879; provides support for the husbands, wives, and partners of people who are chronically ill or disabled.

Self-Help Resources

Beat the Nursing Home Trap: A Consumer's Guide to Assisted Living and Long-Term Care, 3rd ed. (Joseph L. Matthews, Berkeley, CA: Nolo Press, 1999).

Caregiver's Handbook (Visiting Nurse Association of America, New York: DK Publishing, 1998).

Caregiver's Reprieve: A Guide to Emotional Survival When You're Caring for Someone You Love (Avrene L. Brandt, San Luis Obispo, CA: Impact Publishers, 1998).

Caring for Yourself While Caring for Your Aging Parents: How to Help, How to Survive, 2nd ed. (Claire Berman, New York: Henry Holt & Co., 2001).

The Complete Guide to Eldercare (Anita Jones-Lee and Melanie Callender, Hauppauge, NY: Barron's Educational Series, 1998).

The Inside Guide to America's Nursing Homes: Rankings and Ratings for Every Nursing Home in the U.S., 1998–1999 (Robert N. Bua, New York: Warner Books, 1997).

The Nursing Home Choice: How to Choose the Ideal Nursing Home (Marian R. Kranz and Adolph Caso, Boston: Branden Publishing, 1998).

The Nursing Home Decision: Easing the Transition for Everyone (Lawrence M. Martin, New York: John Wiley & Sons, 1999).

References

Conte, H. R., Plutchik, R., Wild, K. V., and Karasu, T. B. (1986). Combined psychotherapy and pharmacotherapy for depression. *Archives of General Psychiatry, 43,* 471–479.

Koenig, H. G., Lamar, T., and Lamar, B. (1997a). *A Gospel for the Mature Years: Finding Fulfillment by Knowing and Using Your Gift.* New York: Haworth Press.

Koenig, H. G., and Weaver, A. J. (1997). *Counseling Troubled Older Adults: A Handbook for Pastors and Religious Caregivers.* Nashville: Abingdon Press.

Koenig, H. G., and Weaver, A. J. (1998). *Pastoral Care of Older Adults.* Minneapolis: Fortress Press.

Koenig, H. G., Weiner, D. K., Peterson, B. L., Meador, K. G., and Keefe, F. J. (1997b). Religious coping in the nursing home: a biopsychosocial model. *International Journal of Psychiatry and Medicine, 27(4),* 365–376.

Nores, T. H. (1997). What is most important for elders in institutional care in Finland? *Geriatric Nursing, 18(2),* 67–69.

Preston, J., O'Neal, J. H., and Talaga, M. C. (1994). *Handbook of Clinical Psychopharmacology for Therapists.* Oakland, CA: New Harbinger Publications.

Rolland, J. S. (1987). Chronic Illness and the life cycle: A conceptual framework. *Family Process, 26,* 203–221.

Terminal Illness

"The Cancer Began to Spread Rapidly"

Ruby is a sixty-seven-year-old widow and lifelong active member of her church. She had a cough that persisted over several weeks. When she saw her physician, he sent her to a specialist, who found two malignancies on her lungs. The oncologist advised aggressive treatment with chemotherapy and radiation. At first, the cancer responded to treatments, and the size of the growths was reduced. However, the disease proved to be especially virulent and began to spread. Over the next several months, a woman of great spirit and dignity lost her hair and her strength. As Ruby's health deteriorated, her immune system became compromised, and she contracted childhood measles. She began to have considerable discomfort and pain as the cancer progressed. Her pastor, the Reverend Marvin Harris, had prior experience as a hospital chaplain and was able to assist Ruby in finding the resources she required to receive proper care.

Pastoral Assessment

The diagnosis of cancer challenged every dimension of Ruby's life—physical, emotional, and spiritual. It shattered her sense of invulnerability and control of her life, engendering anxiety and fear. Ruby had maintained good health and exercise habits, yet out of nowhere, the cancer struck her. It seemed unfair, and at first she was in a state of shock. Compounding her anxiety were the unknowns about the outcome of treatment, which increased her feelings of losing control over her life.

Reverend Harris helped Ruby through the natural course of grief, given the sudden and unexpected loss of her health and the gravity of her illness. Grieving is a natural psychological process that involves working through the pain of loss, typically, in several stages. The first reaction is often marked by shock, disbelief, numbness, and denial. This distances a grieving person from the loss, providing protection from overwhelming emotions.

The second phase is the turn from disbelief to feeling, releasing the pain of the situation. This process may take several forms. Natural emotions of sadness, hopelessness, and helplessness emerge as a person clearly recognizes the extent of the loss. The final stage of grief is characterized by acceptance and resolution. During the last phase, the grieving person is able to accept the reality of the situation.

Reverend Harris knew the value of being a good listener. He encouraged Ruby to express her feelings. The pastor avoided being judgmental or telling Ruby what she should feel. He didn't minimize her suffering or offer pat answers. Reverend Harris affirmed Ruby's faith in God and gave her assurance of God's love and closeness, even in suffering. He prayed with her on each visit.

Care for a suffering person is stressful, and those who cope successfully are able to recognize their own need for self-care. Religious professionals need skills to identify stress within themselves, acknowledge and accept their limitations, develop self-help resources, and seek assistance from others. Stress may increase due to unresolved grief issues in one's personal life or the unrealistic expectation that one will always be able to help. Support groups and discussions with colleagues are valuable resources. Clergy must recognize their need to grieve a loss, providing themselves opportunities to express their feelings to other persons, such as trusted friends, colleagues, or a pastoral counselor.

Relevant History

Ruby was a gentle, guileless soul who expected the best of others. She tended to defer to persons in authority, such as medical doctors. Reverend Harris had extensive experience as a hospital chaplain, so he understood the need for patients to be direct and assertive with the medical system to ensure good care. One of his roles with Ruby and other parishioners was to teach them to ask questions and to insist upon adequate attention to their medical issues.

Diagnostic Criteria

Cancer is among the most feared of all diseases. It is the product of immeasurable, cumulative lifestyle and environmental factors that place everyone at risk for the disease. Cancer is the general term used to describe a large group of diseases whose primary trademark is the uncontrolled growth of cells in body tissue. It is predominantly a disease of the elderly, and the incidence increases with age. Half of all cancers occur in individuals over sixty-five years of age (American Cancer Society, 1994). In the United States, cancer is the second leading cause of death after heart disease, resulting in more than 550,000 deaths annually (Burton, 1998).

Response to Vignette

Cancer patients and their families may be intimidated and confused by the health-care delivery system and by the technology of modern treatment. Although there have been improvements, the current health care system consists largely of fragmented, specialized-care episodes for specific problems, rather than a holistic approach to illness. Cancer patients may need guidance and support to be able to share responsibility with medical personnel in making decisions about their treatment. A crucial element of patient and family satisfaction with medical care is involvement in the decision-making process (Chesler and Barbarin, 1984). Family members value information in understandable language about the status of their loved one and honest answers about patient care and prognosis.

The problem of pain in elderly cancer patients has been seriously neglected. Cancer-related pain afflicts more than one million Americans annually and is often inadequately addressed. As a result, many persons spend the last weeks or months of their lives in unnecessary discomfort and suffering (Bonica, 1990).

Fortunately, Ruby's family physician had experience with palliative care (an approach that focuses on relieving pain and symptoms for the dying). Its goal is the achievement of the best possible quality of life for persons in the dying process and for their families. Ruby chose to receive hospice care at home and later in a residential hospice setting if the demands became too great on her family and friends. Hospice is a medically coordinated interdisciplinary team approach that focuses on compassionate methods of caring for the terminally ill. It places special emphasis on palliative care with strict limits on invasive procedures.

It is the goal of hospice that persons live their last days with dignity and comfort, either at home or in a homelike environment. Hospice care neither prolongs life nor hastens death, but deals with the emotional, social, and spiritual impact of disease on a patient and the patient's family and friends. Hospices offer a variety of bereavement and counseling services to families before and after a patient's death. They cared for 540,000 people in the U.S. in 1998 in over 3,100 separate programs (Hospice Foundation of America, 2000). About 70 percent of persons served by a hospice are sixty-five years of age or older, and the great majority of hospice patients have terminal cancer.

Ruby gave legal authorization (durable power of attorney for health care) to her son, John, to make decisions regarding her treatment if she became unable to do so for herself. The "durable power of attorney for health care" appoints another individual to make decisions regarding health care on one's behalf should one become incompetent, i.e., unable to make such decisions on one's own. A person would, of course, discuss a "living will" with their proxy, clearly expressing preferences ahead of time, so that the proxy can adequately carry out a person's wishes. Ruby's living will included her specific instructions for when to use and refuse medical treatment and when she was to be placed in hospice care. She also made her wishes known to her medical doctor, family members, and pastor.

The advantage of having some form of advance directive is that individuals have the opportunity to state their preferences related to their health care in critical situations, thus relieving family members of having to guess what they would want. In the case of a durable power of attorney, persons can appoint someone that they feel will adequately express their beliefs and choices to act on their behalf. Such documentation may give individuals and families peace of mind.

Living will and durable power of attorney documents exist in standard form and can be obtained from such places as social service agencies or health care facilities. A person may prefer to consult with an attorney, physician, or clergyperson prior to completing such a form. Some faith communities have developed guidance on this subject. In a study in Ohio involving hospital outpatients and their family members, only 12 percent had completed a living will (VandeCreek, Frankowski, and Johnson, 1995).

Treatment Within the Faith Community

Most individuals, particularly older adults, express their faith through religious community. There is a strong relationship between reliance on religious beliefs and practices and effective coping with cancer (Holland et al., 1999). In a study at the University of Michigan Medical Center of 108 women at various stages of cancer, about half felt they had become more religious since having cancer, and none of the patients said they had become less religious since they were diagnosed (Roberts, Brown, Elkins, and Larson, 1997). A high 93 percent of the patients said their faith had increased their capacity to be hopeful.

Faith can help give a person suffering from cancer a framework for finding meaning and perspective through a source greater than self. Faith provides a sense of control over feelings of helplessness along with the natural social support of community. In a study of 100 older adults with an average age of seventy-three who had been diagnosed with cancer, a consistent positive relationship was discovered between religious practice, spiritual well-being, hope, and lower anxiety and depression (Ferhring, Miller, and Shaw, 1997).

Other studies have found that the most common coping strategy for cancer patients is praying alone and with others, as well as having others pray for them (Soderstrom and Martinson, 1987). Cancer patients place a high value on interactions with their pastors, noting that pastoral visits and prayers help them maintain hope and optimism (Johnson and Spilka, 1991). When 231 patients with end-stage cancer were asked what maintained their quality of life, "their relationship with God" was the most often endorsed among twenty-eight choices (McMillian and Weitzner, 2000).

There are numerous ways that congregations can provide spiritual, emotional, and practical support for the terminally ill and their families. For example, Genoa United Methodist Church in Houston, Texas, assigns a Care Leader to each person in the church who is dying. When the death occurs, the Caring Team of several persons visits the bereft family. On the day of the funeral, a meal is taken to the family's home. The Caring Team continues to contact the family to give support after the death (O'Hara, 1995).

St. Mary's Catholic Parish in Colts Neck, New Jersey, has mobilized its members to meet the needs of grieving persons through its Lazarus Ministry. Teams of laypersons in the parish are trained to respond to families who have lost a loved one. They are taught to understand the dynamics of normal and complicated grief and to provide care and support to mourning families (Dewey, 1988).

If members of Ruby's family are not coping well with her impending death, an assessment for complicated bereavement is needed. Complicated bereavement involves being "stuck" in the early stages of grief for several months or more and not being able to move from denial to acceptance and resolution. A person is often preoccupied with thoughts of the deceased, lacks control over weeping, feels stunned by the death, and does not accept the loss of their loved one. For a full discussion of complicated bereavement, see Case 1 in *Counseling Troubled Older Adults: A Handbook for Pastors and Religious Caregivers* (Koenig and Weaver, 1997).

Indications for Referral

The dying process should be a relatively peaceful one. When it is not and emotional distress interferes with a dying person's ability to relate to loved ones, referral to a mental health specialist becomes necessary. A psychiatrist with experience in treating the mental disturbances of the dying and a thorough knowledge of appropriate medications should be sought. Symptoms of pain, depression, and anxiety frequently overlap, and some medications prescribed for the relief of depression (the tricyclic antidepressants) can also help relieve both anxiety and pain.

Treatment by Mental Health Specialist

African-Americans are more likely to develop cancer and less likely to survive it than other groups of Americans. During the period from 1990 to 1996, the incidence rates were 442.9 per 100,000 among African-Americans, 402.9 per 100,000 for European-Americans, and 275.4 per 100,000 among Hispanic-Americans (American Cancer Society, 2000). Research has found that the participation of clergy and key lay members in church-based cancer control programs can improve access to, and participation in, screening for cancer in African-Americans and Hispanic-Americans (Davis et al., 1994).

Cross-Cultural Issues

National Resources

Resources

—American Cancer Society; 1599 Clifton Road, NE, Atlanta, GA 30329-4251; (800) ACS-2345; is a nationwide, community-based voluntary health organization dedicated to eliminating cancer as a major health problem by preventing and diminishing suffering from cancer through research, education, advocacy, and service.

—Candlelighters Childhood Cancer Foundation; 3910 Warner Street, Kensington, MD 20895; (800) 366-2223; www.candlelighters.org; was founded in 1970 as an international foundation with 400-plus groups. It offers support for parents of children and adolescents with cancer, their family members, and adult survivors of childhood cancer. Health and education professionals are also welcomed as members.

—Hospice Foundation of America; 2001 S Street, NW, Suite 300, Washington, DC 20009; (800) 854-3402; www.hospicefoundation.org.

—Kidney Cancer Association; 1234 Sherman Avenue, Suite 203, Evanston, IL 60202-1375; (847) 332-1051; www.nkca.org; was founded in 1990 and has eight affiliated groups. It provides information about kidney cancer to patients and to doctors and advocates on behalf of patients. It offers information and referrals, literature, and conferences.

—Leukemia Society of America; Family Support Group Program, 600 Third Avenue, 4th floor, New York, NY 10016; (212) 450-8834; www.leukemia.org; is a national program of 125 professionally run groups, founded in 1949. It offers mutual support for patients, family members, and friends coping with leukemia, lymphoma, multiple myeloma, and Hodgkin's disease.

—Make Today Count; c/o St. John's Regional Health Center, Mid-America Cancer Center, 1235 East Cherokee Street, Springfield, MO 65804-2263; (800) 432-2273; was founded in 1974 as a national mutual support for persons facing a life-threatening illness. It is open to relatives and friends and provides chapter development guidelines.

—Man to Man Program of the American Cancer Society, (800) ACS-2345, www.cancer.org, provides support and education for men with prostate cancer to enable them to better understand their options and to make informed decisions. It offers phone support, information, referrals, support group meetings, education, support visitation programs, and a newsletter. Wives and partners are invited quarterly. Assistance is available for starting new groups.

—National Coalition for Cancer Survivorship; 1010 Wayne Avenue, Suite 770, Silver Spring, MD 20910-5600; (301) 650-9127; www.cansearch.org; was founded in 1986 as a national grassroots network that works on behalf of persons with all types of cancer. Its mission is to strengthen and empower cancer survivors and to advocate for policy issues. It provides information on employment and insurance issues, referrals, and publications.

—National Ovarian Cancer Coalition; 500 NE Spanish River Boulevard, Suite 14, Boca Raton, FL 33432; (561) 393-0005; www.ovarian.org; is a national organization with twenty-three affiliated groups.

It promotes educational activities about ovarian cancer for patients, families, and the medical community. It provides information, referrals, literature, conferences, phone support, and networking.

—Patient Advocates for Advanced Cancer Treatment; P.O. Box 141695, Grand Rapids, MI 49514-1695; (616) 453-1477; www.osz.com/paact; is an international organization with 150 affiliated groups. It provides support and advocacy for prostate cancer patients, their families, and those at risk. It offers information about advancements in the detection, diagnosis, evaluation, and treatment of prostate cancer, referrals, phone help, conferences, and newsletters.

—The Center to Improve Care of the Dying; 2175 K Street, NW, Suite 820, Washington, DC 20037; (202) 467-2222; is an interdisciplinary organization committed to research, education, and advocacy to improve the care of dying patients and those suffering from severely disabling diseases.

—Us Too, International; 5003 Fairview Avenue, Downers Grove, IL 60615; (800) 808-7866; www.ustoo.com; is an international organization with more than five hundred affiliated groups founded in 1990. It offers mutual support, information, and education for persons with prostate problems (including cancer) and for their families and friends.

—Y-ME National Breast Cancer Organization; 212 West Van Buren Street, Chicago, IL 60607-3908; (800) 221-2141 (24 hrs) or Spanish: (800) 986-9505 (24 hrs); www.y-me.org; is a national organization with twenty-three affiliated groups founded in 1978. It provides information and peer support for breast cancer patients and their families during all stages of the disease. It offers community outreach to educate people on early detection.

Self-Help Resources

Counseling People with Cancer (Jann Aldredge-Clanton, Louisville: Westminster John Knox Press, 1998).

Dying Well: The Prospect for Growth at the End of Life (Ira Byock, New York: Riverhead Books, 1997).

Fading Away: The Experience of Transition in Families with Terminal Illness (Betty Davies, Amityville, NY: Baywood Publishing, 1995).

Final Gifts: Understanding the Special Awareness, Needs, and Communications of the Dying (Maggie Callanan and Patricia Kelley, New York: Poseidon Press, 1992).

The Good Death: The New American Search to Reshape the End of Life (Marilyn Webb, New York: Bantam Books, 1997).

The Hospice Choice: In Pursuit of a Peaceful Death (Marcia E. Lattanzi-Licht, John J. Mahoney, and Galen Miller, New York: Simon & Schuster, 1998).

The Hospice Handbook: A Complete Guide (Larry Beresford, Boston: Little, Brown & Co., 1993).

How to Go on Living When Someone You Love Dies (Therese A. Rando, New York: Bantam Books, 1991).

The Last Dance: Encountering Death and Dying, 5th ed. (Lynne Ann DeSpelder and Albert Lee Strickland, Mountain View, CA: Mayfield Publishing, 1996).

Living with Life-Threatening Illness: A Guide for Patients, Their Families, and Caregivers (Kenneth J. Doka, San Francisco: Jossey-Bass Publishers, 1998).

She Came to Live Out Loud: An Inspiring Family Journey Through Illness, Loss, and Grief (Myra MacPherson, New York: Scribner, 1999).

Straight Talk About Death for Teenagers: How to Cope with Losing Someone You Love (Earl A. Grollman, Boston: Beacon Press, 1993).

Surviving Grief—and Learning to Live Again (Catherine M. Sanders, New York: John Wiley & Sons, 1992).

Transcending Loss: Understanding the Lifelong Impact of Grief and How to Make It Meaningful (Ashley Davis Prend, New York: Berkley Books, 1997).

References

American Cancer Society. (2000). *Cancer Facts and Figures 2000*. Atlanta: American Cancer Society.

American Cancer Society. (1994). *Facts and Figures*. Atlanta: American Cancer Society.

Bonica, J. J. (1990). Cancer pain. In J. J. Bonica (ed.), *The Management of Pain* (pp. 123–128). Philadelphia: Lea & Febiger.

Burton, L. A. (1998). The spiritual dimension of palliative care. *Seminars in Oncology Nursing, 14(2)*, 121–128.

Chesler, M. A., and Barbarin, O. A. (1984). Relating to the medical staff: How parents of children with cancer see the issues. *Health Social Work, 9*, 49–65.

Davis, D. T., Bustamante, A., Brown, C. P., Wolde-Tsadik, G., Savage, E. W., Cheng, X., and Howland, L. (1994). The urban church and cancer control: A source of social influence in minority communities. *Public Health Reports, 109(4)*, 500–508.

Dewey, D. (1988). When a congregation cares: Organizing ministry to the bereaved. *Death Studies, 12*, 123–135.

Ferhring, R. J., Miller, J. F., and Shaw, C. (1997). Spiritual well-being, religiosity, hope, depression, and other mood states in elderly people coping with cancer. *Oncology Nursing Forum, 24(4)*, 663–671.

Johnson, S. C., and Spilka, B. (1991). Coping with breast cancer: The role of clergy and faith. *Journal of Religion and Health, 30*, 21–33.

Holland, J. C., Passik, S., Kash, K. M., Russak, S. M., Gronert, M. K., Sison, A., Lederberg, M., Fox, B., and Baider, L. (1999). The role of religious and spiritual beliefs in coping with malignant melanoma. *Psycho-Oncology, 8*, 14–26.

Hospice Foundation of America (2000). *What Is Hospice?* www.hospicefoundation.org, Washington, DC: HFA.

Koenig, H.G., and Weaver, A. J. (1997). *Counseling Troubled Older Adults: A Handbook for Pastors and Religious Caregivers.* Nashville: Abingdon Press.

McMillian, S. C., and Weitzner, M. (2000). How problematic are various aspects of quality of life in patients with cancer at the end of life? *Oncology Nursing Forum, 27(5)*, 817–823.

O'Hara, R. P. (1995). Congregations offer hope. *Circuit Rider, Sept.,* 10–11.

Roberts, J. A., Brown, D., Elkins, T., and Larson, D. B. (1997). Factors influencing views of patients with gynecological cancer about end-of-life decisions. *American Journal of Obstetrics and Gynecology,176(1)*, 166–172.

Soderstrom, K. E., and Martinson, I. M. (1987). Patients' spiritual coping strategies: A study of nurse and patient perspectives. *Oncology Nursing Forum, 14*, 41–46.

VandeCreek, L., Frankowski, D., and Johnson, M. (1995). Variables that predict interest in and the completion of living wills. *Journal of Pastoral Care, 49(2)*, 21–220.

Case 17

Infertility

"It's Not Fair"

Ayla and Kevin Rodrigues have been trying to have a baby for the two years that they have been married. At first, they thought that having a child would be easy, but as the months passed and Ayla did not get pregnant, they became anxious. Ayla read books on fertility, and they tried everything they could to conceive. Then they consulted a specialist. Thirty-year-old Ayla went to speak with Reverend Sadorra because of her unhappiness. She reported that she and Kevin argue during the time of the month that she is supposed to be most fertile and that sexual relations have become a chore. The couple avoid their friends and family members who have young children because Ayla feels depressed around them. The last incident found her weeping for hours after celebrating Easter with her extended family, in which there are many babies. Both of them come from large families, and they constantly field insensitive comments from relatives as to why they have no children.

The Rodrigueses are a devout couple who are very active in the church. Because of her fertility problems, Ayla sometimes finds herself questioning her religious faith. She wonders why God has singled her out to be infertile when it seems that none of her female relatives and friends have that problem. | **Pastoral Assessment**

As a result of numerous consultations with an infertility specialist, hormone therapy was prescribed for Ayla. Kevin's reproductive system checked out as "normal." Ayla feels like a failure as a woman. She is getting increasingly frustrated and depressed because she feels her biological clock running out. She harbors secret fears that Kevin will one day leave her for a fertile woman. | **Relevant History**

Diagnostic Criteria

Infertility is commonly defined as the failure to conceive after one year of intercourse with no use of birth control. Couples without children are said to have primary infertility. Secondary infertility is defined as the inability to become pregnant or carry a pregnancy to term following the birth of one or more biological children to the same couple, and it is the most common of the two (Simons, 1999). Most research, however, has been conducted on couples experiencing primary infertility.

Estimates for infertility vary from 6.1 million American women and their partners—10 percent of the reproductive-age population (American Society for Reproductive Medicine, 1998)—to 1 in every 6 couples (Morrow, Thoreson, and Penney, 1995). Infertility has been described as a "traumatic crisis" that has a "demoralizing effect" on individuals and couples (Whiteford and Gonzalez, 1995) and that can result in psychological, marital, and sexual dysfunction. Spiritual conflicts may also result (Mcdonald, 1999).

Research suggests that couples feel psychological distress because of their infertility (Morrow et al., 1995). However, it is important to remember that most couples participating in such research have come to seek help about this condition. Thus, we do not know much about infertile couples who do not seek help. Common responses of help-seeking infertile couples include shock and denial, followed by grief and depression (Robinson and Stewart, 1996). Other reactions can be disappointment, disillusionment, anger, guilt, shame, devastation, loss, and mourning (Cooper-Hilbert, 1998; Scharf and Weinshel, 2000; Whiteford and Gonzalez, 1995). The Kubler-Ross model of the stages of acceptance experienced by persons facing their own death has been applied to infertile couples: They first feel denial, followed by anger or depression. The next stage is grief for the children they will never have. Passing through the stages is not a linear process, and individuals may move through them at different speeds. The duration and intensity of the emotions also vary (Harkness, 1992).

Infertility has been likened to a chronic condition that some couples must cope with over a period of many years. This chronic coping model is particularly fitting for couples whose hope of fertility is kept alive as new reproductive technologies are developed or for those who experience secondary infertility (Harkness, 1992).

Female infertility commonly results from hormonal problems that cause such conditions as irregular ovulation and structural problems, manifested in symptoms such as endometriosis or damaged fallopian tubes (Gutman, 1985). In addition to other emotional responses to the diagnosis, the stigma often attached to infertility can cause women to feel defective.

Male infertility commonly results from problems with sperm production, maturation, motility, or a combination of these. Men can react to infertility by feeling personally or sexually inadequate, depressed, hostile, and guilty. Sexual dysfunction and a conflicted relationship with the spouse can also result (Irvine and Cawood, 1996), as well as self-blame and avoidance coping (Morrow et al., 1995).

It is commonly believed that infertility is more stressful for women because of societal and cultural expectations about their roles as wives and mothers. An analysis of the literature indicates that men and women also cope differently (Jordan and Revenson, 1999). Men sometimes feel that they must be strong for their wives and shield them from pain (Phipps, 1998). Infertility can negatively affect both partners' identities as women and men (Davisson, 1995). Furthermore, as in the Rodrigueses' case, the relationship the couple have with each other and with their families and friends may be negatively affected, depriving them of a support network (Davisson, 1995).

Infertile couples generally have the following options available to them: seeking medical help, becoming parents through alternative means (such as foster care or adoption), or choosing to remain childless. One study in the Netherlands found that more than 80 percent of infertile couples sought medical help for their problem initially and then examined the other options later (Van Balen, Verdurmen, and Ketting, 1997). Medical help in the form of new reproductive technologies can offer hope for infertile couples. Unfortunately, these procedures can be stress-inducing, expensive, and unsuccessful, disrupting couples' careers, privacy, and lifestyle (Robinson and Stewart, 1996).

Response to Vignette

Clergy who counsel infertile couples must be able to recognize and address the psychological impact that infertility has on the man and woman as individuals and as a couple. Reverend Sadorra and Ayla examined the shame, guilt, and feelings of defectiveness and inadequacy she was experiencing. He validated her emotions of grief and loss and encouraged her to communicate with her husband about her feelings. The pastor and Ayla discussed ways that she and Kevin could acknowledge their emotions to each other and keep the lines of communication open. Reverend Sadorra wanted Ayla to try to put infertility in perspective by looking at other important aspects of their lives that they take pride in, such as their marriage, their careers, and other accomplishments. He also explored ways that her religious faith could provide help in coping. Although Ayla sometimes questions her faith in God, she still believes that if it is God's will, she will have children.

Another way to put infertility into perspective was to help Ayla clarify her motivations to have children. The pastor discussed the options that the Rodrigueses' have at this point in their lives, including continuing the hormone therapy, pursuing other medical solutions, examining alternative ways to become parents, or remaining childless. He encouraged her to become educated about infertility and the new reproductive technologies that are available and what the procedures entail, including side effects, costs, and success rates. Additionally, to address Ayla's fears of her biological clock running out, he suggested that she develop a time line with options and steps to take along the way as they learn more about treatment or as other options become available to them.

Reverend Sadorra educated himself about the moral and legal issues related to scientifically assisted conception and encouraged the couple to do the same. As they examined the different techniques available, he discussed corresponding ethical issues: procreation outside of marriage, risks associated with medical procedures, and parenting experiences and expectations. Other matters considered included what information should be given to future children and others about the methods used to conceive. Specific procedures such as surrogate motherhood, sperm donation, in vitro fertilization, and other techniques raise specific moral issues to be discussed (Cavanaugh, 1994).

Treatment Within the Faith Community

Infertile couples can benefit from social support (Amir, Horesh, and Lin-Stein, 1999). Childless couples often isolate themselves from others because of the difficulty of being around children and the perceived or actual insensitivity on the part of others. The faith community can be supportive by being sensitive to childless couples. This can be as simple as not asking questions or making comments about childlessness and not giving advice on how to conceive. To this end, the Rodrigueses were encouraged to reach out to family members and friends who could be supportive. If this was not adequate, the Rodrigueses were encouraged to ask their physician for a referral to an infertile couples support group.

Indications for Referral

In some cases, sexual dysfunction may be the cause of infertility. More commonly, sexual dysfunction is a consequence of infertility. Clergy who do not feel qualified or comfortable working with couples on this and other symptoms associated with infertility are encouraged to refer them to mental health professionals with expertise in these matters.

Treatment by Mental Health Specialist

A therapist may aim to help a couple realize that their emotional needs are just as important as the goal of conceiving a child. Depending on orientation, a therapist may assess them as individuals and as a couple, and as to their coping styles and skills, forms of communication, and problem-solving strategies. Additionally, family and social networks may be evaluated. With the couple's input, a treatment plan will be developed by the therapist, which may include elements of education about infertility and potential solutions and about facilitating communication and problem solving and increasing intimacy in the marriage. Joining a support group for infertile couples may be suggested, since hearing others' stories and sharing experiences can help alleviate a couple's feelings of isolation (Christie and Morgan, 2000).

African-American women have a risk of infertility that is 1.5 times higher than European-American women do (Kalmuss, 1987). Infertility may be especially difficult for African-American couples because families are traditionally child-centered, and the roles of mothers and fathers are very important (Crosbie-Burnett and Lewis, 1993). One study found eight African-American couples coping by strengthening their relationship as a couple (Phipps, 1998). At the same time, they distanced themselves from others, including extended family, which is a traditional source of support (Thornton, 1998). Seeking infertility treatment often was not an option for financial reasons (Phipps, 1998). A qualitative study of two African-American women revealed coping strategies that centered around their isolation and the internalization of racist stereotypes of African-American women's ability to have children. The women found strength in religious beliefs and values (Ceballo, 1999).

Cross-Cultural Issues

National Resources

Resources

—American Infertility Association; 666 Fifth Avenue, Suite 278, New York, NY 10103; (888) 917-3777; www.americaninfertility.org; provides information, referral lists, resources, and support. Website has links to other sites.

—InterNational Council on Infertility Information Dissemination, Inc; P.O. Box 6836, Arlington, VA 22206; (703) 379-9178; www.inciid.org; on-line resource, formed in 1995, to provide comprehensive infertility information, including new reproductive technologies and treatments. Website has forums on infertility, pregnancy loss, parenting, and adoption.

—RESOLVE: The National Infertility Association; 1310 Broadway, Somerville, MA 02144; National help line (617) 623-0744; www.resolve.org; nonprofit organization, founded in 1974, that provides support and information for people experiencing infertility and increases awareness of infertility through public education and advocacy. Has publications, a national newsletter, local chapters around the nation, and physician referral lists.

Self-Help Resources

Experiencing Infertility: An Essential Resource (Debby Peoples and Harriette Rovner Ferguson, New York: W. W. Norton & Co., 2000); written in question-and-answer format addressing medical, financial, and emotional issues couples must work through.

The Infertility Book: A Comprehensive Medical and Emotional Guide (Carla Harkness, Berkeley, CA: Celestial Arts, 1992); divided into three parts: The Infertility Experience; Diagnosis, Causes, and Treatments; and Resolution. Also contains a resources chapter listing medical information, referrals, and emotional support.

Resolving Infertility: Understanding the Options and Choosing Solutions When You Want to Have a Baby (The staff of RESOLVE with Diane Aronson, New York: HarperResource, 1999); comprehensive book on medical, emotional, financial, and decision-making aspects of infertility.

References

American Society for Reproductive Medicine. (1998). *Fact Sheet: Infertility*. www.americaninfertility.org/asrm/infertility.html.

Amir, M., Horesh, N., and Lin-Stein, T. (1999). Infertility and adjustment in women: The effects of attachment style and social support. *Journal of Clinical Psychology in Medical Settings, 6(4),* 463–479.

Cavanaugh, M. (1994). Genetic science and pastoral care. *Pastoral Psychology, 42(5),* 335–344.

Ceballo, R. (1999). "The only Black woman walking the face of the earth who cannot have a baby": Two women's stories. In M. Romero and A. J. Stewart (Eds.), *Women's Untold Stories: Breaking Silence, Talking Back, Voicing Complexity* (pp. 3–19). New York: Routledge.

Christie, G., and Morgan, A. (2000). Individual and group psychotherapy with infertile couples. *International Journal of Group Psychotherapy, 50(20),* 237–250.

Cooper-Hilbert, B. (1998). *Infertility and Involuntary Childlessness: Helping Couples Cope.* New York: W. W. Norton & Co.

Crosbie-Burnett, M., and Lewis, E. A. (1993). Use of African-American family structures and functioning to address the challenges of European-American post divorce families. *Family Relations, 42,* 243–248.

Davisson, D. (1995). Infertility. In M. W. O'Hara and R. C. Reiter (Eds.), *Psychological Aspects of Women's Reproductive Health* (pp. 149–160). New York: Springer Publishing.

Gutman, M. (1985). Fertility Management: Infertility, Delayed Childbearing, and Voluntary Childlessness. In D. C. Goldberg (Ed.), *Contemporary Marriage: Special Issues in Couples Therapy* (pp. 120–165). Homewood, IL: Dorsey Press.

Harkness, C. (1992). *The Infertility Book: A Comprehensive Medical and Emotional Guide.* Berkeley, CA: Celestial Arts.

Irvine, S., and Cawood, E. (1996). Male infertility and its effect on male sexuality. *Sexual and Marital Therapy, 11(3),* 283–290.

Jordan, C., and Revenson, T. (1999). Gender differences in coping with infertility: A meta-analysis. *Journal of Behavioral Medicine, 22(4),* 341–358.

Kalmuss, D. S. (1987). The use of infertility services among fertility-impaired couples. *Demography, 24,* 575–585.

Mcdonald, D. (1999). The experiences of couples with infertility: A phenomenological study of infertility treatment participants. *Dissertation Abstracts International, Section B: The Sciences and Engineering 59 (90B).* March, 1999, 5098.

Morrow, K. A., Thoreson, R. W., and Penney, L. L. (1995). Predictors of psychological distress among infertility clinic patients. *Journal of Consulting and Clinical Psychology, 63(1)*, 163–167.

Phipps, S. A. A. (1998). African-American couples lived experience of infertility. In H. McCubbin, E. A. Thompson, A. I. Thompson, and J. A. Futrell (Eds.), *Resiliency in African-American Families* (pp. 245–258). Thousand Oaks, CA: Sage Press.

Robinson, G. E., and Stewart, D. E. (1996). The psychological impact of infertility and new reproductive technologies. *Harvard Review of Psychiatry, 4(30)*, 168–172.

Scharf, C. N., and Weinshel, M. (2000). Infertility and Late-life Pregnancies. In P. Papp (Ed.), *Couples on the Fault Line: New Directions for Therapists* (pp. 104–129). New York: Guilford Press.

Simons, H. F. (1999). Secondary Infertility. In L. H. Burns and S. N. Covington (Eds.), *Infertility Counseling: A Comprehensive Handbook for Clinicians* (pp. 313–322). Pearl River, NY: Parthenon Publishing Group.

Thornton, M. C. (1998). Indigenous resources and strategies of resistance: Informal caregiving and racial socialization in Black Communities. In H. I. McCubbin, E. A. Thompson, A. I. Thompson, and J. A. Futrell (Eds.), *Resiliency in African-American Families* (pp. 49–66). Thousand Oaks, CA: Sage.

Van Balen, F., Verdurmen, J., and Ketting, E. (1997). Choices and motivations of infertile couples. *Patient Education and Counseling, 31(1)*, 19–27.

Whiteford, L. M., and Gonzalez, L. (1995). Stigma: The hidden burden of infertility. *Social Science and Medicine, 40(1)*, 27–36.

Severe Mental Illness: Bipolar Disorder

"He Spoke Rapidly and Paced Back and Forth"

Luke's father called the Reverend Garrison Larsen and asked him to come to his house. Luke, a twenty-year-old college junior, had been acting increasingly strangely in recent days, and the family wanted to consult their pastor. The whole family were active and devout members of the Lutheran Church. Luke was a single, high-energy, industrious young man working on a degree in engineering. As the pastor drove into the driveway, Luke rushed out to meet him. Although usually meticulous in his appearance, Luke looked somewhat disheveled and was unshaven. Reverend Larsen, who knew him to be levelheaded and thoughtful, listened as Luke spoke rapidly while pacing back and forth. He began to explain about a book he was writing on the spiritual insights he had gained from the Internet. Luke claimed to have found a unique relationship between website listings and important clues to God's special message to him. Luke kept so busy with his work that he had little time to eat or sleep. He was spending his savings to buy all the books and documents he needed to prove his theory and gain recognition for his ideas.

Reverend Larsen had received clinical pastoral education training in a mental hospital as a seminary student, and he recognized the signs of the acute manic state of bipolar disorder (also known as manic-depressive illness). This condition is not self-induced, but it is caused by a major change in the chemistry of the brain.

The illness typically has episodes of both depression with low energy, and mania with abnormally high energy. The mood swings can last for days, weeks, or even months. During manic episodes, persons may sleep very little; talk rapidly, loudly, and continually; experience racing thoughts; and take little time to eat. They often exhibit poor judgment and

Pastoral Assessment

may lose touch with reality. Persons can be wildly overconfident and grandiose in their thinking, even becoming delusional (having fixed, false beliefs from which a person cannot be dissuaded). They often become impulsive, making serious financial, social, and occupational blunders. The predominant moods during mania are elevated, expansive, elated, or irritable.

The risk of suicide is very high among persons suffering from manic-depressive illness. One in 4 persons with this disorder attempts suicide, and more than 1 in 10 will die at their own hand (Prien and Potter, 1990).

Relevant History

Luke was under a great deal of academic pressure and had been somewhat distressed at college in the past semester. He had been seen as irritable and anxious with an inability to concentrate on his work. Sometimes mild or moderate signs of depression and high stress are present before a manic state (Hammen and Gitlin, 1997).

Diagnostic Criteria

About 1 in 100 individuals in the U.S. has manic-depressive illness or bipolar disorder (American Psychiatric Association, 1994). There is no cure, but with proper treatment, the frequency and severity of the episodes can be reduced and the person's quality of life can be significantly improved. Manic-depressive illness occurs equally among men and women with the early twenties being the most common time of onset. Twin and adoption studies offer evidence for a genetic link in bipolar disorder. The majority of persons with the illness return to a fully functioning life after treatment, although 20 to 30 percent continue to have problems with mood and interpersonal difficulties (APA, 1994). The stress of this disorder can cause serious problems in a marriage and occupational life. Divorce rates are two to three times higher for couples in which one of the spouses has this illness, and an individual with manic-depressive illness is at higher risk of losing employment than is a person not suffering from bipolar disorder (Coryell et al., 1993).

Response to Vignette

This is an acute episode of mania that requires immediate medical attention. Luke needs to be admitted to inpatient hospital care without delay so that a psychiatrist can give him medications that will reduce, or possibly end, his symptoms. These prescription drugs can also be effective in reducing the risk of future episodes. Medications include those that decrease symptoms of mania and depression (such as lithium, valproate, and carbamazepine) and those that control other symptoms (such as antipsychotics and benzodiazepines). Prescription drugs also substantially lower the risk of suicide in bipolar patients (Muller-Oerlinghausen, Muser-Causemann, and Volk, 1992). When Luke's symptoms have decreased, he will begin to function better and benefit more from other forms of treatment, such as individual, group, and family therapy.

Luke and his family are fortunate to have the pastoral care of Reverend Larsen, who is knowledgeable about mental illness and cares enough to intervene. In a survey of five hundred members of the National Depressive and Manic-Depressive Association (NDMDA), more than half of those suffering from bipolar disorder waited five years to seek care after experiencing the first symptoms, and 36 percent waited for more than ten years (1993). According to the survey, the correct diagnosis was not made until an average of eight years after persons initially sought treatment. Those suffering from mental illness often deny they need medical care because of the societal stigma of having such conditions.

Individuals suffering from mental health problems report that faith is an important positive resource in their lives. Lindgren and Coursey (1995) surveyed a group of psychiatric patients in a psychosocial rehabilitation setting in Maryland. Fifty-seven percent of the patients attended religious services and reported praying at least daily. More than 8 in 10 felt spiritual beliefs had positive effects on their illnesses through the comfort they provided, the feelings of being cared for, and the feelings that they were not alone. Regrettably, almost 4 in 10 of the patients expressed discomfort with the idea of talking to their therapists about their spiritual/religious concerns.

In a study conducted in a Chicago medical center, researchers discovered that 3 in 4 psychiatric patients identified their faith as an important source of comfort and support. Unfortunately, it found that these patients were less likely to have talked to a clergyperson than to a comparable group in a general medical/surgical hospital. Moreover, while 80 percent of the psychiatric patients considered themselves spiritual or religious, only 20 percent had a pastor or spiritual adviser to consult (Fitchett, Burton, and Sivan, 1997). Nancy Kehoe (1999), a Roman Catholic sister and psychologist at Harvard Medical School, has shown that therapy groups based on spiritual issues for patients with chronic mental illness can be useful in fostering coping and self-awareness, as well as in helping to bring meaning to suffering.

Self-help groups for those with a chronically mentally ill relative are increasing in number and can be supported by congregations that are seeking to help these families. Such groups may serve to meet social needs, foster hope, and provide emotional support. Information and knowledge can be exchanged, and models of successful coping can be shared. Group organization and cooperation allow for the pooling of resources and information. There are freedom and empowerment in knowing that everyone in the group is facing similar issues and renewed hope in discovering that others have found ways to sustain their lives while caring for mentally ill family members.

Some organizations (see Resources) have developed outreach programs to help clergy and congregations support and care for those with mental illnesses such as bipolar disorder and schizophrenia. These groups can also

Treatment Within the Faith Community

help combat the stigma and the stereotype often associated with mental illness by presenting accurate, factual information about the diseases.

In a nationwide survey of mental health consumers, respondents indicated that they had experienced societal stigma from several sources, including communities, families, churches, coworkers, and mental health caregivers (Wahl, 1999). The majority had tried to conceal their disorders and worried a great deal that others would find out about their psychiatric condition and treat them unfavorably. They reported discouragement and lowered self-esteem as a result of their experiences, and they urged public education as a means of reducing stigma. Some reported that involvement in advocacy and speaking out when discrimination was encountered helped them cope with those experiences.

Indications for Referral

Occasionally, people have manic episodes caused by undetected medical disorders or by the use of certain illicit drugs. For this reason, a complete medical history and physical examination should be conducted to rule out other possible causes of Luke's symptoms before concluding he has manic-depressive illness.

Treatment by Mental Health Specialist

Since bipolar disorder is a long-term episodic illness, continued medical care and medication are required. It is important to find a psychiatrist who is well-qualified, interested in the illness, and can establish and maintain a strong therapeutic alliance with the patient and loved his or her loved ones. Families are a valuable source of information on symptoms, medication compliance, and general adjustment. They, in turn, need information concerning the course of the illness, treatment options, expected prognosis, and goals for the patient.

Denial is often a major part of bipolar disorder, which can interfere with a person's ability to make sound treatment decisions. The psychiatrist, other members of the treatment team, and loved ones need to observe changes in mood or behavior that can be early signs of an impending episode of the disorder. Individuals frequently lack insight into their illness, and most benefit from information about it. Feedback and education over a period of time can assist in strengthening a patient's role as collaborator in the treatment. It is important to help a person in a manic state avoid engaging in embarrassing behaviors and making major life decisions. Patients will need help to bolster their morale and encouragement to enlist the help of others in their support networks.

Luke's family may need help accepting the fact of mental illness and learning how best to manage it. Research has shown that a good family environment can be a major factor in improving the chances of stabilizing persons with bipolar disorder and in preventing relapse (Miklowitz, Goldstein, Nuechterlein, Snyder, and Mintz, 1988). Families that are supportive and nonjudgmental can do much to foster a person's recovery, while harsh or unstable families can increase the risk of relapse.

Unfortunately, many in the U.S. who suffer from bipolar disorder, schizophrenia, or other severe forms of mental illness do not receive treatment, and they become homeless, use alcohol and/or illegal drugs, and may end up in prison. The National Law Center on Homelessness and Poverty estimates that at least 25 percent of our nearly one million homeless suffer from some form of mental illness. There are now far more mentally ill in the nation's prisons (approximately 250,000) than in state hospitals (approximately 58,000). Until recently, state mental hospitals served as the last resort for those who could not find adequate treatment in the private sector. The increasing closure of these institutions has become a major reason for the lack of treatment for the severely mentally ill (Lamb, 1998).

The incidence of manic-depressive illness appears to be the same across all races and ethnic groups (APA, 1994).

Cross-Cultural Issues

National Resources

Resources

—Consumer Organization and Networking Technical Assistance Center (CONTAC); c/o WVMHCA, 1036 Quarrier Street, Suite 208-A, Charleston, WV 25301; (888) 825-8324; www.contac.org; is a nationwide resource center for mental health consumers and consumer-run organizations that promotes self-help, recovery, and empowerment. It provides technical assistance for organizing and maintaining self-help groups and conducts leadership training and on-line peer support.

—Depression and Related Affective Disorders Association (DRADA); Meyer 3-181, 600 North Wolfe Street, Baltimore, MD 21287-7381; (410) 955-4647; www.med.jhu.edu/drada; is an international organization, founded in 1986, with sixty affiliated groups. It aims to alleviate the suffering arising from depression and manic-depression by assisting self-help groups, providing education and information, and supporting research. It offers a newsletter, literature, phone support, and assistance in starting new groups.

—Dual Recovery Anonymous (DRA); P.O. Box 128232, Nashville, TN 37221-8232; (877) 883-2332; www.draonline.org; is an international organization, founded in 1989, with 130 chapters. It offers self-help programs for individuals who experience the dual disorder of chemical dependency and psychiatric illness. It is based on twelve-step principles and the personal experiences of individuals in dual recovery. It has a newsletter and provides assistance in starting local groups.

—Federation of Families for Children's Mental Health; 1101 King Street, Suite 420, Alexandria, VA 22314; (703) 684-7710; www.ffcmh.org; is a national parent-run organization with 122 affiliated groups. It focuses on the needs of children and teens with mental health problems, providing information and advocacy. Its website is also available in Spanish.

—National Alliance for the Mentally Ill (NAMI); Colonial Place Three, 2107 Wilson Boulevard, Suite 300, Arlington, VA 22201-3042; (800) 950-6264; www.nami.org; is a network of self-help groups for relatives and friends affected by mental illness that was founded in 1979. It has a section devoted to giving support and information to siblings and children of persons with mental illness. NAMI has a newsletter and runs an anti-discrimination campaign on behalf of the mentally ill. It provides educational materials to clergy and religious organizations.

—National Depressive and Manic-Depressive Association (NDMDA); 730 North Franklin Street, Suite 501, Chicago, IL 60610; (800) 826-3632; www.ndmda.org; is a national organization with 275 chapters. It offers mutual support and information for persons with depressive and manic-depressive illness and their families, as well as public education services. It has annual conferences, chapter development guidelines, a newsletter, and a catalog.

—National Empowerment Center; 599 Canal Street, Lawrence, MA 01840; (800) 769-3728; www.power2u.org; is a consumer-run center that provides information on self-help resources and conferences. It also offers networking, conference calls, and workshops.

—National Mental Health Consumers' Self-Help Clearinghouse; 1211 Chestnut Street, Suite 1207, Philadelphia, PA 19107; (800) 553-4KEY; www.mhselfhelp.org; is a consumer self-help resource offering information geared toward meeting the needs of mental health consumers. It offers assistance in advocacy, listing of publications, on-site consultations, training, and educational events.

—Pathways to Promise; 5400 Arsenal Street, St. Louis, MO 63139; (314) 644-8400; www.pathways2promise.org; helps to develop outreach programs for the mentally ill through religious communities. It offers information, educational materials, and other resources for clergy.

Self-Help Resources

Bipolar Disorder: A Guide for Patients and Families (Francis Mark Mondimore, Baltimore: Johns Hopkins University Press, 1999).

A Brilliant Madness: Living with Manic-Depressive Illness (Patty Duke and Gloria Hochman, New York: Bantam Books, 1992).

Clinical Psychopharmacology Made Ridiculously Simple, 4th ed. (John Preston and James Johnson, Miami: MedMaster, 2000); offers the layperson a succinct, practical guide to medications used when treating mental health problems, including bipolar disorder.

Living Without Depression and Manic Depression: A Workbook for Maintaining Mood Stability (Mary Ellen Copeland, Oakland, CA: New Harbinger Publications, 1994).

A Stranger in Our Midst (Ruth Fowler, St. Louis: Pathways to Promise,

1987); a congregational study guide on prolonged mental illness. It offers a continuing education curriculum and training manual designed for pastors and churches.

An Unquiet Mind (Kay Redfield Jamison, New York: Random House, 1997).

Why Am I Up, Why Am I Down? Understanding Bipolar Disorder (Roger Granet and Elizabeth Ferber, New York: Dell Publishing, 1999).

References

American Psychiatric Association. (1994). *Diagnostic and Statistical Manual of Mental Disorders* (4th ed.). Washington, DC: APA.

Coryell, W., Schefter, W., Keller, M., Endicott, J., Maser, J., and Klerman, G. L. (1993). The enduring psychosocial consequences of mania and depression. *American Journal of Psychiatry, 150(5)*, 720–727.

Fitchett, G., Burton, L. A., and Sivan, A. B. (1997). The religious needs and resources of psychiatric inpatients. *The Journal of Nervous and Mental Diseases, 185*, 320–326.

Hammen, C., and Gitlin, M. (1997). Stress reactivity in bipolar patients and its relation to prior history of disorder. *American Journal of Psychiatry, 154(6)*, 856–857.

Kehoe, N. C. (1999). A therapy group on spiritual issues for patients with chronic mental illness. *Psychiatric Services, 50(8)*, 1081–1083.

Lamb, H. R. (1998). Deinstitutionalization at the beginning of the new millennium. *Harvard Review of Psychiatry, 6(1)*, 1–10.

Lindgren, K. N., and Coursey, R. D. (1995). Spirituality and serious mental illness: A two-part study. *Psychosocial Rehabilitation Journal, 18(3)*, 93–111.

Miklowitz, D. J., Goldstein, M. J., Nuechterlein, K. H., Snyder, K. S., and Mintz, J. (1988). Family factors and the course of bipolar affective disorder. *Archives of General Psychiatry, 45*, 225–231.

Muller-Oerlinghausen, B., Muser-Causemann, B., and Volk, J. (1992). Suicides and parasuicides in a high-risk patient group on and off lithium long-term medication. *Journal of Affective Disorders, 25*, 261–269.

National Depressive and Manic-Depressive Association (NDMDA). (1993). National survey of National Depressive and Manic-Depressive Association members finds long delay in diagnosis of manic-depressive illness. *Hospital and Community Psychiatry, 44(8)*, 800–801.

Prien, R. F., and Potter, W. Z. (1990). National Institute of Mental Health workshop report on treatment of bipolar disorder. *Psychopharmacology Bulletin, 26*, 409–427.

Wahl, O. F. (1999). Mental health consumers' experience of stigma. *Schizophrenia Bulletin, 25(3)*, 467–478.

Schizophrenia

Bipolar disorder and schizophrenia are the most common severe mental illnesses. Schizophrenia is a psychotic disorder that is marked by "gross impairment in reality testing and the creation of a new reality" (APA, 1994). As in bipolar disorder, about 1 person in 100 develops the illness.

Schizophrenia has a biological basis; there are numerous studies documenting changes in brain structure and function. Like bipolar disorder, schizophrenia carries a high risk of suicide. One in 10 individuals with the illness ends his or her life, especially in the first six years after the initial psychotic episode (Westermeyer, Harrow, and Marengo, 1991).

People in the acute stage of schizophrenia often report hearing voices others do not hear (auditory hallucinations) and have fixed and false beliefs from which they cannot be dissuaded (delusions). They can speak without apparent connections between their thoughts (loosening of associations) and express emotions that are inappropriate to the situation (e.g., smiling broadly while telling a sad story). The symptoms can also involve impairment in behavior (disorganization), concentration, motivation, and judgment. This condition usually negatively affects occupational, educational, and social activities. Living in a world of distortions is frightening and highly confusing.

Individuals in the active stage of schizophrenia need immediate medical attention, prescription drugs, and hospitalization. Antipsychotic medications help to reduce delusions, hallucinations, agitation, confusion, and distortions, and most people show substantial improvement within a few weeks. These drugs also reduce by half the risk of future episodes (Carpen-ter et al., 1990).

American Psychiatric Association. (1994). *Diagnostic and Statistical Manual of Mental Disorders* (4th ed.). Washington, DC: APA.

Carpenter, W. T., Hanlon, T. E., Heinrichs, D. W., Summerfelt, A. T., Kirkpatrick, B., Levine, J., and Buchanan R. W. (1990). Continuous versus targeted medication in schizophrenia outpatients: Outcome results. *American Journal of Psychiatry, 147,* 1138–1148.

Westermeyer, J. F., Harrow, M., and Marengo, J. T. (1991). Risk for suicide in schizophrenia and other psychotic and non-psychotic disorders. *The Journal of Nervous and Mental Disease, 179,* 259–266.

Alcohol Dependency

"He Began Lying to Her About His Drinking Habits"

Pastor Langi received the call late on a Friday night. There had been a serious automobile accident, and he was asked to meet the family at the hospital. Over the next two weeks, he made regular visits to see Diana and Larry, a young couple who came to church occasionally. Larry had serious injuries from a single car accident—he lost control of his vehicle while driving under the influence of alcohol. The full story of his drinking problem came out during conversations when Pastor Langi visited him in the hospital.

Larry began drinking with buddies in high school. He liked the feeling of getting high when he partied with friends. Alcohol made him feel more self-confident and less anxious. He gradually drank more and more to celebrate a victory or grieve a hurt. During college, his drinking became heavier, and his tolerance for alcohol increased. Larry had to drink more to get the same feeling, and he began to crave alcohol. Following a particularly painful hangover, he managed to stay sober for a few weeks with the encouragement of Diana, who had growing concerns. His sobriety didn't last, however, and he began hiding his drinking from his wife.

After that, he became increasingly defensive about his drinking and began lying to Diana about it. He rationalized his excessive use of alcohol, blaming it on stress at work and her nagging. On the night of the accident, he lied to her about needing to work late and went to a bar to have a few at Happy Hour. He lost track of time and the number of drinks he had consumed. It was long past the time he had told Diana he would return, and he was very intoxicated. Larry sped to get home and lost control of his car. The vehicle was totalled, and he ended up in the hospital in serious condition.

Larry has several of the key signs of a person addicted to alcohol. He continues to drink, despite serious problems in his life resulting from its

Pastoral Assessment

use. He has developed a tolerance and needs increasing amounts to achieve the desired effect. He frequently consumes more beverages over longer periods of time than he intended. He craves the anesthetic effects of alcohol and makes unsuccessful attempts to control its use.

It is important for Pastor Langi to assess Larry's motivation to deal with his alcohol addiction. The time Larry spent in the hospital gave him two weeks of sober thinking and a chance to seriously reflect on his life. Pastor Langi listened to his story and responded empathetically, seeking to build trust in their relationship and self-worth in Larry. Research indicates that a supportive, respectful confrontation of a person who is addicted improves the chance of getting positive results with less resistance (Miller, Benefield, and Tonigan, 1993). Effective pastoral counseling, combined with the gravity of the accident, moved Larry from denial of his alcoholism to a consideration of how he could do something about his addiction, and finally to reaching out for help. Pastor Langi recognized that Larry's new attitude was a window of opportunity and that action needed to be taken. The pastor, Larry, his physician, and Diana discussed several treatment options. The couple chose intensive outpatient treatment through a local university hospital.

It is valuable to assess a person's assets when developing a pastoral care evaluation. Several strengths point to a positive prognosis for Larry. He has a spouse and extended family who are actively interested in his welfare and willing to work with him on his addiction. He also has good vocational skills, a college education, high personal resilience, and insight into his illness. Larry will need help to focus on his strengths, successes, and resources during his recovery.

Relevant History

Diana grew up in a church where the emphasis was on a loving God who is gracious and forgiving. Larry, however, was raised in a rigid church environment that discouraged members from having any doubts about faith. He rejected the punitive religion of his youth while in college, but many of his religious beliefs were stuck in the concepts of his childhood. He heard the words of mercy and grace, but the heavy overlay of moralistic and judgmental attitudes he had learned as a child added to the guilt, fear, and shame experienced while he was in the hospital. Part of his recovery will require caring, gentle pastoral counseling that is sensitive to these issues.

Diagnostic Criteria

Dependence is characterized by a group of symptoms that indicate an individual's continual use of a substance despite significant resulting problems. Persons suffering alcohol dependence have a pattern of compulsive use, usually leading to tolerance and withdrawal; a "craving" for alcohol is present. According to the *Diagnostic and Statistical Manual of Mental Disorders, 4th Edition* criteria, at least three of the following symptoms must be present at the same time over a twelve-month period:

- Tolerance has developed, evidenced by the need for increased amounts of alcohol to achieve the desired effect or the markedly diminished effects with continued use of the same amount.
- Withdrawal symptoms, such as physical discomfort, illness, or severe complications, are experienced by a person when alcohol is not available.
- Alcohol is frequently consumed in larger amounts, or over longer periods of time, than intended.
- There is a recurrent desire or unsuccessful attempts to control or cut down alcohol use.
- A lot of time is devoted to activities related to obtaining alcohol, using it, and recovering from its effects.
- Important social, occupational, or recreational activities are reduced or stopped as a result of alcohol consumption.
- Alcohol is used in spite of persistent psychological or physical problems caused or exacerbated by its use.

Response to Vignette

The intensive outpatient treatment that Larry and Diana chose is modeled after a program designed at Harvard Medical School (Rotunda and O'Farrell, 1997). It combines marital therapy and traditional alcohol treatment methods: family education, client education, group therapy, AA and AL-ANON meetings, the prescription drug Antabuse, activity therapy, and spiritual counseling. Families with an alcoholic member typically have poorer communication and problem-solving skills with higher levels of negativity, conflict, and estrangement than non-alcoholic families have (Rotunda, Scherer, and Imm, 1995). Improving relationships and promoting good communication skills have been shown as important goals of treatment for couples affected by alcoholism.

In the program, Larry and Diana are seen together to help them build teamwork and collaborative support for his sobriety, to enhance relationship cohesion, to increase positive feelings, and to learn effective communication skills. The therapist emphasizes structured listening and speaking techniques to minimize the blaming, hostility, and avoidance that often occur in alcoholic relationships. Abstinence and acceptance of the disease of alcoholism are emphasized. Education helps instill new attitudes toward alcoholism—that it is an illness with recognizable signs, and like other diseases, it is treatable. A common feature of alcohol dependence is a warped perception of reality. Group therapy and twelve-step programs can provide accurate feedback, lessen shame, and reduce isolation. A common problem for those in recovery is how to fill the time that was previously used for drinking. Many alcoholics come to think of drinking as their only leisure activity. Planning and engaging in shared enjoyable times that do not involve alcohol is essential.

The couple made a sobriety contract, and Larry takes Antabuse each day at an agreed upon time with the support of Diana. Antabuse, which is widely used in the treatment of alcoholism, alters the way the body uses an enzyme, which affects the normal metabolism of alcohol. It creates adverse effects for anyone drinking alcohol, including throbbing in the head and neck, nausea, vomiting, sweating, weakness, and vertigo. Antabuse cannot cure alcoholism, but it is a strong deterrent to impulsive drinking. Continued sobriety can help Larry build confidence that he can stop drinking, giving Diana assurance, which will build trust and decrease conflict about alcohol over time.

Through ongoing contact, Pastor Langi provides support, reassurance, and praise for the couple's recovery work. He encourages cooperation with the treatment and perseverance in difficult times. A pastor who has an ongoing relationship with parishioners may be able to recognize the early signs of a relapse, thereby preventing or minimizing its negative effects. The clergyperson can help a recovering person gain perspective when a relapse occurs and reframe it as an opportunity to learn. It is a reality of human nature that people will backslide, especially in the first year of abstinence, and a plan to deal with that is realistic. Pastors have professional training and experience in using the powerful resources of faith, hope, and compassion to help sustain the healing process. The underlying cause of an addiction such as alcoholism is often a spiritual crisis, the resolution of which can be a turning point in Larry's understanding of himself and his marriage, as well as helping to renew meaning in his life.

Treatment Within the Faith Community

Alcoholism is a major social problem that often goes untreated. It is estimated that 2.7 percent of Americans twelve years of age or older experience problems associated with alcohol and substance abuse that require treatment, although only a small minority of them receive it (Edwards and Steinglass, 1995). Substance abuse results in considerable costs for the sufferer, his or her family, and society—lost jobs, family disruption, financial instability, accidental injury, and death. Four of 10 highway fatalities in this country involve drivers who have been drinking (Special Report of the U.S. Congress on Alcohol and Health, 1987).

There is solid scientific evidence that, across the life span, individuals involved in nurturing, nonpunitive religion are less likely than the general population to abuse alcohol and other substances, to take part in the excessive use of addictive substances, and to suffer the adverse effects of dependence (Larson, Sawyers, and McCullough, 1998). Religious practice and strength of religion in the family are inversely associated with antisocial behavior in young people, including fewer drug and alcohol problems (Weaver, Preston, and Jerome, 1999).

One way that churches and synagogues can help persons in recovery from addictions is to provide space and support for twelve-step self-help groups that provide a spiritually based supportive fellowship in which a major source of strength is a member's Higher Power. In 1989, it was estimated that ten to fifteen million people in the U.S. participated in twelve-step or other mutual help groups (Goldsmith, 1989). About 9 percent of the adult population reported attending an Alcoholics Anonymous (AA) meeting in their lifetimes, and 13 percent had attended a twelve-step program of some type (Room and Greenfield, 1993). Active involvement in twelve-step programs, such as AA, Narcotics Anonymous (NA), and Al-Anon, is helpful for persons with chemical dependence. The programs work equally well for addicts of all economic and educational levels (Miller and Verinis, 1995). These groups can function as caring environments in which members feel safe and secure, offering a natural bridge in the process of reconnecting with the community when addicts are tempted to withdraw and isolate themselves.

In a survey of members of the American Academy of Family Physicians, most physicians indicated that they accept clergy and pastoral professionals in the care of their patients. More than 8 in 10 had referred or recommended patients to clergy for counseling, and 2 in 10 of the physicians listed substance abuse counseling as the reason for their referral to clergy (Daaleman and Frey, 1998). In 1991, the University of Texas Medical Center surveyed 75 percent of the clergy in Galveston, Texas, and found that no congregation in the community had a specific ministry for addicted persons or their families (Turner, 1995). The majority of those contacted expressed interest in learning more about addiction and increasing their counseling skills. The Medical Center developed a successful monthly training program for pastors responding to alcohol and drug addiction, which has increased congregational and clergy involvement in the issue.

Indications for Referral

A key question for clergy dealing with persons with alcohol and drug problems is when to help. Larry had a rapid conversion after his life-threatening automobile accident that moved him quickly from denial that he had a drinking problem to acceptance that he did and to the point of seeking help. Most addicted persons will change much more slowly.

William Miller, a psychologist and Presbyterian layman, has divided the process into stages (Miller and Jackson, 1995). It begins with "precontemplation," when a person is not considering change, and then moves to "contemplation," when an individual begins to consider it, wavering between favoring and resisting action. The third stage in which a person acknowledges the problem and recognizes the need for action is called "determination." At this critical point where motivation is reached and a decision to act is made, an immediate intervention is required.

It is important to prepare a list of professional and community resources for addiction problems before being faced with an immediate need to assist someone. Develop appropriate plans of action with mental health colleagues before an emergency occurs.

Treatment by Mental Health Specialist

It is estimated that 30 to 50 percent of alcoholics suffer from a major depression, and possibly one third have an anxiety disorder, such as agoraphobia. Because persons who suffer from alcohol dependence may have other mental health problems, they will need a specialist to evaluate them and offer treatment if other issues are found.

An assessment will need to be made as to whether inpatient detoxification is required for individuals who are alcohol dependent. The following indicate inpatient care may be the treatment of choice: alcohol use is associated with imminent danger to self or another, other antisocial behavior, severe mental illness (e.g., major depression, psychosis, post-traumatic stress, suicidal thinking), failure in previous attempts at outpatient treatment, or the lack of a support system.

Cross-Cultural Issues

The ethnic minority community is disproportionately affected by alcohol and drug abuse problems. For example, the non-Caucasian mortality rates for cirrhosis of the liver are twice as great as those of Caucasians. Lack of education, poverty, and the psychological impact of racism may increase the likelihood of chemical dependence among African-Americans and other ethnic minority groups. Specialized treatment programs, including faith-based treatment, need to be explored when working with ethnic-minority persons (Closser and Blow, 1993).

Resources

National Resources

—Al-Anon Family Group Headquarters, Inc.; 1600 Corporate Landing Parkway, Virginia Beach, VA 23454-5617; (888) 4AL-ANON; www.al-anon.alateen.org; is an international organization with 32,000-plus groups. It was founded in 1951 as a fellowship of men, women, children, and adult children whose lives have been affected by the compulsive drinking of a family member or friend. The program is based on the twelve steps of AA. Literature is available in twenty-nine languages.

—Alcohol and Substance Program of the Indian Health Service; 5300 Homestead Road, NE, Albuquerque, NM 87110; (505) 248-4121; wilbur.woodis@mail.ihs.gov.

—Alcoholics Anonymous World Services, Inc.; General Service Office, P.O. Box 459, Grand Central Station, New York, NY 10163; (212) 870-3400; www.alcoholics-anonymous.org; is a worldwide fellowship of women and men. The only requirement for membership is a desire to stop drinking. Members observe personal anonymity at the public level, emphasizing AA principles rather than personalities. For more information, check the local phone directory or newspaper.

—Alcoholics Victorious; c/o International Union of Gospel Missions, 1045 Swift Street, Kansas City, MO 64116-4127; (816) 471-8020; www.av.iugm.org; is a Christian-oriented twelve-step support group for recovering alcoholics. Information, referrals, literature, phone support, conferences, support group meetings, and a newsletter are available.

—American Council for Drug Education; 164 West Seventy-fourth Street, New York, NY 10023; (800) 488-DRUG; www.acde.org.

—American Society of Addiction Medicine (ASAM); 4601 North Park Avenue, Upper Arcade, Suite 101, Chevy Chase, MD 20815; (301) 656-3920; is a medical society dedicated to educating physicians and improving the treatment of individuals suffering from alcoholism and other addictions.

—Calix Society; 7601 Wayzata Boulevard, Minneapolis, MN 55426; (800) 398-0524; dhackl@isd.net; is an international fellowship of Catholic alcoholics maintaining their sobriety through Alcoholics Anonymous. It is concerned with total abstinence, spiritual development, and sanctification of the whole personality of each member.

—Dual Recovery Anonymous (DRA), P.O. Box 121376, Nashville, TN 37212; (888) 869-9230; is an international twelve-step self-help program for individuals who experience a dual disorder of both chemical dependency and psychiatric illness. It provides literature, a newsletter, and assistance in starting local groups.

—Hazelden Foundation; P.O. Box 11 C03, Center City, MN 55012-0011; (800) 257-7100; www.hazelden.org.

—JACS (Jewish Alcoholics, Chemically dependent persons and Significant others); 850 Seventh Avenue, New York, NY 10019; (212) 397-4197; www.jacsweb.org; was founded in 1980 for alcoholic and chemically dependent Jews, their families, friends, and associates, and the community. It provides networking, community outreach, retreats, a newsletter, literature, spiritual events, and a speaker's bureau.

—Mothers Against Drunk Driving (MADD); P.O. Box 541688, Dallas, TX 47354-1688; (800) 438-6233; www.madd.org; is an educational and advocacy organization with four hundred chapters. It is devoted to heightening awareness of the dangers of impaired driving.

—National Center on Addiction and Substance Abuse at Columbia University; 633 Third Avenue, 9th floor, New York, NY 10017-6706; (212) 841-5200; www.casacolumbia.org.

—National Clearinghouse for Alcohol and Drug Information (NCADI); P.O. Box 2345, Rockville, MD 20847; (800) 729-6686; TDD: (800) 487-4899; www.health.org; provides free materials about many aspects of alcohol and drug abuse treatment and prevention. Several of these publications are designed for the faith community.

—National Council on Alcoholism and Drug Dependence (NCADD); 20 Exchange Place, Suite 2902, New York, NY 10005; www.ncadd.org.; is a nonprofit organization that offers information and referral services through two hundred state and local affiliates. It provides preventive educational programs for community organizations such as churches and temples. Persons seeking assistance can contact their area affiliate or call a national toll-free help line: (800) 622-2255.

—National Families in Action; Century Plaza II, 2957 Clairmont Road, Suite 150, Atlanta, GA 30329; (404)248-9676; www.emory.edu/NFIA.

—National Institute on Alcohol Abuse and Alcoholism (NIAAA); 6000 Executive Boulevard, Willco Building, Bethesda, MD 20892-7003; (301) 443-3860; supports and conducts research on the causes, consequences, treatment, and prevention of alcoholism and alcohol-related problems.

—Overcomers Outreach is a Christian-oriented twelve-step support group found in most states; 520 North Brookhurst, Suite 121, Anaheim, CA 92801; (800) 310-3001; www.overcomersoutreach.org.

—Recovered Alcoholic Clergy Association; (800) 944-2979; www.geoc-ities.com/HotSprings/8872/index.html; is a national network for clergy of the Episcopal Church supporting one another in their recovery from alcoholism. Also provides assistance to clergy (and their families) who are dealing with drinking issues.

—SMART Recovery Self-Help Network (Self Management And Recovery Training); 7537 Mentor Avenue, Suite 306, Mentor, OH 44060; (440) 951-5357; www.smartrecovery.org; is a national network of self-help groups for individuals wanting to gain their independence from addictive and compulsive behaviors. It is an abstinence program based on cognitive-behavioral principles, especially those of rational-emotive-behavior therapy. It provides information, referrals, literature, and assistance in starting local chapters.

—The Salvation Army, P.O. Box 269, Alexandria, VA 22313; (703) 684-5500; www.salvationarmyusa.org.

—United Methodists in Recovery, www.Winternet.com/webpage/umr.html, is an anonymous mailing list to share experience, strength, and hope.

Self-Help Resources

Another Empty Bottle, www.alcoholismHELP.com/emptybottle.com, is a website for the friends and families of alcoholics.

Center for Substance Abuse Information, Treatment, and Treatment Referral Hotline, (800) 622-HELP.

Counseling Troubled Older Adults: A Handbook for Pastors and Religious Caregivers (Harold G. Koenig and Andrew J. Weaver, Nashville: Abingdon Press, 1997); has chapters on alcohol abuse and dependence and on over-the-counter and prescription drug abuse and dependence.

Counseling Troubled Teens and Their Families: A Handbook for Pastors and Youth Workers (Andrew J. Weaver, John D. Preston, and Leigh W. Jerome, Nashville: Abingdon Press, 1999); has chapters on alcohol and drug abuse and dependence and tobacco and gambling addiction.

Practical Psychology for Pastors, 2nd ed. (William R. Miller and Kathleen A. Jackson, Englewood Cliffs, NJ: Prentice Hall, 1995); offers very helpful chapters on the process of addiction from a faith perspective and how clergy can help.

Understanding and Counseling Persons with Alcohol, Drug, and Behavioral Addictions: Counseling for Recovery and Prevention Using Psychology and Religion, rev. ed. (Howard Clinebell, Nashville: Abingdon Press, 1998); is a comprehensive look at addiction from a pastoral care perspective by a pioneer in the field.

References

American Psychiatric Association. (1994). *Diagnostic and Statistical Manual of Mental Disorders* (4th ed.). Washington, DC: APA.

Closser, M. H., and Blow, F. C. (1993). Special populations: Women, ethnic minorities, and the elderly. *Psychiatric Clinics of North America: Recent Advances in Addictive Disorders, 16(1)*, 199–209.

Daaleman, T. P., and Frey, B. (1998). Prevalence and patterns of physicians referral to clergy and pastoral care providers. *Archives of Family Medicine, 7*, 548–553.

Edwards, M. E., and Steinglass, P. (1995). Family therapy treatment outcomes for alcoholism. *Journal of Marital and Family Therapy, 21(4)*, 475–509.

Goldsmith, M. F. (1989). Proliferating "self help" groups offer wide range of support, seek physician rapport. *Journal of the American Medical Association, 261*, 2474–2475.

Larson, D. B., Sawyers, J. P., and McCullough, M. E. (1998). *Scientific Research on Spirituality and Religion*. Rockville, MD: National Institute for Healthcare Research.

Miller, N. S., and Verinis, J. S. (1995). Treatment outcome for impoverished alcoholics in abstinence-based programs. *International Journal of Addictions, 30*, 753–763.

Miller, W. R., Benefield, G., and Tonigan, J. S. (1993). Enhancing motivation for change in problem drinking: A controlled comparison of two therapists' styles. *Journal of Consulting and Clinical Psychology, 61(3)*, 455–461.

Miller, W. R., and Jackson, K. A. (1995). *Practical Psychology for Pastors*. Englewood Cliffs, NJ: Prentice Hall.

Room, R., and Greenfield, T. (1993). Alcoholics Anonymous, other twelve-step movements and psychotherapy in the U.S. population, 1990. *Addiction, 88*, 555–562.

Rotunda, R. J., Scherer, D., and Imm, P. (1995). Family systems and alcohol misuse: Research on the effects of alcoholism on family functioning and effective family interventions. *Professional Psychology: Research and Practice, 26*, 95–104.

Rotunda, R. J., and O'Farrell, T. J. (1997). Marital and family therapy of alcohol use disorders: Bridging the gap between research and practice. *Professional Psychology: Research and Practice, 28(3),* 246–252.

Special Report of the U.S. Congress on Alcohol and Health. (1987). Rockville, MD: National Institute on Alcohol Abuse and Alcoholism.

Turner, N. H. (1995). Bridging the gap: Addressing alcohol and drug addiction from a community health perspective. *American Journal of Public Health, 85(6),* 870–871.

Weaver, A. J., Preston, J. D., and Jerome, L. W. (1999). *Counseling Troubled Teens and Their Families: A Handbook for Pastors and Youth Workers.* Nashville: Abingdon Press.

The Homeless Family

"Nowhere to Turn for Help"

A twenty-five-year-old woman named Darlyn appeared at Pastor Mitchell's church office with four-year-old Keri in tow. She and her daughter were dressed in wrinkled but clean clothing. Darlyn asked for food and prayers. She had been living in her car for several days while she drove from another state. Darlyn had grown up in a Baptist family, so she went to a Baptist church for help. She was fleeing a battering husband, who was a police officer in their small town. Darlyn had stayed with her parents for a few days after the last beating, but her father was gambling and drinking heavily and thought she should return to her husband. She fled the small town and left her part-time waitressing job, feeling unsafe after her husband continued to harass her and threatened to take Keri. Darlyn had no other family or friends to turn to and not enough money to afford housing. She and her daughter had slept the previous night in her car in the church parking lot. She wanted to find work as a waitress.

Darlyn is not unlike many women with children who experience crisis poverty and homelessness. The average homeless female head of household is in her late twenties, is not a high school graduate, and has two or three preschool-age children. Events associated with family homelessness include job loss, eviction or inability to pay rent, and conflict with those with whom the family lived prior to becoming homeless. Many such women have had extremely traumatic childhoods and/or adult relationships. They are more likely than housed low-income women to have lived in foster care, been runaway youth, suffered physical or sexual child abuse, and to have limited social contacts (Shinn, Knickman, and Weitzman, 1991).

Pastoral Assessment

Domestic violence contributes greatly to homelessness among families. When a woman leaves an abusive relationship, she often has nowhere to go. This is particularly true of women with few financial resources. In a study of homeless parents (the majority of whom were mothers) in ten U.S. cities, 22 percent said they had left their last place of residence because of domestic violence (Homes for the Homeless, 1998).

Despite the overwhelming difficulties that homeless mothers face, they also possess strengths deserving of recognition and affirmation. One study found that personal qualities such as pride, determination, clarity of focus, a positive attitude, and moral structure guide the lives of homeless women. These mothers are committed to the well-being of their children, generally hold religious beliefs, and find purpose in helping others (Montgomery, 1994).

Relevant History

Four in 10 Americans living in poverty are children. The poverty rate of 20 percent for children is almost twice as high as the rate for any other age group (U.S. Bureau of the Census, 1998). Homeless youngsters are subject to stark poverty and a set of risk factors that severely affect their health and well-being. The average age of homeless children is six years. Severe poverty and housing instability are especially harmful during early childhood. Research links homelessness among children to hunger, poor nutrition, medical problems, lack of health care and mental health care, developmental delays, anxiety, depression, behavioral problems, lowered educational achievement, psychological problems, and academic difficulties (Lindsey, 1998). School-age homeless children face barriers to enrolling in and attending school, including transportation problems, residency requirements, inability to obtain previous academic records, and lack of appropriate clothing and school supplies.

Diagnostic Criteria

Homelessness is a devastating experience that disrupts virtually every aspect of family life, damaging the well-being of persons, interfering with children's education and development, and frequently resulting in the separation of members. Families with children constitute approximately 40 percent of the homeless, and among families, this condition is on the rise (Lindsey, 1998). A survey of thirty U.S. cities found that in 1998, children accounted for 25 percent of the homeless population (U.S. Conference of Mayors, 1998). These proportions are likely to be higher in rural areas where families, single mothers, and children make up the largest group of people who are homeless (Vissing, 1996).

The lack of affordable housing is a major factor underlying the growth of homelessness. The gap between the quantity of affordable housing units and the number of people needing them is at a record level, estimated to be 4.4 million units (Daskal, 1998). The affordable housing crisis has had a particularly severe impact on poor families with children because of soaring rent (U.S. Department of Housing and Urban Development, 1999). As a result, increasing numbers of families are in need of housing assistance. With less income available for food and other necessities, many are only an accident, an illness, or a paycheck away from becoming homeless. Recent changes in American welfare programs threaten to create a new wave of family homelessness. With public assistance no longer an entitlement but a limited benefit of two to five years (depending on the state), it is likely that the number of homeless families will increase, especially when the economy dips.

Response to Vignette

Pastor Mitchell was in a good position to help Darlyn because he had a working relationship with the homeless network in his community. His church actively supports a ministry that offers transitional housing for homeless families, providing up to four months of rent and utilities. The program offers an environment that can help Darlyn become self-supporting and self-reliant. Along with housing, the ministry provides services such as haircuts; dental care; medical treatment; legal aid; GED training; car repair; employment skills; community living training; and classes in budgeting, nutrition, and parenting. An aftercare program for graduate families provides basic needs such as domestic goods, furniture, and counseling services.

The transitional housing made all the difference for Darlyn and her daughter. They were able to reestablish their lives. Keri was given a scholarship to attend the church preschool, and Darlyn found employment. With counseling, she eventually was able to recover from the psychological trauma of domestic violence and losing her home. Darlyn gained renewed confidence in herself, found an apartment, and began to complete her GED. She became an active member of the congregation and a productive member of her new community.

Treatment Within the Faith Community

Working directly with homeless people is one of the best ways to learn about homelessness. Many of the members of Pastor Mitchell's congregation do volunteer work for the program. While the causes of homelessness are complex, there is much that a person of faith can do to help. No matter what a person's skills, interests, or resources, there are ways he or she can make a difference. Volunteer work, advocacy efforts, and contributions of money, clothes, food, and services are all needed. Several church members help with clerical work (answer phones, type, file, sort mail), and others serve food, wash dishes, and sort or distribute clothes. A number of others offer services directly or assist in job training, including secretarial, catering, plumbing, accounting, management, carpentry, tutoring, public relations, fund-raising, legal, medical, dental, writing, child care, and counseling.

The church runs a thrift shop that collects clothing for the homeless and donates its proceeds to the food bank. The lack of clean, well-fitting shoes and clothes poses a great hardship as the homeless are exposed to the elements. It also hurts their self-image and limits their opportunities for employment. At job interviews, a poorly dressed person has little chance for success. Homeless people must travel light, with few opportunities to safely store or adequately clean what they can't carry. Items such as new clothes, diapers, children's toys, and food are in high demand among homeless families, offering an excellent opportunity for a valuable ministry.

Faith communities have an essential moral role as advocates for the poor and homeless. Cohen and colleagues (1992) have documented the substantial involvement of several faith communities in addressing this problem. Attempts to remedy homelessness cannot be fully effective if they are isolated from a broader community strategy designed to address the problems of the poor, including the lack of affordable housing. Only a concerted effort to ensure jobs that pay a living wage, and to provide adequate support for those who cannot work, affordable housing, and access to medical and mental health care will bring an end to the national scandal of homelessness.

Indications for Referral

Darlyn was a mother experiencing homelessness as a result of family disruption and crisis poverty. Pastor Mitchell's intervention and referral to transitional housing meant that her situation was transient and not a long-term disruption of family life. Unfortunately, for many with chronic disabilities, living on the streets becomes a way of life. Although a minority of those who become homeless each year, this group is the most visible and tends to dominate the public's image of homelessness.

According to the U.S. Department of Veterans Affairs, about one third of the adult homeless population has served in the armed services. On any given day, as many as 250,000 veterans (mostly males living alone) are on the streets or in shelters, and perhaps twice as many experience homelessness at some point during the course of a year. Alcohol and other drug abuse, severe mental illness, chronic health issues, or long-standing family difficulties may compound whatever employment and housing problems persons have. Lacking financial resources and having exhausted family support make homelessness more likely to be long-term. Disability coupled with the toll of street-living make the situation more complex than that of those who are homeless because of crisis poverty. Persons with chronic disabilities require not only economic assistance, but also rehabilitation and ongoing support.

The U.S. Department of Veteran Affairs provides resources for veterans and their dependents. It offers an array of programs specifically designed to help homeless veterans live as self-sufficiently and independently as possible. The programs offer a continuum of services that include: outreach to veterans living on streets and in shelters; assessment and referral to needed medical treatment for physical and psychiatric disorders, including substance abuse; long-term sheltered transitional assistance, case management, and rehabilitation; employment assistance and linkage with available income supports; and supported permanent housing. Contact the local Veterans Affairs office for assistance.

Homelessness for a family is a crisis with multiple stressors. Given the many difficulties, it is not surprising that homeless mothers have a high risk of depression and their children are at a greater risk for behavioral problems than those in the general public (Conrad, 1998). The interaction of distressed mothers and children can also lead to problems for the parent-child relationship. Mental health professionals need to screen homeless children and parents for these problems.

It is important to recognize the distinction between the mental health needs of a mother like Darlyn, who experienced an episode of moderate depression related to a crisis, and those of a long-term homeless person, who has a chronic mental illness or long-term addiction. A situational depression can usually be helped by lowering the level of stress, offering supportive therapy, and prescribing antidepressant medications.

Homeless individuals with major psychiatric disorders such as schizophrenia, bipolar disorder, and/or substance abuse problems require intensive evaluation, inpatient treatment, medications, and/or specific drug treatment programs. The National Law Center on Homelessness and Poverty estimates that at least 25 percent of the nearly one million homeless persons suffer from some form of severe and persistent mental illness. Obtaining proper care for the seriously mentally ill became exceedingly difficult after over 95 percent of state mental hospital beds were closed between 1955 and 1995 (Lamb, 1998).

Ethnic minorities are disproportionately represented among the homeless, especially among homeless families (Burt, 1992). African-Americans, for example, consistently form a larger fraction of the homeless population than of the general population and are less likely than Caucasians to find permanent housing (Rocha, Johnson, McChesney, and Butterfield, 1996).

National Resources

—Habitat for Humanity International; 121 Habitat Street, Americus, GA 31709-3498; (800) 422-4828; www.habitat.org; is a nonprofit ecumenical organization dedicated to eliminating substandard housing and homelessness worldwide and to making adequate, affordable shelter a matter of conscience and action. It is founded on the conviction that every person should have a simple, decent, affordable place to live in dignity and safety. Habitat invites people of all backgrounds, races, and religions to build houses together in partnership with families in need. It has built

Treatment by Mental Health Specialist

Cross-Cultural Issues

Resources

more than 80,000 houses around the world, providing more than 400,000 people in more than 2,000 communities with shelter.

—Homeless Providers Grant and Per Diem Program Office; Mental Health Strategic Health Care Group (116E), U.S. Department of Veterans Affairs, 810 Vermont Avenue, NW, Washington, DC 20420; (877) 332-0334. This office can assist faith communities in gaining grants to help homeless veterans.

—National Alliance to End Homelessness; 1518 K Street, NW, Suite 206, Washington, DC 20005; (202) 638-1526; www.endhomelessness.org; is a nationwide federation of public, private, and nonprofit organizations working together to form a network advancing practical, community-based solutions to homelessness. It is a nonprofit membership organization dedicated to solving the problems of homelessness and to preventing its continued growth.

—National Center for Homeless Education at Serve (NCHE); 915 Northridge Street, 2nd floor, Greensboro, NC 27403; (800) 755-3277; www.serve.org/nche; funded by the U.S. Department of Education, it was established to provide information to improve educational opportunities for homeless children and youth. Its goal is to disseminate resource and referral information related to the complex issues surrounding the education of homeless children.

—National Coalition for the Homeless; 1012 Fourteenth Street, NW, Suite 600, Washington, DC 20005-3410; (202) 737-6444; nch@ari.net; is a national advocacy network of homeless persons, activists, service providers, and others committed to ending homelessness through public education, policy advocacy, grassroots organizing, and technical assistance.

—National Health Care for the Homeless Council, Inc.; HCH Clinicians' Network, P.O. Box 60427, Nashville, TN 37206-0427; (615) 226-2292; www.nhchc.org; is a membership organization of health care providers working with homeless people across the United States. It exists to help bring about reform of the health care system to best serve the needs of people who are homeless. The Council works in alliance with others whose broader purpose is to eliminate homelessness and provide support to members. The network provides opportunities for education, information sharing, peer support, and networking. Membership in the Clinicians' Network is open to any hands-on provider of care to homeless individuals.

—National Law Center on Homelessness and Poverty; 1411 K Street, NW, Suite 1400, Washington, DC 20005; (202) 638-2535; www.nlchp.org; is committed to solutions that address the causes of homelessness, not just its symptoms. It addresses homelessness in the larger context of poverty and advocates to protect the rights of homeless people and to implement solutions to end homelessness. It was established in 1989 and is governed by a board of directors that includes lawyers, activists, researchers, and homeless and formerly homeless people.

—National Low Income Housing Coalition (NLIHC); 1012 Fourteenth Street, NW, Suite 610, Washington, DC 20005; (202) 662-1530; www.nlihc.org; was established in 1974 and is dedicated to ending America's affordable housing crisis. The NLIHC is committed to educating, organizing, and advocating to ensure decent, affordable housing within healthy neighborhoods for everyone. It provides up-to-date information, formulates policy, and educates the public on housing needs and the strategies for solutions.

—National Resource Center on Homelessness and Mental Illness; Policy Research Associates, Inc., 262 Delaware Avenue, Delmar, NY 12054; (800) 444-7415; nrc@prainc.com; provides technical assistance, identifies and synthesizes knowledge, and disseminates information. It links policy makers, service providers, researchers, consumers, and other interested parties to findings from federal demonstration projects and research on homelessness and mental illness.

Self-Help Resources

Confronting Homelessness Among American Families (Madelyn DeWoody, Washington DC: Child Welfare League Of America, 1992).

The Friends in Action Manual: A Model for Establishing a Volunteer Program to Build Caring, Supportive Relationships with Poor and Homeless Families (Carolyn Dow Parker, Rockville, MD: Community Ministry of Montgomery County, 1992).

The New Poverty: Homeless Families in America (Ralph da Costa Nunez, New York: Insight Books, 1996).

Out of Sight, Out of Mind: Homeless Children and Families in Small-Town America (Yvonne M. Vissing, Lexington: University Press of Kentucky, 1996).

References

Burt, M. (1992). *Over the Edge: The Growth of Homelessness in the 1980s.* Washington, DC: Urban Institute Press.

Cohen, E., Mowbray, C. T., Gillette, V., and Thompson, E. (1992). Preventing homelessness: Religious organizations and housing development. In K. I. Pargament, K. I. Matson, and R. E. Hess (Eds.), *Religion and Prevention in Mental Health: Research, Vision and Action* (pp. 317–333). New York: Haworth Press.

Conrad, B. S. (1998). Maternal depressive symptoms and homeless children's mental health: Risk and resiliency. *Archives of Psychiatric Nursing, 12(1)*, 50–58.

Daskal, J. (1998). *In Search of Shelter: The Growing Shortage of Affordable Rental Housing.* Washington, DC: Center on Budget and Policy Priorities.

Homes for the Homeless. (1998). *Ten Cities 1997-1998: A Snapshot of*

Family Homelessness Across America. New York: Homes for the Homeless and the Institute for Children and Poverty.

Lamb, H. R. (1998). Deinstitutionalization at the beginning of the new millennium. *Harvard Review of Psychiatry, 6(1)*, 1–10.

Lindsey, E. W. (1998). The impact of homelessness and shelter life on family relationships. *Family Relations, 47*, 243–252.

Link, B. G., Susser, E., Stueve, A., Phelan, J., Moore, R. E., and Struening, E. (1994). Lifetime and five-year prevalence of homelessness in the United States. *American Journal of Public Health, 84(12)*, 1907–1912.

Montgomery, C. (1994). Swimming upstream: The strengths of women who survive homelessness. *Advances in Nursing Science, 16(3)*, 34–45.

Rocha, C., Johnson, A. K., McChesney, K. Y., and Butterfield, W. H. (1996). Predictors of permanent housing for sheltered homeless families. *Families in Society, 77*, 50–57.

Shinn, M., Knickman, J. R., and Weitzman, B. C. (1991). Social relationships and vulnerability to becoming homeless among poor families. *American Psychologist, 46(11)*, 1180–1187.

U.S. Bureau of the Census (1998). *Poverty in the United States, 1996*. Washington DC: U.S. Department of Commerce.

U.S. Conference of Mayors (1998). *A Status Report on Hunger and Homelessness in America's Cities: 1998*. Washington, DC: U.S. Conference of Mayors.

U.S. Department of Housing and Urban Development, Office of Policy Development and Research. (1999). *Waiting in Vain: An Update on America's Housing Crisis*. Rockville, MD: HUD.

Vissing, Y. M. (1996). *Out of Sight, Out of Mind: Homeless Children and Families in Small-Town America*. Lexington: University Press of Kentucky.

PART THREE

Summary

Summary and Conclusions

Religion plays a vital role in the lives of families across the life span, especially in times of stress and crisis. Given the increasing diversity of family forms (e.g., blended families, single parents) and the strains of social and economic changes, growing numbers of people will ask clergy and the community of faith for counseling and guidance. For this reason, those in ministry need to know about key issues over the life span of a family, along with the most common mental health problems that may occur. Information is needed about how to diagnose and assess problems, types of treatment that can be initiated in the faith community, when referral is required, and to whom to refer. This text identifies twenty transitional issues along with common mental health conditions that can occur within the life of a family, provides illustrative cases, lists resources available for help, and suggests when and from whom to seek additional professional assistance. There is an emphasis on self-help resources available on the Internet, an increasing source of information today.

Because of the important role that religion plays in the lives of many, it is essential that pastors, chaplains, and others in ministry have knowledge about the protective aspects of faith for families as they cope with change and adversity. Studies link religious practice to many positive social benefits. Active faith involvement increases marital commitment and can be a strong deterrent to instability and divorce. Well-functioning families often adhere to deeply felt values based on religious principles. The beliefs and practices of faith are helpful to older adults when facing the psychological stress of poor health and disability. Family caregivers of the chronically ill cope better if they have a strong religious faith. Youth who practice their faith show more prosocial values and caring behaviors, and their families are more stable. Commitment to nonpunitive, nurturing religious beliefs and activities reduces alcohol and drug abuse, depression, suicide, and antisocial behavior in young people. Faith communities are powerful preventive and healing resources that will increasingly be relied upon to help meet the emotional needs of families.

Pastoral care is a responsibility of the whole religious community. Clergy can offer guidance and direction, but the task of caring for families requires a larger group of helpers. Much emphasis has been given to preventive mental health care through education within the community of faith. The book offers concrete suggestions about how the issues addressed can be understood as forms of ministry for the entire congregation.

Glossary of Terms

Acting out: The indirect expression of feelings through behavior that attracts the attention of others.

Active listening: Alert listening with an attitude of wanting to hear what the person is saying.

Acute illness: A severe illness of short duration.

Addiction: The condition that arises when increasing amounts of prescription or illegal drugs are required to achieve the desired effect (physical tolerance), and unpleasant symptoms (withdrawal) occur when their use is stopped. A person who is addicted to alcohol or drugs is also dependent on the substance.

Adolescence: The developmental transition between childhood and adulthood; generally considered to begin around age twelve or thirteen and end in the late teens or early twenties.

Adult daycare: A day care center offering health-related and rehabilitation services to physically and/or mentally impaired adults.

Affective disorder: A mental disorder involving mood.

Agoraphobia: A fear of open spaces, which can lead to an inability to function independently outside the home.

Al-Anon: An organization dedicated to helping the families of alcoholics through a support group and twelve-step program.

Alzheimer's disease: A form of dementia that causes a severe, progressive, irreversible deterioration of intellectual functioning.

Anxiety: The state of feeling apprehension, agitation, uncertainty, and fear from an anticipated event.

Aphasia: Loss of the capacity to use or understand language.

Behavior disorder/emotional disturbance: These terms are used interchangeably to describe children who exhibit extreme and chronic behavior problems. These children lag behind their peers in social development. They are isolated from others either because they withdraw from social contact or because they demonstrate antisocial behaviors.

Benzodiazepine: A minor tranquilizer, such as diazepam (Valium), that can be addictive for some persons, particularly for those who have a past history of drug or alcohol abuse.

Bereavement: A normal emotional reaction to the loss of anyone who is important to a person; this usually refers to the grief that follows the loss of a family member or other loved one.

Bipolar disorder/manic-depressive illness: A serious mental disorder that involves extreme mood swings and sometimes psychosis.

Blended family: A new family unit formed by the marriage of divorced persons and their children from former marriages.

Boundary: A central concept in family systems theory. It indicates the degree of separateness between individuals or groups of family members within the family unit. Boundaries change over time as the family goes through various stages of development.

Brief family therapy: A form of therapy that uses short-term interventions that are solution-oriented. The emphasis is on resolving present issues rather than exploring underlying problems.

Child abuse: Maltreatment of a minor involving physical, sexual, or emotional injury.

Child neglect: The withholding of adequate care from a minor. It usually refers to physical needs such as food, clothing, medical care, and supervision.

Chronic illness: An illness that has a long duration, as opposed to an acute illness.

Cognitive: Relating to the ability to think or reason; sometimes used to describe the memory process; the operation of the mind, as distinct from emotions.

Cognitive behavior therapy (CBT): A form of psychological therapy that focuses on directly modifying both thought processes and behaviors.

Collaboration: The shared planning, decision making, problem solving, and goal setting by persons who work together.

Compulsion: An intrusive, repetitive, and unwanted urge to perform an act that is counter to a person's usual conduct.

Conduct disorder: A persistent pattern of behavior that involves violations of the rights of others with little sense of guilt, such as disobedience and destructiveness.

Confidentiality: A principle of ethics in which professionals may not disclose personal information about a patient without the person's permission.

Conjoint therapy: Treatment of two or more persons in therapy sessions together.

Coping: The process of using personal, spiritual, and social resources to manage stress.

Countertransference: Feelings that a counselor or therapist develops toward a client, such as overconcern, sexual attraction, or anger. Such feelings can interfere with the process of counseling if not recognized and addressed.

Crisis: A disturbance caused by a stressful event or a perceived threat to the self.

Crisis intervention: Emergency assistance that focuses on providing guidance and support to help mobilize the resources needed to resolve a crisis.

Culture: An ordered system of shared and socially transmitted symbols, values, and meanings that give a worldview and guide behavior.

Delusions: Fixed, false beliefs from which an individual cannot be dissuaded.

Dementia: A clinical term describing a group of brain disorders that impair thinking, memory, mood, and judgment.

Depression: Emotional disturbance in which a person feels unhappy and often has trouble sleeping, eating, or concentrating.

Developmental transitions: The movement of persons or families from one life phase to another. This can be a time of increased stress and conflict until the transition is completed.

Diagnosis: The process of collecting data for the purpose of identifying a problem.

Diagnostic and Statistical Manual of Mental Disorders, 4th Edition (DSM-IV): The official manual of mental health problems developed by the

American Psychiatric Association. This reference book is used by mental health professionals to understand and diagnose psychological problems.

Disengaged family: A family in which members are isolated from each other.

Disorder: A mental health problem that impairs an individual's social, educational, or mental functioning or significantly interferes with her or his quality of life.

Durable power of attorney for health care: The legal authorization given to a person of one's choosing (usually a spouse, close relative, or trusted clergy) to make decisions about his or her health care treatment if he or she becomes unable to do so. It may include such matters as when to use and refuse medical treatment or provisions about nursing home placement.

Dysfunctional: Abnormal or impaired functioning.

Empathic listening: Listening that conveys genuine concern for the feelings of the speaker.

Empathy: The ability to put oneself in another's place and feel what another person feels.

Empowerment: The process of assisting a person or family to enlarge their influence over the circumstances of their life.

Enabling: Acting in such a way that another person's dysfunctional behavior is supported.

Enmeshment: A family dynamic in which personal boundaries become blurred and members become overinvolved in one another's lives.

Entitlement: The belief that one has a rightful claim to special privileges.

Family life span: Stages of family life from leaving the parental home to marriage, having children, growing older, retirement, and death.

Family of origin: Refers to the original nuclear family of an adult.

Family therapy: A therapeutic method that involves assessment and treatment with immediate family members present. This model emphasizes the family as a whole, rather than focusing on one person.

Genogram: A structured procedure for drawing a family map.

Geriatrics: The branch of medicine that specializes in treating the conditions of the elderly.

Gerontologist: A psychologist who specializes in the mental and behavioral aspects of aging.

Grandiosity: Overappraisal of one's value and ability.

Group dynamics: Interactions among group members, which develop as a result of relationships within the group rather than of simply individual personalities.

Hallucinations: Abnormal perceptions that occur as symptoms of schizophrenia or other severe forms of mental illness; mostly in the form of hearing voices or seeing objects.

Holistic: A person or family is seen as more than the sum of the parts. Physical, psychological, spiritual, social, and cultural influences are considered in one's assessment and treatment.

Hospice care: Warm, personal patient and family-oriented care for an individual with a terminal illness.

Hyperactivity: A condition in which activity is haphazard and unorganized.

Hypervigilance: Increased watchfulness.

Learning disabilities: A specific set of problems that cause an individual to have difficulties understanding and may lower academic achievement.

Living will: Written instructions making known what one wants done if, for example, he or she is gravely ill and the only way to be kept alive is by artificial means.

Maladaptive behavior: Behavior that does not adjust to the environment.

Mania: A symptom of bipolar disorder marked by exaggerated excitement, physical overactivity, and rapid changes in ideas. A person in a manic state feels an emotional high and often follows his or her impulses.

Meals-on-Wheels: A program of delivering nutritious meals to housebound seniors for little or no cost.

Medicare: A federal health insurance program for Americans over the age of sixty-four and some disabled individuals, which helps to defray medical expenses.

Normalizing: A therapeutic strategy that depathologizes problems in a way that changes perceptions of the situation and defuses the difficulty.

Norms: Unspoken standards of acceptable behavior in a society.

Nuclear family: Parents and their children.

Nursing home: Facility that provides twenty-four-hour care and medical supervision. They are divided into intermediate-care facilities (for patients who require periodic, low-level nursing care and physician input) and skilled-care facilities (for patients who require continuous nursing supervision and physician care).

Obsession: The mental state, occurring in obsessive-compulsive disorder, of having recurrent thoughts about something or someone. The recurrent thoughts are difficult to stop and difficult to control.

Ombudsman: A person designated to advocate for, and protect the rights of, persons living in long-term care facilities. She or he is given authority to investigate elder or dependent adult abuse and initiate corrective action.

Oncologist: A medical doctor who specializes in the treatment of patients with cancer.

Paranoid thinking: Exaggerated belief or suspicion that one is being persecuted, harassed, or unfairly treated.

Parish nurse: A nurse working in a congregation to promote all aspects of wellness. Parish nurses train and coordinate volunteers, develop support groups, liaison within the health care system, refer to community resources, and provide health education.

Phobia: An intense, irrational fear of a harmless object or situation that the individual seeks to avoid.

Projection: Attributing one's own thoughts or impulses to another.

Post-traumatic stress disorder (PTSD): An anxiety disorder in which symptoms develop following a psychological trauma. The essential features of PTSD include increased physical arousal, intrusive reexperiencing of the traumatic event, and avoidance.

Prognosis: A forecast of the outcome of a disorder, including an indication of its probable duration and course.

Psychiatrist: A medical doctor with special training (medical residence in psychiatry) to handle psychological problems. A psychiatrist can hospitalize patients and may treat them with medications, psychotherapy, or both.

Psychoanalysis: An approach to psychotherapy that emphasizes unconscious motives and conflicts. In this therapy, the effort is to bring unconscious material to awareness and to increase conscious choice.

Psychologist: A doctor with an advanced degree (Ph.D. or Psy.D.) who is trained to use a variety of treatment modalities, including individual and group psychotherapy, cognitive therapy, behavior modification, psychodynamic psychotherapy, and family systems. She or he also does psychological testing.

Psychopharmacology: The management of mental illnesses using medications.

Psychosis: A mental condition that involves hallucinations, delusions, or paranoia.

Psychosomatic: A physical disorder of the body caused or aggravated by chronic emotional stress.

Psychotherapy: A process in which an individual seeks to resolve problems or achieve psychological growth through verbal communication with a mental health professional.

Regression: A process in which a person exhibits behavior that is more appropriate to an earlier stage of development.

Resilience: The capacity to endure and rebound from adversity.

Scapegoat: A member of the family or group who is the object of displaced conflict.

Schizophrenia: A chronic mental disorder associated with a loss of contact with reality exhibited in the form of hallucinations and delusions.

Self-esteem: A person's positive self-evaluation or self-image.

Self-help groups: Therapeutic groups without the leadership of health professionals.

Social worker: A professional with an advanced degree (M.S.W.) who is trained to understand and emphasize the impact of environmental factors on mental health problems. He or she often works with individuals and families to access available community services.

Stepfamily: A linked family created by the marriage of two people, one or both of whom have been married before, in which children from the former marriage live with the remarried couple.

Stress: Tension resulting from a person's response to the environment.

Stroke: The blockage or rupture of blood vessels that suddenly interrupts the supply of blood to the brain.

Substance abuse: Excess, abnormal, or illegal use of drugs or alcohol.

Reframing: Relabeling behavior by putting it into a new, more positive perspective, thus changing the context in which it is understood.

Transference: A term for distorted emotional reactions to present relationships based on unresolved family-of-origin relations.

Triangulation: When a conflict between two people uses a third person to stabilize their relationship. Most commonly it involves two parents and a child.

Visiting nurse: A trained nurse who visits persons in their homes to monitor their physical condition and implement medical care.

Index